DUBLIN

with David Sheehan

www.**HERO**BOOKS.digital

HERO BOOKS

PUBLISHED BY HERO BOOKS
1 WOODVILLE GREEN
LUCAN
CO. DUBLIN
IRELAND

Hero Books is an imprint of Umbrella Publishing
First Published 2021
Copyright © David Sheehan 2021

A CIP record for this book is available from the British Library

ISBN 9781910827383

Cover design and formatting: jessica@viitaladesign.com
Ebook formatting: www.ebooklaunch.com
Photographs: Sportsfile

★ DEDICATION ★

To all those who have worn the famous Blue

★ CONTENTS ★

★ ACKNOWLEDGEMENTS ★

WHEN I WAS approached about writing this book, as a proud Meath man I had to consider my options very carefully! But it was an easy decision. I've spent most of my life supporting my own county and, because of that, have become very familiar with several generations of Dublin players. Those I hadn't seen in person were familiar to me from the likes of the *Kerry's Golden Years* video.

The first big game I attended as a young Meath fan was the 1989 Leinster final, a game that still resonates with me today. Even though my own county lost that one, the noise and the colour on Hill 16 was something I'll never forget. The game itself was a typical Meath-Dublin clash from that era – frantic, physical and incredibly dramatic. It's fair to say Dublin have come out on top more often than not in the years since then!

The most difficult part of putting this book together was trying to narrow down the list to just 25 players. There are so, so many Dublin footballers who would warrant inclusion, such is the length of the list of legendary players in the county. Even during the lean years when Dublin weren't winning All-Irelands, their teams were generally full of household names and huge characters.

Thanks to Hero Books and Liam Hayes for again trusting me with an important project. We got there in the end… *just!* A huge thanks as always to my parents Eddie and Monica for instilling the interest in GAA in me from an early age. The seed was sown when I was a child and has grown into something far greater than I probably ever anticipated.

Of course, I must reserve my biggest thank you for all the former Dublin players who gave so generously of their time for this book. It was a real pleasure to be able to listen to the story of the game that stood out from your career. While I hope most of you enjoyed the experience, a special word of praise must go to

Shane Ryan, who put himself through awful trauma for his chosen game!

While we all have our own personal allegiances, GAA players the country over are all cut from the same cloth. They put their lives on hold for their county, they enjoy the highs of victory, and endure the torment of defeat more than any of us probably realise.

I hope this book provides an insight into what made these players tick, what playing for Dublin meant to them, and why the game they chose was the *Game of their Life*.

David Sheehan
October 2021

JIM CROWLEY

DUBLIN 2-7 GALWAY 1-9
All-Ireland SFC Semi-Final
Croke Park
AUGUST 17, 1958

Jim Crowley (left) with his 1958 All-Ireland winning teammate, the late St Vincent's legend Johnny Joyce, attending a GPA former players celebration in Croke Park.

★ **DUBLIN:** P Flaherty: L Foley, M Wilson, Joe Timmons; C O'Leary, **J Crowley**, S O'Boyle: John Timmons, S Murray: P Haughey (0-1), O Freaney (0-4), D Ferguson: P Farnan, J Joyce (2-2), K Heffernan. Sub: M Whelan for Brennan.

★ **GALWAY:** J Mangan: J Kennedy, G Daly, T Dillon: J Kissane, M Greally, J Mahon: F Evers (0-1), M McDonagh (0-1): G Kirwan (1-0), S Purcell (0-5), S Colleran (0-1): W O'Neill, F Stockwell, J Young (0-1).

THE ACTION

DUBLIN MADE IT back to the All-Ireland final for the first time since 1955 with a dramatic win over Galway at a packed Croke Park. The Dubs, who hadn't lifted the Sam Maguire Cup since 1942, inflicted late heartbreak on their opponents when Ollie Freaney's free with the last kick of the game proved decisive.

Things didn't start well for the eventual winners, who found themselves three points to no score behind after 20 minutes. Dublin found their feet in the run-up to half-time though, and two points from Johnny Joyce before the interval meant that the westerners led by just a point (0-3 to 0-2) at the break. To be fair to both sets of players, heavy rain that morning made the conditions tricky, meaning that scores were always likely to be hard come by.

Although Freaney levelled the scores from a free a minute after the restart, Galway then seized control of the game with points from Seán Purcell and Mattie McDonagh either side of a goal from Gerry Kirwan. They had a five-point lead with 20 minutes remaining. In a game of few scores, it looked like a decisive advantage.

However, Dublin hit back immediately when Joyce got on the end of John Timmons' free and finished to the net. Another Freaney free on 45 minutes left just a point between the sides once again. One minute later Joyce found the net for a second time. Galway weren't done yet though, and two quick-fire points from the imperious Purcell levelled the scores. Freaney and Pádraig Haughey put Dublin two points to the good before Purcell brought it back to the minimum.

With three minutes remaining, Purcell's long-range free dropped into the goalmouth and was gathered by Stockwell. He passed to Frank Evers, who looked to have the goal at his mercy. The big midfielder set himself, but sent his shot crashing against the post, and referee Liam Friel awarded Dublin a free out in the scramble which ensued. Dublin gifted the ball to Galway from that free however, and Séamus Colleran kicked the equaliser.

With a replay looking likely, Dublin were awarded another free, this time within scoring distance of the Galway goal. The clocked ticked past the hour mark as Friel told Ollie Freaney that this would be the last kick of the game. The St Vincent's man stepped up as the crowd held its breath. The ball sailed between the posts.

★★★★★

66

IF IT HADN'T been for the Wall Street Crash, who knows if I'd ever have ended up playing for Dublin at all! I was born in New York in October 1929, around the time it happened. My parents were from Cork, and they moved back to Ireland when I was four… I've been in Dublin since.

I played all my adult football with St Vincent's, who were extremely dominant around that time. Dublin famously won a National League in 1953 with all the outfield players from Vincent's and Tony O'Grady the odd man out in goal! I don't know if players from other clubs resented the fact that they weren't getting a look-in but, given that we won the league with that team, I suppose nobody could argue too much.

The league is nice, but we were desperate for an All-Ireland. We hadn't won it since 1942, so that was the goal. In 1955 we got to our first final since that win in '42. Kerry were our opponents. You could say it was the beginning of that Dublin vs Kerry rivalry in a way, even though it didn't get going properly until the 70s.

We lost that game, which was a huge disappointment for all of us. It was our first final and we had such high hopes that we would win. I know Kevin Heffernan often said that loss hit him really hard and had a huge role in what he went on to do subsequently, both as a player and a manager.

The one consolation from losing that game was that we got invited over to New York afterwards. It was my first time being back there.

We got kitted out with nice blazers and all… that kind of thing was rare back then. It was a fantastic trip because this was a time long before team holidays. John Kerry O'Donnell was the one who invited us, so we were all delighted. We'd have preferred to have won the game of course, but it was brilliant to get back to New York again.

Having lost the final in 1955, the expectation was that we'd push on in '56, but it didn't work out that way. We lost to Wexford in the Leinster semi-final and then in '57 Louth beat us in the final. At the start of 1958, Heffo – who was captain of the team – got us all together and he made it clear that we were going to give it everything that year.

People always ask me if I could see the manager in him even then. I absolutely could. He was such a great leader… someone who lads really respected and could get behind. His words that day set the tone for the year. And we won all there was to win.

We beat Kildare in the National League final, which was always a great way to go into the championship. We would have felt a certain amount of pressure that season. I had been in there since 1950, and a lot of the other lads had been around a good few years too. Some of us were getting towards the end of the line, so that was where the pressure came from.

We didn't know how many more chances we were going to get.

In Leinster that year, we played Meath in Drogheda and we were lucky to come out of that one. We didn't play that well but won by two points. We beat Carlow in the semi-final and then got a bit of revenge on Louth in the final. Ollie Freaney was great for us that day… he kicked a lot of frees.

We had Galway in the semi-final, who had won the All-Ireland in 1956 and had Seán Purcell playing centre-forward for them. Seán is one of the all-time greats of gaelic football and was named on the Team of the Millennium. In Galway, he was as close to royalty as you could get.

I remember hearing one story about how he was getting the bus home to Tuam one night, and the inspector told the driver to take the bus back to the depot and get a double decker… because… 'Seán might want to have a smoke upstairs!' That's how revered he was. He was a fantastic footballer.

I knew I was going to have my work cut out marking him. I had played midfield for much of my career but went to centre-back for the replayed All-Ireland semi-final in 1955 as we had a couple of injuries. I didn't mind playing there, but I preferred midfield because you had a bit more freedom to go forward.

In those days defenders didn't really attack much; their job was to mark their man and put the ball into the forward line as quickly as possible. I wouldn't say we had tactics, as you'd call them today, but we tried to get the ball into the full-forward line as often as possible. There was far more kicking done then than now.

Cathal O'Leary was wing back on that team and also my brother-in-law.

We'd been at a dance some years before and I brought my neighbour's daughter. I saw Cathal coming in a little bit later with this lady, whom I was quite taken with! I said to him at one stage, 'Who's that?'

'That's my sister, Mary,' he replied. That was it!

We were married not too long after that. So, I have football to thank for finding my wife, as well as everything else. Cathal was a great player and a wonderful man. Dublin GAA hosted an event in December 2018 to mark the 60 years since our All-Ireland. Cathal sadly passed just before that, and I said a few words about him to the room.

It was a great evening… it was a shame he wasn't there to see it. With all the success Dublin has had since 1958, particularly in the last 10 years, it's nice to have our achievements recognised. I think the GAA is very good at that kind of thing, and there's great respect between Dublin players past and present.

Another example of this is that Tommy Drumm organised for a framed No 6 jersey, signed by all the Dublin All-Ireland-winning centre-backs, to be presented to me. It's hanging in my house in Santry. Pride of place. It means a lot that we are remembered so fondly.

The supporters would almost be hanging from the rafters in those days. They'd be spilling onto the pitch in some games. I remember coming off after winning a game and some fella shouted, 'HEY JIM!' I was delighted with myself after winning the game, so I looked around as if to say… *'What?'*

The response that came wasn't what I was expecting! It was related to my lack of hair… that's as much as I can say! So that fairly brought me back down to earth with a bump! But it was all in good spirits really, you wouldn't ever have people shouting much abuse at players or anything like that.

The Galway game was a very tight one, played in front of a huge crowd. We were behind for most of it, but we got level near the end… and then we got a free in, with what was going to be the last kick of the game. Seán Purcell rested his head on my shoulder. He didn't want to look because I think he knew Ollie Freaney would put the ball over the bar… which he did.

I suppose people might ask was the All-Ireland final against Derry not the best day of my Dublin career?

Of course it was very special to finally win Sam Maguire, but the Galway game was the bigger test in my view. They had been champions only two years earlier and had some fantastic players. We knew that getting over them was going to be difficult. For the final, it was Derry's first time to be there, and we had the experience from 1955 under our belts. We were expected to win, and we did.

It wasn't as close or as tense as the semi-final… we won relatively comfortably.

The lead-up to the game went a lot differently for us than it would for players now. The night before, I went out for a walk with the dog at around 11pm.

A Dublin supporter spotted me and let out a shout that I should be in bed! The truth was that I couldn't sleep. I was very nervous about the game. The next morning, I got the bus to the game… with my gear bag!

Paddy Farnan, who went on to score a goal in that final, almost didn't make it into the ground! He was held up on his way to Croke Park and then the man on the gate wouldn't believe he was a player and didn't want to let him in. Someone in the crowd recognised him and he got in then.

Could you imagine that happening today? Things have changed a lot.

The celebrations after were brilliant. We went on an open-top bus tour around town… thousands of fans came out to greet us. We had put the disappointment of 1955 behind us and ended that long wait for an All-Ireland.

It's a long time ago now, but that Dublin team still holds a special place in the county's history. I was hugely proud to be a part of it.

BERNARD BROGAN SNR

DUBLIN 1-11 OFFALY 0-13
Leinster SFC Quarter-Final
Croke Park
JUNE 16, 1974

Bernard Brogan Snr and his son Bernard walk up Jones' Road and towards Croke Park, the scene of so many memorable family celebrations.

★ **DUBLIN:** P Cullen; D Billings, S Doherty, R Kelleher; P Reilly, A Larkin, G Wilson; S Rooney (0-1), B Mullins (0-1); F Ryder, T Hanahoe (0-1), D Hickey (0-1); J McCarthy, J Keaveney (0-5), A O'Toole (0-1). Subs: L Deegan (1-1) for Ryder, **B Brogan** for McCarthy, G O'Driscoll for Billings.

★ **OFFALY:** M Furlong; R. Allen, M Ryan, M O'Rourke; E Mulligan, S Lowry, M Wright (0-1); W Bryan (0-1), L Claffey; P Fenning, K Kilmurray (0-2), T McTague (0-7); S Cooney, M Connor (0-1), S Darby (0-1). Sub: S Evans for Cooney.

THE ACTION

DUBLIN SPRUNG A huge upset in dethroning defending Leinster champions Offaly in a thrilling encounter in Croke Park. Leslie Deegan's late winner for Kevin Heffernan's men was the perfect finish to a game that had swung both ways.

The Dubs' form coming into this game did not suggest that they had a performance like this in them. Underwhelming displays against Wexford and Louth meant that Offaly were rightly favourites to advance to the Leinster semi-final.

The victory owed much to the bravery shown both on the field, and on the line. Heffo threw Leslie Deegan on inside the opening quarter-hour, with Fran Ryder making way. Deegan's impact was almost immediate, as he deflected a long delivery from Paddy Reilly to the Offaly net in the 20th minute.

That helped the underdogs to a 1-5 to 0-7 lead at the break, at which time Heffo made another decisive intervention. Gay O'Driscoll and Bernard Brogan entered the fray from the start of the second-half, meaning that the manager had played all his cards. The 15 on the field would have to get the job done without any further assistance from the bench.

Both changes proved masterful, with O'Driscoll tightening up the defence and Brogan making smart use of the ample possession he got, before picking up an injury in the closing stages which rendered him almost motionless.

The second-half proved just as competitive as the first. Offaly were left to rue the chances they missed in the opening 12 minutes after the restart, at a time when Dublin looked under most pressure.

With less than five minutes to go, back-to-back points from Jimmy Keaveney put Dublin two to the good, and they looked like certainties to win. Offaly weren't done yet though, with Mick Wright and Kevin Kilmurray levelling the scores for the seventh and final time.

Just when a replay looked likely, Stephen Rooney dispossessed Seán Lowry, fed his midfield partner Brian Mullins, who in turn knocked it to Deegan. The Supersub swung over the winning score with a coolness that belied the pressure of the occasion.

★★★★★

66

THIS WAS A difficult game for us... Offaly were the team to beat in Leinster at the time. For me personally, I was 20 and it turned out to be a day of mixed emotions.

To put things in context, at the end of 1973 nobody wanted to play for Dublin. We had been beaten that year by Louth, and I didn't have much interest in even watching Dublin play... they had won nothing in so long... they were going nowhere.

Kevin Heffernan came and asked me to play, and I pretty much refused. I was going into my last year in college... I actually ended up doing my finals around the time of the Offaly game. So, I told him I had no interest in playing.

But then he came back and asked me a second time.

Dublin were training out in a gym in Finglas at the time, and Heffo invited me to come out and have a look. I remember a lot of lads passed through that gym... there was a high turnover of players. Mickey Whelan wasn't there in person, but he was advising Kevin in the background on what we should be doing. This was a time when circuit training was just coming into fashion.

This was completely new to everyone, even for the lads who had been around the panel for a few years. It was new to me as well, because I'd never played minor or under-21 football for Dublin. I was on the minor hurling panel, but hadn't made the cut in the football. It wasn't that I was too far off; I would have gone to trials, but didn't make the final panel. Lads develop in different ways and at different speeds. Brian Fenton is a good example of that in the modern era. I probably would have played with the under-21s in 1974, but I was involved with the seniors at that stage.

I never played Sigerson in UCD either, because they played in the Dublin leagues at the time, and you obviously couldn't play for two clubs in the league. The UCD team at that time would have been made up of lads from around the country, most of whom were inter-county footballers.

My first formal game for the county was coming up to Christmas 1973, when we played the Combined Universities... I was marking John O'Keeffe. John was

fairly established footballer at that stage, even though he was relatively young. I played very well, but I twisted my left knee and had to come off.

From that point on, I started to take it all very seriously.

There was great momentum behind the scenes, and everyone was giving a big commitment. Everyone who was in there, with the exception of Brian Mullins and myself, had played inter-county football in the previous years… even though it looked like we came out of nowhere. Jimmy Keaveney had retired in 1971, in spite of the fact that he was still very young.

When the Leinster Championship came around, I started at full-forward against Wexford in Croke Park. There was nobody at the match! We didn't play well at all, and I think a lot of the media wrote us off after that performance. Keaveney came out of retirement before the next game… so I was dropped! That was against Louth in Navan, and we won relatively easily.

The Offaly game was next, and nobody gave us much of a chance. They were going for four in-a-row in Leinster… they had won the All-Irelands in 1971 and '72. I came on at half-time along with Gay O'Driscoll and was marking Kevin Kilmurray, who was one of the best players around. I played well, but unfortunately, I twisted my right knee, and had to spend the last 10 minutes or so of the game standing in the corner. We had used all our substitutes, which meant I couldn't come off.

I was barely able to walk, but someone had to stand beside me, so I kept one of the Offaly lads occupied. But I wasn't in good shape at all.

I had ruptured my cruciate ligament and damaged cartilage in the knee as well. Kevin came to me after the game and congratulated me on my performance. Even though I got injured, I felt I contributed significantly to the win. Getting over Offaly was a huge milestone for us. I don't recall there being a huge crowd at that one either, but by the time we got to the final four weeks later, Croke Park was full.

The momentum of the whole thing had changed in a really short space of time, both for us as a team, and for the supporters in terms of what they were seeing happen.

That game was pivotal for us, and also for me in terms of what happened after. I went to see a surgeon called Niall Mulvihill and was operated on in Cappagh about three weeks later. When I went in, he took a look at my right knee... my cruciate ligament had withered. Nowadays, you can do an MRI scan to find out what the problem is, but back then they had to cut you open and have a look. The way it worked was, once you were in there, they'd fix everything they could... to save you going back again. They removed some cartilage and tried to fix me up the best they could.

This is how things have change compared to now – I was in hospital for two weeks, and I was in plaster for six weeks. I was in hospital for the Leinster semi-final, and was back in the dugout for the final, but in plaster. That's a significant change from today, where you probably wouldn't be allowed in the dugout if you were injured... you'd be up in the stand.

For that year, even though I was injured, I felt a part of everything that went on.

I was studying Engineering in UCD, and I told my tutor that I wanted a job in Dublin because I was playing football. Prior to that I had been looking at jobs in England and around Europe.

What ended up happening was... I did a Masters in Engineering Science, which kept me in college for another year. All of that basically came out of the Offaly game and my desire to play for Dublin.

Leslie came on in that game and got a goal in the first-half, but what he's best remembered for is getting the winning point right at the end. I was standing in the corner on one leg, so I had a great view of it. Stephen Rooney knocked the ball away from one of the Offaly guys, and it came to Leslie via Brian Mullins.

I was standing quite close to him, probably hoping he wasn't going to pass to me! I needn't have worried, because he let fly with a shot from about 30 yards out on the Hogan Stand side and it sailed over the bar.

That was a huge point for us.

You could feel that everyone in the group knew we were on the brink of something. Sometimes when you're in a squad, one result or one training session can change everything. It's hard to put it into words, but there was a buzz around the squad, and the interest from the public fuelled that to a certain extent. Heffernan had our fitness levels through the roof, and we went after every team we played that year. The training had us fit enough to last the full game without any problems. We didn't have GPS trackers, but we were very fit and that gave us a huge advantage.

The training really was state-of-the-art for that time. I don't think the other teams were doing the same as we were. This was at a time when championship games lasted 80 minutes, so we really had to be in great shape to last. That really had an impact against Offaly, because I think they would have expected us to die… but we didn't.

Being out for the rest of the year was tough, but I was kept involved. I never felt marginalised or outside of things. Sometimes I feel that when lads are injured, they are almost forgotten about and ignored, not just in GAA but in other sports too.

The win over Offaly was a real springboard; that's why it's so significant for me and why I chose it. We went from being no-hopers before that game to winning an All-Ireland and competing at the highest level for most of the next 10 years. There were a couple of other games I could have picked… like the All-Ireland semi-final in 1977 or the Leinster final in '79 where I got a goal.

By then though, we expected to win every game. Prior to 1974, we hoped we might win. Once we beat Offaly, we knew we had as good a chance of winning a Leinster and then the All-Ireland.

One notable thing about that squad was there was a big age difference between a lot of us. I went in at 20… and Jimmy Keaveney and Paddy Cullen were 28 or 29. They were experienced guys, but they weren't really well-known, because Dublin hadn't won anything. I wouldn't even have known them, because I didn't go to Dublin matches. Plus, I think I was the first guy from Plunketts to play senior football for Dublin, so we weren't going along to watch someone from the club playing for the county. That's not to say I didn't go to Croke Park, but I would have gone to sell programmes… not to watch a match! We were really in the doldrums at that stage.

Getting back playing after the injury was difficult, but I played a good bit of the 1975 championship and started in the All-Ireland final. I marked Pat McCarthy and was taken off. I marked him again in 1976 and *he* was taken off!

I don't recall feeling much different when I came back than I did before the injury. I played until the winter of 1982, didn't play in the championship of '83… then played league in '84. In my mind, I always believed I was fine in terms of playing. But I was working at the time in Plattin outside Drogheda as a consultant engineer. I worked there from 1976 until '82, and I remember playing matches and going to work the next day, and I couldn't walk up the stairs. I had to go up the stairs sideways, because I couldn't bend my knee.

That made me realise I wasn't one hundred percent, even though I told myself I was. My last involvement with Dublin was that league in '84.

I was never dropped… I was just never told to come back!

I had an amazing time playing football. The group that I played with, we still go to Portugal every year. Football stopped me doing other stuff, but you can't do it all.

Once I started playing for Dublin, I basically did nothing else for six years. I didn't go on a holiday that I organised myself from 1974 to '79. We got a few All Star trips to the US… they were the only holidays I was on. The league started in October, so we were going pretty much all year.

When we went to the game in 1974, we went on our own steam. I walked up to the door at the back of the Nally Stand and knocked.

I used to drive down the New Cabra Road. I remember the change from the first time we went down the road against Wexford, when there was nobody there, to the Leinster final when the place was jammed. Everybody had flags, and to park the car and walk down among the crowd… it was an amazing experience.

The economy wasn't great at the time. When I finished my Masters, my tutor came to me and said he had a job for me as a cost engineer with a company on Upper Mount Street. I worked there for three months, then got a call that someone was after quitting down in Kerry, and they needed me down there in a hurry.

I went down around June or July of 1975. We were beaten in the All-Ireland final that year and I went back to Kerry on the Monday… because I wanted to get the abuse over with!

Jimmy Deenihan was a PE teacher down there, and I trained with him over the winter of '75. We'd run the golf course in Ballybunion, and we'd use the gym in the school. We were in there one night climbing the ropes and John O'Keeffe walked in.

He asked Jimmy, 'Who's that?'

Jimmy said, 'That's Bernard Brogan from Dublin'.

John just laughed… 'I hope we don't regret this, Jimmy!'

Jimmy introduced me to my wife too... to Maria, so the trip to Kerry was worth it!

We beat Offaly out of nowhere, and then played in six All-Ireland finals. You had lads who had been plugging away with Dublin and didn't even have a Leinster. I was involved in an All-Ireland in my first year, so I came along at the right time.

You couldn't write the script.

ALAN LARKIN

DUBLIN 2-11 CORK 1-8
All-Ireland SFC Semi-Final
Croke Park
AUGUST 11, 1974

Dublin's breakthrough 1974 All-Ireland winning team (with Alan Larkin second from right in the back row).

★ **DUBLIN:** P Cullen: G O'Driscoll, S Doherty, R Kelleher: P Reilly, **A Larkin**, G Wilson: B Mullins (1-1), S Rooney (0-1): B Doyle (0-2), T Hanahoe (0-1), D Hickey: J McCarthy (0-2), J Keaveney (0-4), A O'Toole (1-0). Sub: B Pocock for Wilson.

★ **CORK:** B Morgan: B Murphy, H Kelleher, D Hunt: K O'Sullivan, J Coleman, C Hartnett: D Long (0-1), D Coughlan: E Kirby, D Barron, D McCarthy: J Barry Murphy (1-2), R Cummins (0-4), J Barrett (0-1). Subs: M Doherty for Kirby, K Kehilly for O'Sullivan.

THE ACTION

DUBLIN MADE LIGHT of their rank outsiders tag when they trounced favourites Cork in front of 42,000 spectators at Croke Park. The Rebels came into the game as near-certainties to progress to their second successive All-Ireland final and defend the title they won in convincing fashion against Galway 12 months earlier.

Perhaps complacency got the better of the Leesiders, who had no answer to the power and fury of Dublin's play.

The Dubs got off to the ideal start with points from Jimmy Keaveney and Brian Mullins, and the latter's dominance at midfield alongside Stephen Rooney provided the platform for much of their success. Declan Barron was ploughing a lone furrow for Cork, but was well-shackled by Alan Larkin.

At the other end, John Coleman's physicality curbed Tony Hanahoe's influence to a certain extent, but Bobby Doyle and David Hickey were causing problems on the wings. Anton O'Toole had a glorious chance of a goal on the half-hour mark, but his shot was well-blocked by Brian Murphy. Dublin finished the half well, and points before the break from John McCarthy and Keaveney gave them a three-point interval lead (0-7 to 0-4).

Cork moved Barron to midfield in a bid to gain primary possession, but the switch made little difference. Billy Morgan made a wonderful save from Mullins early in the second-half, but shortly after he was powerless to prevent O'Toole finding the net as Dublin strengthened their grip on the game. Cork received a lifeline on 55 minutes when referee Patsy Devlin awarded a penalty when substitute Martin Doherty was fouled in the square, and Jimmy Barry Murphy fired the resultant kick into the left corner of the net.

In spite of that score, the expected rally from Cork never materialised and when Morgan fouled Keaveney with 14 minutes to go, Dublin were awarded a penalty of their own. Mullins made no mistake with his kick, which gave his side a six-point lead which they never relinquished.

Dublin advanced to their first All-Ireland final in 11 years.

★★★★★

66

AFTER THE DIVISION Two league final in 1974, where we were beaten by Kildare, we had a meeting in The Hollybrook Hotel. We'd been beaten by Louth in the Leinster Championship the previous season, so we knew something needed to change.

Kevin Heffernan got everyone in, and we were asked to make a commitment that we'd give it everything we had for the upcoming championship. In other words, lads were to look after themselves off the field… and train properly. Training would be hard, because the championship games were 40 minutes each half at the time. So, we were going from 60-minute games in the league to 80 minutes in the championship.

Heffo decided that peak fitness was going to be a massive requirement, especially for a team that wasn't playing outstanding football. We all made that commitment.

As it transpired, I got a call around April of that year to join a League of Ireland team… I had played a bit of soccer in the Civil Service and had come to the attention of some people in Home Farm. Dr Brendan Menton called me up asking would I consider playing with them. It was certainly of interest, but I told him that I'd already made a commitment to play with Dublin, but that if we got knocked out of the championship… whenever that was, that we could look at it again.

The upshot was that after the All-Ireland final that year he came back to me and asked me again. I had to say to him, 'I don't think I can walk away from this now'. The following year, Home Farm won the FAI Cup, which I was glad to see.

But to go back to the start of that season, we committed to training two nights a week in Parnell Park… then either training or playing a game on the Saturday morning or Sunday afternoon. That might not sound like much now, but for those who hadn't been used to a structured training regime, it was a bit of a challenge.

We had 25 originally selected in the squad… one had to step away due to illness, but aside from that I think we kept everyone. We didn't start the year off well at all. We were winning games but by objective standards, we were poor. What was helping us to win was our fitness. We were able to keep going in the last 20 minutes of games, when our opponents were wilting.

In that 1974 Leinster campaign, we beat Wexford comfortably.

Next up was Louth, and we obviously wanted to put the defeat from the previous year to bed. We won by five points, but the key to the year was really the Offaly game in the quarter-final. We were facing the reigning Leinster champions, and we needed to go out and perform. Fortune favours the brave.

We went out and had a go, got a bit of luck… and then there was an inspired substitution, when Les Deegan came on and got the winning point. We scraped through. However, that gave us a real sense of belief and confidence that things were going in the right direction.

In the semi-final, we had Kildare. They had beaten us in the league final, so that was another little edge we had that we wanted to make good on that, which we did.

It was Meath in the final, who were always tough opponents, but we managed to overcome them. That gave us a huge sense of achievement… we had done something that no Dublin team had done for a long time in winning a Leinster.

It had been nine years. At that stage, we had something to show for the year and anything after that was a bonus.

The pressure was off us going into the semi-final against Cork. There was a great spirit within the group, everyone was working hard for one another, and the determination was growing all the time.

One of the things that was introduced, which would be par for the course now, was a degree of self-reflection among the team…. looking back on the previous match, analysing the performance, the errors we made… where can we improve, all that kind of thing.

We'd discuss what we did well too, of course, but people had to be open to criticism, because it was criticism for the sake of improving the performance the next day. Heffo encouraged that. He might say a few words, but then he'd leave the room… it'd be left to us to toss around the various aspects of the game.

That was how we approached it and it definitely helped.

There was greater trust, because players were open and honest about their performances and any failings they may have had. When you combine that trust… the win over Offaly, atoning for previous defeats against Louth and Kildare, and then the crowning glory of a Leinster title… all of those things helped to really tighten the bond between those players. It meant that we were going into the semi-final against Cork feeling really good about ourselves.

For all that, we were massive underdogs for that game. I think some people got odds of 8/1 in the bookies. I know my brother would have a bet… and he got us at 4/1. Needless to say, Cork were odds-on.

Normally, on the day before a game, we'd have a little 15-minute practice match. It was just a kickaround really, the only purpose was to quell the butterflies in the stomach and just get lads thinking about the game. Part of it too would have been to kill a bit of time, because the eve of a game was always a time when you'd be nervous… and not really knowing what to do with yourself.

After we finished up and came in and showered, Heffo would come in and say a final few words. Then he'd head off, and we'd be left to it. Everyone would make their own contribution and commit to giving everything to the game… to the team.

When we walked out of Parnell Park that day, we felt like we were unbeatable. We couldn't wait to get out and take on Cork.

There were no team buses at that time… we'd arrive at Croke Park and park the cars off Clonliffe Road. We'd then walk across and congregate, waiting for everyone to arrive. Once all the players were accounted for, we'd make our way in through the gates.

We'd watch a bit of the minor game, and have a bit of a chat. That particular day, Paddy Cullen, who had befriended me when I first joined the panel, came over and asked me was I okay? I said I was fine.

Then he asked if I had been reading any papers. I said that I hadn't… which was in keeping with what I'd always done. I never read papers the week of a game, and I never gave interviews… not that anyone was asking me!

I'd wait until after games to read anything.

I knew something derogatory must have been said just from the way the guys were acting. They all seemed concerned about me. But I just ignored it, and didn't inquire about it. I was focused on going out and getting on with the game.

Two of the smallest men on our team were the wing-backs Paddy Reilly and George Wilson, and we knew we were going to be up against it with the Cork half-forward line, particularly Declan Barron, who won a couple of All-Star awards. It was always going to be very difficult to compete with them in the air. We knew Cork would kick the ball high into Declan as much as they could, so we discussed how I would try to spoil it and break it… so the lads could come in and pick up the loose ball.

That worked out well… the two lads were alert to that.

Later in the game our midfielders Brian Mullins and Stephen Rooney were playing so well that Cork had to bring Declan out to midfield, to try and win some ball there. I ended up marking Denis Coughlan, who came in on me from midfield.

At the end, there was just relief and joy that we had made it through. But that match was played on the 11th of August. The All-Ireland final was almost six weeks away!

We took a break for about two weeks and then came back, and started getting ready for the final. In that sense it was a bit different to most All-Ireland finals where you wouldn't have such a gap and you'd keep training right through. It worked out well because it gave us a little bit of time to recharge the batteries, relax and enjoy what had gone before… but not too much!

Unfortunately, RTÉ didn't deem the semi-final worthy of televising.

The Horse Show was on that weekend, and all available cameras were over in the RDS, with the exception of one little brownie. They managed to get some footage, but I don't think there's anything with the full game.

Tape back then was an expensive commodity, and often the reels would be used again. There was no such thing as downloading the recording and having it forever. As a result, a lot of stuff was missed which was a pity in some ways.

Somebody on the Sunday night then mentioned the newspaper article, and I said, 'Look, I'll read it tomorrow!'

The paper was at home… *The Sunday Independent.*

I picked it up on Monday morning. That was when I saw what had been written by their GAA writer at the time, Gerry McGuigan.

I am afraid the Achilles heel of the Dublin side is at centre half-back. Alan Larkin is not the ideal man for the job, and much of the time of Reilly and Wilson is taken up in covering off for the man in the middle, who tends to be caught out of position. Against

Declan Barron I would say Larkin will have his toughest ever test and may not come out with flying colours.

There was an accompanying picture of me with the caption…*ALAN LARKIN… Dublin weak link?* underneath. I was glad I hadn't read it before the game, because it certainly wouldn't bolster your confidence. But after the game, because I knew something bad had been written, I gave two fingers to the press box.

It wouldn't even have been noticed, but I just turned around out of frustration. It was something that obviously upset my friends on the team, so in turn it upset me. When I actually read it on the Monday, I wasn't too happy about it, but I felt that I had proved them wrong. As a team we had proved everyone wrong. But definitely the fact that I hadn't read anything before the game was a blessing.

Kevin Heffernan was manager of the team in 1972, when I made my debut for Dublin. He was gone then for the following season, but after we lost to Louth in a replay in 1973, Jimmy Gray (Dublin chairman) had the idea to bring Kevin back in as manager and bring two other selectors along with him. Those two selectors were Donal Colfer and Lorcan Redmond.

By all accounts, they weren't that well-known to Heffo at the time. Jimmy brought the three of them together. Heffo then called in his good friend Mickey Whelan. Mickey was in the States at the time, he was doing a Masters in physical education.

Mickey drew up a training plan which would have included gym work, and then carried through to the on-field stuff. Mickey was a very influential person in the set-up behind the scenes and gave a lot of good information to Heffo in terms of the physical preparation of the team.

We saw the changes very quickly when that management team came in.

We started doing a lot of indoor winter training, which consisted of what you'd call circuit training. Small groups at each station and moving around doing different exercises. That might not seem like a big thing now, but it was a big leap forward for us because it was a much more professional way of doing things and it replaced the haphazard approach of the previous years.

For example, in 1973, there was no real structure to things. I remember being asked to take training one night. Another player might have been asked to do it another night. There was no game plan… Heffo introduced that in the shape of a third midfielder, and also the roving centre-forward in Tony Hanahoe. These were things that were never done before.

As the championship progressed, we got the filmmaker Tiernan McBride to come to our games. Tiernan would go up to the back of the Hogan Stand and he'd have a camera with a wide-angle lens that would cover the whole pitch so you could see everything that was going on.

When we were doing our analysis of the games, we'd have his film on one screen… and we might also have clips of what RTÉ had shown. We focused more on our own game than the opposition, because what we were trying to do was minimise the mistakes that we made in previous games and see where we could improve our play.

Having that wide angle was great… you could see everything and there was no hiding place for anyone. It added to that open and honest environment for us, and there were plenty of forthright exchanges between the players. But you learned to accept that because it was all for the betterment of the team.

Heffo was brilliant at coming up with new ideas.

He was always open to things. If you look at Jim Gavin and Pat Gilroy, one of their key principles was that they wanted to empower the players and help them to be the best they could be. By doing that, you explain what you're looking for and how you expect players to perform. But the bottom line is that the players on the field are the only ones who can play the game… *They take charge.*

They take control.

Basically, as a manager, all you're trying to do is give your players some sense of a plan, and to have them anticipate certain things that might happen so the reaction is automatic rather than lads looking at each other perplexed. All of this started with Heffo.

When we won the All-Ireland in 1976, Heffo had taken up a role in the Middle East. All of a sudden, we had no manager. Rather than bringing someone in from the outside, we decided to keep the status quo… and Tony Hanahoe was moved up to the position of manager, as well as being captain. Donal Colfer took charge of training and co-ordinated all of that.

We were taking responsibility, but we were getting guidance from Tony, Donal and Lorcan. We were really just continuing on as we had been doing, with some small variations. As it was, that worked successfully because we won the All-Ireland again in 1977, and Tony became unique in management.

Getting back to the Cork game, it was a no-lose situation for us.

We'd done something that no Dublin team had done for almost 10 years in winning a Leinster. So, there was a degree of freedom about the semi-final… we could go out and have a go. If you look at where Cork were coming from… they had just hammered Kerry in the Munster final, they were defending All-Ireland champions.

They seemed almost invincible at that time.

Maybe they took us for granted a small bit, and they weren't prepared for the onslaught and didn't seem to know how to react. We started off at a fierce pace and kept it going right through to the end. I think that was what really flummoxed them… the intensity of the game. Eighty minutes is a long time, and there was no such thing as players going down and play being stopped for a few minutes while they received attention.

If you got hit, your immediate reaction was to get up and show that it hadn't affected you. Nowadays for some, it's an Oscar performance… as if they're doing a screen test for *Casualty*!

We ended up winning that game very comfortably, and a lot of that was, without a doubt, down to our fitness. That was one of the things that Mick O'Dwyer picked up on when he took charge of Kerry. He was driven to beat Dublin the following year and got rid of a lot of older players.

He brought in a new generation, who he thought he could get to a certain level of fitness so that it wouldn't be a consideration anymore when they came to play Dublin. A lot of teams then tried to do the same. Everyone had to get to that level of fitness that would allow them to compete physically with Dublin for 80 minutes.

I still remember coming out of Parnell Park the day before the Cork game. We didn't have great facilities. There was a little hut where we had all of our meetings… and when fellas were leaving, you could see them bouncing out the door.

We were really up for it.

Paddy Gogarty was a teammate of mine and often brought me to and from training, and the two of us were buzzing in the car on the way home. There was a great expectation that we could really do something here and do ourselves justice.

There were 24 of us on the panel, and ninety percent of the lads would contribute to the conversation. Everyone was encouraged to speak, especially the lads on the bench because they were the ones looking on… *They saw everything!* I look at some guys on the bench that day and a lot of them went into management in the county.

We had a highly intelligent group of players, who understood what was needed. We had a huge self-belief, and everyone had confidence in the guys around them. Heffo used to say… and this always stuck with me… *One third of the team will play above themselves, one third will perform as we expect… And one third will struggle.* But if those five lads who are struggling keep going and keep fighting, it encourages those around them.

I used to say that to the underage teams that I managed. At the end of a game, I'd ask… 'Which third do you think won the game for you?' They'd be looking at each other, thinking… *This is a trick question!*

And I suppose it was. The answer though, to my mind, was the lads who were struggling but who were still working hard. It might only take one interception, or one block from a lad who is being beaten up a stick by his man, that can turn a game.

That sums up the attitude within that Dublin team, because nobody can perform well every day. We're amateurs, so you can't expect that… but what you can expect is for everyone to give one hundred percent.

I had played corner-back in the National League of 1974.

Pat O'Neill was centre-back most of the time. But then Pat was unwell for a period, so I was tried there, and I must have done okay. One of my first games there was in the Corn na Casca game which was a fundraiser for the Dublin schools. We played Sligo and I was marking Mickey Kearins… and the GAA had just introduced the personal foul rule.

I became one of the first to fall foul of the new rule, and got my marching orders. You could get sent off before that, but you would have had to strike someone or do something really dangerous.

But then, you see incidents like what happened in the 1975 Munster final when Páidí Ó Sé decks Dinny Allen… and the ref tells them to shake hands and off they go!

The ref in that Corn na Casca game was a Brother Frawley, and he was the first one to apply the rules. Unfortunately, I was on the wrong end! That was the only time I was sent off in my career, which someone once commented was some achievement, because I wouldn't have been a wilting flower.

I would say I was *robust*.

Awards wouldn't have been a big deal for me, but I was nominated for an All Star later that season… but was ruled out because I had been sent off in that game.

Nonetheless, I finished that season with Leinster and All-Ireland medals. Not bad for a fella who was the *Achilles heel!*

99

PADDY CULLEN

DUBLIN 0-14 GALWAY 1-6
All-Ireland SFC Final
Croke Park
SEPTEMBER 22, 1974

Paddy Cullen brilliantly turns the penalty from Galway's Liam Sammon around the post in the historic 1974 All-Ireland final victory.

★ **DUBLIN:** P Cullen; G O'Driscoll, S Doherty, R Kelleher; P O'Reilly, A Larkin, G Wilson; B Mullins (0-2), S Rooney; B Doyle, T Hanahoe, D Hickey (0-2); J McCarthy (0-1), J Keaveney (0-8), A O'Toole (0-1).

★ **GALWAY:** G Mitchell; J Waldron, J Cosgrave, B Colleran; L O'Neill, TJ Gilmore, J Hughes (0-1); W Joyce, M Rooney (1-1); T Naughton (0-2), J Duggan (0-1), P Sands; C McDonagh, L Sammon, J Tobin (0-1).

THE ACTION

PADDY CULLEN WAS the hero for Dublin as they bridged an 11-year gap to reclaim the All-Ireland title in front of their delirious supporters at Croke Park. Galway couldn't complain about suffering their third final defeat in four years, as they had no answer to Dublin's brilliant second-half performance. Indeed, the final margin of victory for Kevin Heffernan's men could have been far greater.

It's worth noting how far Dublin has come. This, remember, was a Dublin team who lost a Division Two final to Kildare earlier in the season and not many people would have backed them to even win a Leinster Championship, much less the All-Ireland.

Galway, on the other hand, had been so close so often in previous seasons. Perhaps that cumulative pressure got to the Connacht champions, who never looked comfortable and underperformed badly... in stark contrast to their opponents' freedom of movement. The Dublin forwards interchanged positions on a regular basis, which often appeared to cause confusion in the Galway defence.

For all that, things were looking reasonably good for the Tribesmen at half-time. Aided by Michael Rooney's 31st minute goal, they led at the break. Jimmy Keaveney made it a one-point game just after the resumption, and the key moment of the match arrived soon after.

Referee Patsy Devlin awarded a penalty after Liam Sammon was fouled, and Sammon himself stepped up to take the kick. He put it to Cullen's left, but the Dublin keeper reacted brilliantly to touch the ball around the post for an inconsequential '50'.

That save seemed to inspire the Dubs, who played with a pace and verve that their more fancied opponents just couldn't match. Keaveney kicked scores off left and right, Bobby Doyle popped up all over the field, while Stephen Rooney and Brian Mullins dominated around the middle. Allied to that was the fact that Dublin only conceded two points, and only one from play, in the entire second-half, with captain Seán Doherty imperious at full-back.

★★★★★

66

THE MOST EXCITING win is the first. You only ever win something for the first time once, and we just came along at the right time. Whatever happened to our team at that time, it just came together.

Kevin Heffernan was a major factor in that because he was plucking guys from all over the place. I was with a junior club, and we had three or four others who were also playing junior football at the time. We were made up of a lot of different clubs. Anton O'Toole, Lord rest him, was just plucked from relative obscurity. Some might have said he had an unconventional style, but Heffernan saw something in him, and he turned out to be a fantastic player for us.

We had the backbone of a few St Vincent's lads in fairness, but there was a good spread of players from around the county. It was great that we could gel. He selected very large lads too. We had a lot of tall, strong men in that team. Even though we had a few smaller men like Paddy O'Reilly and George Wilson, in general we were a big team.

We'd lost to Kildare in a Division Two league final in 1974, and we were all down in the dumps because we thought we were getting somewhere. Heffo got us all together in a hotel in Clontarf after that. It was a miserable enough evening because nobody was smiling or laughing.

Groups of lads were getting together and the general feeling was... *We can't keep going like this...we have to break through.* Heffo knew we all wanted to turn things around, so when we were done talking amongst ourselves, he sat us all down. He basically told us that we were going to be taking this thing really seriously from now on, and that it was going to take up a lot of our time. If anyone was unwilling or unable to commit to the Dublin cause, then that was the time to say it, and there'd be no hard feelings. That was the simple message!

For those who wanted to stay, Kevin said that the management group were going to get us fit enough to go for 80 minutes, which was how long championship games lasted in those days. We knew from that night on that we were going to be in real trouble in training!

In previous years, we'd have run around and done a few laps, done a few press-ups and jumped in the shower. It was a bit of a joke. You wouldn't call it training at all. There was no real plan, but then that was what every team was doing at that stage. But in 1974, Heffo had car tyres out and we were running in and out of those.

We'd be going over and under ropes. Exercises that we had never seen before. He'd have us doing sprints in groups of three and four, then he'd swap us around. This was *real* stuff. You got into the shower afterwards and you were wrecked. He brought us to a level of fitness that other teams couldn't live with.

We kept going when our opponents didn't.

Heffo used to also get the games filmed, so he could pick things out after and ask lads… 'What were you doing there?' It was a brilliant idea, because we were able to see it ourselves. Even with the Mikey Sheehy goal in 1978, Seán Doherty and two other lads were walking back, and they swore blind in the dressing-room after that they were covering fellas!

I was like… 'Hang on lads, you're there on camera strolling along!'

We had our little hut in Parnell Park too, which was basically an open forum. Kevin would turn to me and say, 'Right Paddy, what do you think about this?'… on whatever the subject was. I was outgoing, so I didn't mind talking up, but a lot of fellas would be shy and wouldn't be that comfortable talking, even in front of their own teammates.

We had a fair few arguments, too!

We played Derry in the semi-final in 1975, and the arrangement we had was that if I left my goal area, someone else would get back into it, if they could. A Derry player came in along the end-line, and I had to go out to him to try to close him down, because he had beaten his man.

He handpassed the ball across the goal, and I couldn't block it, but I was full sure there'd be someone covering me in the square.

I was wrong… the full-forward got it and stuck it in the net. I had a big row with Heffo after because he was asking me what I came out for? I said that I *had* to come out. The argument went on for a few minutes and in the end I said, 'You weren't a goalkeeper anyway, so what would you know about it!' He got you riled up, but he loved that. He wanted to see lads standing up to him and fighting their corner.

As a keeper, I had to make spilt-second decisions. If you thought about something for a second, you were *gone*. If you decided to go, you had to go one hundred percent.

In 1977 we were caught with everyone up the field and Mikey Sheehy was in behind on his own. I came off my line as quickly as I could, and he played it on the ground. I just about got my studs on the ball… it went just outside the post.

I was well out of my goal, but if I didn't go, Mikey Sheehy would have put it by me no problem. After that game, Kevin said, 'Well, you were right to come out there!'… which was as close to a compliment as I was going to get!

Kevin had Lorcan Redmond and Donal Colfer with him as selectors… lovely blokes and excellent men. Quiet. Heffernan did all the talking, but when the three of them got together it was serious stuff. They were so smart… they knew what football was all about. They scoured the county and a lot of lads came and went during that time, a lot of good men who just didn't fit in with what the three lads wanted.

My first year on the panel was 1967.

At the back end of 1966, about a week before that year's All-Ireland final, I was called in for a challenge match in Parnell Park. There were a good few of the victorious 1963 team still around then. John Timmons was full-forward, but he got the flu. I got a call two days before the game asking me would I come in and play full-forward. I nearly had a heart attack! But I said I would.

I was only on the pitch about 10 minutes when I went for a ball and stepped into this hole in the ground and snapped my ankle. That kept me out for a few months.

When I got back fit, Dublin were looking for a goalkeeper. Keaveney reckons he got me in… we knew each other since we were kids, but I don't believe that!

I played in goals for the soccer team in the company that I worked for in East Wall. We were in the AUL at the time. I used to play soccer on a Saturday and gaelic on a Sunday. One of the lads in O'Connell's Boys said to me, 'I think you're going to get called in. Would you do me a favour and give up the soccer for a few weeks? This could be a chance to get in as goalie for Dublin'.

I think they were going through a few goalkeepers at the time. I was called up… I got a little card in the post asking me to bring my boots to Croke Park, basically!

This was for the Corn na Casca game on Easter Sunday against Galway. I knew Croke Park inside out, but only from going through the turnstiles. I had no idea where the players went. I turned up and banged on a few doors, until someone answered.

'I'm due to play for Dublin today,' I told him.

He looked at me funny, but he let me in and told me where to go. I walked into a room full of lads with All-Ireland medals, which was pretty daunting.

There was a trip to New York for the winners. Back then, that was as good as going to the moon! Unfortunately, it didn't happen. We lost by two points. No goals though! So, a clean sheet… but no trip to New York.

I played against Westmeath in that year's Leinster Championship, which didn't go to plan. At one stage in the game, I came out for a long ball. At the last minute I realised I'd misjudged it slightly. Next thing… the ball was in the net. We lost and I thought that was the end of me, but they left me there and I got away with it.

The Ban (Rule 27) was still around at this time remember, and the fact that I had played soccer didn't go down well with certain people. Some of the County Board lads lost their heads. They'd nearly be asking… 'What the hell is that fella doing here? He's playing soccer.' It was a load of bulls**t.

You tell your kids to get out and play sport. It doesn't matter what it is. That talk died down quickly enough because I was committed to the Dublin team.

In 1974, we gradually improved. We started badly against Wexford in the first round. It was dreadful. I don't know if we were just shaky or what it was.

When I started playing in 1967, we were beaten by Westmeath.

Longford beat us in '68. Things like that were happening every year. But in 1974, you could see a bit of light at the end of the tunnel with the way Heffo was approaching things. The game that changed everything for that team was the win over Offaly, who were Leinster champions at the time. Leslie Deegan, one of our great players, got the winning point from about 40 metres.

Stephen Rooney in the middle of the park came in and blocked one of the Offaly fellas, and it bounced into Leslie's arms. I remember it well because I was standing up at the other end with my heart in my mouth. The scores were level… time was nearly up. I could see the shot turning, and I was nearly turning the imaginary wheel myself… willing it to go over! The kickout came and the game was over. That was a huge win… it felt like a weight had been lifted off our backs and we were making real progress. We went on from there and won Leinster.

We took on a Cork team in the semi-final that should have won two or three All-Irelands on the trot. They were a super team. I mean, my God… when you read through that Cork team, they were all really top-class and established. It was our speed that day that got the better of them. We were delighted to have a Leinster title, but we were determined to give Cork a good go. We chased them down and hunted in packs. Every time they got a ball, there were two or three Dublin shirts around them.

We were so fit, and there were little things that we did which mightn't have been seen before. Bobby Doyle was rambling in and around midfield, and picking up loose ball and pulling lads out of position. Hanahoe was pulling out of the middle and leaving space for the ball to be popped in to Keaveney.

It all came together against Cork, and I think they were caught by us. I don't think that they really believed that we could beat them. They should have won much more than they did, and that defeat finished them really, because a bunch of whippersnappers from Kerry came along the following year!

When Cork won the All-Ireland in 1973, they were the team going to America to play the All Stars. But because Billy Morgan was the Cork keeper and also an All Star winner, I was asked to go to be goalkeeper for the All Stars. I was only delighted! We got lovely green blazers with a crest on it… and we went to New York, LA and San Francisco. It was magic. I couldn't believe I was going to America. It was a great trip and I got to know the Cork lads really well, and the Galway lads. You got to know fellas that otherwise you'd never get to know. It was wonderful.

All the lads were taking penalties on me.

'Go on Cullen, stand in the goal there!' We'd have a training session and then after it the lads would all hit a few penalties. In the final of 1974, I saved a penalty from Liam Sammon. There was a suggestion after the game that I had made a note of what he did when he took a penalty on me in training on the All Stars trip. That's not quite true.

He had taken penalties on me, but I didn't pay any attention to where he put them. I'm sure he took several on that trip, as plenty of others did. My theory in facing penalties in gaelic football and soccer is that you don't move until the ball is kicked… because you have a chance once you see which way it's going.

I used to step out of the goal.

I'd let the player put the ball down, and then lift his head and see an empty goal. Then, I walked into the middle… and he sees a 6'2" man standing there. All of a sudden, things look a lot different.

I put a little worry into their heads.

Liam hit a good penalty to my left. I had taken maybe a half-step to the right, but I was just about able to react. The ball wasn't along the ground, and I managed to get a bit of my little finger and a piece of my palm to it.

I still thought for a second it was going in, because I was looking at it all the way. It went just past the post. I couldn't believe it.

I made a few saves in the second-half and got Man of the Match in a few of the papers, but the ball was hitting me on the knee and things like that. It was just one of those days. I was involved quite a lot… which is never great!

I don't know where my defenders were! The game was quite open and fast, so there were a lot of chances.

I conceded a goal in the first-half. It was a long ball into the square which was punched in by Michael Rooney. It was sent across the square and he put it to one side of me. He was covered well by our backs, so I'm going to say it wasn't a ball for me to come out for. I'm defending myself there!

He was just in front of one of our lads and got a good punch on it. We were two down at half-time, got one back at the start of the second-half… and then came the penalty save. I'm not blowing my own trumpet here, but if Galway had scored that, it would have put them four in front. I think that miss derailed them a little.

It's amazing what happens when you miss a penalty.

I saw that first-hand in 1992 when Charlie Redmond missed that penalty against Donegal in the All-Ireland final. It was early in the game, and we were flying. It would have given us a four-point lead inside 10 minutes. Something *happened* then. The little quiver came into the team, I still haven't figured it out to this day.

You have to take it on the chin because you can't do anything about it.

Missing that penalty seemed to effect Galway. We were brilliant from that point on and went on to kick some fantastic scores. Jimmy Keaveney gave an exhibition.

It was an unbelievable feeling to win. You have to remember that in the late-60s, you could hear the birds singing in Croke Park when we played. There were so few people following us. I often think back to the first game that year against Wexford in 1974. Someone had a big banner… DUBLIN FOR THE CUP.

That seemed miles off. But as we went through Leinster, bit by bit more people came out. After we won the final, I mean… wow! The town went mad. It's very hard to put into words what that 1974 team did for us… for everyone. The euphoria after we won was incredible… *incredible*. We were back in the hotel after the game, and there were people trying to climb in these tiny windows! The place was jammed, and it was hectic for a good few months afterwards. We were going around with the cup to all the schools. It was great.

When we won the All-Ireland, me and Seán Doherty left Croke Park with the Sam Maguire in the boot of his car. On the way out of town, we stopped at the house of the accountant in the company I worked for at the time, because we were passing on our way to the Blue Haven pub.

We left Sam on the step and rang the bell. He came out and nearly had a canary! He couldn't believe it.

I would walk up to Croke Park back then… walk to the game with the supporters. It was only when we got posh that we arrived on a bus. I was going in for years and people would be talking to me on the way. Everyone was the same.

All of us were making our way to Croke Park on our own steam. Everyone knew us… they'd talk to us, asking us questions.

Different times… *magical times*.

99

ROBBIE KELLEHER

DUBLIN 3-12 KERRY 1-13
All-Ireland SFC Semi-Final
Croke Park
AUGUST 21, 1977

Robbie Kelleher (second from right in the front row) before the All-Ireland final victory over Armagh in 1977, but the semi-final that same year was the 'Game of his Life'.

★ **DUBLIN:** P Cullen; G O'Driscoll, S Doherty, **R Kelleher**; T Drumm, K Moran, P O'Neill: B Mullins, F Ryder: A O'Toole (0-4), T Hanahoe (0-3), D Hickey (1-1); B Doyle (0-1), J Keaveney (0-3), J McCarthy (1-0). Subs: B Brogan (1-0) for Ryder, P Gogarty for McCarthy.

★ **KERRY:** P O'Mahoney: J Deenihan, J. O'Keeffe, G. O'Keeffe (0-1); D Moran, T Kennelly, G Power; P Ó Sé, J O'Shea; J Egan (0-2), P Lynch (0-1), P Spillane; B Walsh, S Walsh (1-2), M Sheehy (0-7). Subs: T Doyle for B Walsh, P McCarthy for O'Shea.

THE ACTION

FOLLOWING ONE WIN apiece in their two previous championship meetings, Kerry and Dublin went head-to-head once again in what was an All-Ireland final in all but name. This eagerly-awaited third instalment promised much and delivered even more.

For much of the second-half, Kerry looked to be cruising comfortably to another All-Ireland final. Dublin had spurned several goal chances, notably Jimmy Keaveney's miss in the game's opening moments, and it looked like that inaccuracy would prove costly.

A crowd of 54,974 (a record for a semi-final in the televised era) were kept on the edge of their seats throughout as an epic tug-of-war unfolded in front of them. Seán Walsh's goal on 22 minutes helped his side to a 1-6 to 0-6 lead at the break. But Dublin began a frenetic second-half in perfect fashion.

Tony Hanahoe got on the end of a loose ball inside the Kerry square, and the ball broke from his grasp into the waiting arms of John McCarthy, who finished from close range to level things up. It was nip and tuck for much of the next 20 minutes. Anton O'Toole was superb for Dublin throughout, with Brian Mullins dominating the midfield exchanges. Kerry rallied to go two up, but Dublin hit back and David Hickey's punched effort tied up the scores again with 14 minutes left. When Hanahoe gave his side the lead, it looked like the momentum was with Dublin, but again Kerry responded. Seán Walsh clipped over a point from a seemingly impossible angle, before Bobby Doyle and Paudie Lynch swapped scores within a minute as the game sped towards its dramatic crescendo. Mikey Sheehy and John Egan kicked defiant points which looked like deciding the contest with 10 minutes left. Kerry now led by two, but would not score again as Dublin surged to the finish line.

First, O'Toole's delivery was punched into the path of Hanahoe by John O'Keeffe. The Dublin centre-forward fed Hickey, who buried the ball to the roof of the net. Moments later, Hanahoe was again instrumental. This time he fed Bernard Brogan, who galloped through from 25 yards out and finished to the net from close range.

Fittingly, Hanahoe added the final gloss on a superb individual performance with the last point of the game.

★★★★★

66

THERE WERE PROBABLY three games in contention for me when I think back to the days that stand out from my career. The 1974 final, because it was my first All-Ireland final win, and the '76 final, because we took revenge on Kerry after losing the previous year. On a personal level though, it has to be the 1977 semi.

I got married the weekend before in San Francisco and had been out there for two weeks before the wedding. I arrived back on the Wednesday morning before the game, and Donal Colfer brought me out to Parnell Park a few times to see what kind of shape I was in, but I'd kept myself in good nick while I was out there.

The wedding was on August 13, and the Leinster final had been on July 31. I headed off straightaway after the Leinster final and got married. It was a fairly short honeymoon! When we were flying back, the first leg was San Francisco to New York. We got off the plane, and everyone in the airport was crying. We went up to the bar and asked the barman what had happened?

'Elvis has died.'

So that's why everyone was so upset. I met my wife on an All-Stars trip. She's a born and bred San Franciscan, albeit her parents are Irish. We met out there after Dublin won the All-Ireland in 1974.

The match in 1977 was regarded for a long time as one of the best ever played, though looking back on it now, I'm not sure many people would say that, given the number of balls that were kicked wide and over the sideline. But every game is of its time, and that game was regarded as an all-time classic.

What made it so dramatic was that we were five behind at one stage and two down with 10 minutes to go… then we got two goals. David Hickey got the first, which put us one up. What you won't see on the highlights is that I got a short free off Kevin Moran in between those two goals, went up field and had a shot. It went about 50 yards wide!

I got forward a bit, but corner-backs wouldn't have attacked much in those days compared to now. I stayed back to cover Paddy Cullen as much as possible, although he would probably say I didn't do much for him for the famous Mikey Sheehy goal in 1978!

We were playing golf down in Lahinch one day, and the fourth hole has a big mound in the middle. On busy days, there's a guy standing at the top of the mound to tell you when it's safe to play.

We were playing it and this guy waved his green flag for us to hit away. Then he came running down the mound and comes up to me.

'Are you Robbie Kelleher?'

'I am!' He was complimenting me on my golf and sure I was only delighted at this. Then, just before he turned to go, he said, 'You're the guy who handed the ball to Mikey Sheehy, aren't you?' I came home and said to my wife that whatever we put on the tombstone about loving father and caring husband, we'll also have to include… *The man who handed the ball to Mikey Sheehy!* If I'm remembered for nothing else, I'll always have that!

I had been there in 1974. There is a bit of a myth with some people that Kevin Heffernan came out of nowhere that year, but he'd been there for a few years before that. Jimmy Gray was the chairman of the County Board at the time, and he never gets the credit he deserves. The County Board used to meet, and choose the selectors for the year ahead.

The manager didn't get to pick them. But Jimmy went to Kevin in '74 and said to him that he was free to pick his own selectors… so Kevin got Lorcan Redmond and Donal Colfer. Mickey Whelan also deserves credit, because he was in the background framing all the training. I'm not au fait with modern training techniques, but I believe that's where modern training started. The SAQ stuff… Speed Agility Quickness. We used to train on a Saturday morning, and it'd be all ball work, which was new. The training was really designed to make you think, which was also different. So, while '74 wasn't Kevin's first year involved, it was a year when a lot of things changed.

We played five games to win Leinster that year, and that was without any replays. I'm not sure that has been done since. Beating Offaly was the big breakthrough. We played Cork in the semi-final, and Jimmy Keaveney used to be great friends with Billy Morgan. One night we were in the little hut in Parnell Park and Jimmy told us a story.

He said he had been down visiting Billy in Cork, and Billy opened this little press under the stairs… and there was the Sam Maguire Cup. Billy said to Jimmy, 'Take a good look at it, because that's the closest you'll ever get to it!'

I've never seen a team as over-confident in my life as Cork were for that semi in 1974. They thought they only had to turn up.

I had played in four Leinster Championships... 1970, '71, '72 and '73. We won two matches in those four years. The only teams we beat in that time were Wexford and Westmeath. We were really in a terrible state. It was pretty much the same team that won the All-Ireland in '74.

Now, the one addition – and it was a hell of an addition – was Brian Mullins. But most of the rest of us had been around for a few years at that stage.

When we played the opening round in Leinster against Wexford in 1974, it was the curtain-raiser to the National League final between Kerry and Roscommon. We beat Wexford, though not very convincingly. The following Tuesday I pulled up in Parnell Park for training. A car pulled up alongside me and Jimmy Keaveney got out of one side and Leslie Deegan the other.

It was hard to tell who had the bigger belly! I nearly put my gear back in the car because I was thinking... *If we're reduced to this, we've no chance!* But both of them went on to be hugely important. Deegan got a goal and the winning point when we beat Offaly, and Jimmy Keaveney was... *Well, Jimmy Keaveney!*

When we beat Kerry in 1976, that was the end of a big hoodoo for Heffo. He had lost several times to them as a player, and then we thought we had them in '75, but they turned us over that day too. That was a real shock to the system. Finally, we beat them in 1976. That was the big monkey off his back, and I remember we all went down to the Gresham Hotel a few weeks after that final.

I assumed it was just a pre-season meeting to get our focus back after celebrating for a few weeks. Kevin walked in and he said he was going... and he went. I was amazed. We had just won the All-Ireland, and the league was starting up soon. But I think getting that victory over Kerry was a huge thing for him, and he decided it was time to step down.

I won't say there was only one man to take over, but it would have been very difficult for someone from the outside to come in and be accepted. So, Tony Hanahoe came in as player-manager. You might think it was difficult for Tony to go from being a teammate to manager, but it wasn't really like that at all. We were a very mature team, and the relationship between the players and Kevin was a mature one. What I mean by that is, there was no doubt who was in charge, but it wasn't a schoolmaster-pupil relationship. If you look at the team, the vast majority were very successful in their own right both at the time and in terms of the careers they pursued since. That kind of relationship was there anyway, and Tony did a great job combining playing and managing.

Donal and Lorcan stayed on, which gave us great continuity. It was a seamless transition. I would also say that if you asked any of the players who they would have wanted to step in from that team… they would have said Tony. He was the obvious choice in many ways.

The training sessions were on Tuesday and Thursday, which was all the physical stuff. Saturday was all football. I was working in the Central Bank in Fitzwilton House on Leeson Street Bridge at the time. I'd start work at nine o'clock. On the days we weren't training, I'd go back home to Stillorgan at lunchtime and go for a run around Belfield. I'd arrive back in work about half two! Home at five o'clock!

You wouldn't get away with it now.

By the time 1977 came around, the Dublin-Kerry rivalry had grown. It was the third year in-a-row that we had played each other. I was marking Barry Walsh, who I think was taken off at half-time and Tommy Doyle came on.

There wouldn't really have been a whole lot of switching going on back then. I'd have gone into my corner and picked up whoever came in. I don't ever remember being switched, though I remember being taken off a few times alright! Myself and Gay O'Driscoll wouldn't have swapped over, ever, as far as I can remember.

I had a good game that day, apart from missing that point! Heffo came into the dressing-room afterwards and told me it was the best game I'd ever played for Dublin, which was fantastic to hear given I'd only arrived back in the country on the Wednesday morning. I don't really know if the management were considering not starting me, but I was certainly expecting to play. I had trained quite a bit while I was in San Francisco, and as I said, I minded myself.

Before heading off, I've a memory of telling Tony in Parnell Park one night before the Leinster final that I'd be flying out straight after it. I don't remember him trying to talk me out of it, but he could hardly have told me I couldn't go either, I suppose. Once I got back and Donal put me through my paces and deemed that I was ready to go, then I was always going to be starting.

It was a very exciting game; the skill-level mightn't be what it is today, but the crowd certainly enjoyed it. Croke Park was heaving. I remember one incident in the second-half when John Egan was running through and Gay O'Driscoll – my God, Gayo was a tough man – absolutely milled John.

John hit the ground, got up, and kicked the ball over the bar. That put them two points up and I thought we were nearly gone at that stage. But shortly after that, David Hickey got the goal.

Before games, I wouldn't say I was relaxed, but I had the right degree of nerves. Heffo always said that if you weren't nervous before a game then there was something wrong. Before I got married in 1977, I lived in Clontarf. I used to go down to St Anne's Park for a walk with the dog on the morning of a game and visualise that first ball. That was my process. I'd imagine arriving for that first ball at the same time as my man and… BANG! We hear a lot about visualisation now, but that was going on back then.

We didn't have a sports psychologist, but Heffo was a psychologist, nutritionist and manager all rolled into one.

Hanahoe did the talking at half-time once he took over. Donal and Lorcan wouldn't say much. Over time, he invited Kevin to come back and take an odd training session, but of course Kevin couldn't stay away and ended up coming back into the fold in the subsequent years. The winning of that game was essentially the winning of the All-Ireland. We beat Armagh comfortably in the final.

Ourselves and Kerry were dominant for those few years and nobody else could really get close to us. That win in 1977 really put the defeat of '75 to bed. That was a real slap in the face for us and we were probably a little overconfident, like Cork were in 1974.

I was on the bench in 1979. I broke my leg in a challenge match with the club at the beginning of that year. I was 28 at the time and was back playing by around May or June, but I wasn't deemed to be sufficiently recovered to start. We were hammered by Kerry in the All-Ireland final that year and a whole host of lads retired… so I did likewise.

I subsequently got a call from Heffo asking would I come back in, and I said I would. I played two more seasons and retired in 1981. By then, Offaly were starting to come good… they beat us in the 1980 Leinster final. In 1981 we lost to Laois, and it was time to say goodbye. I was only 30, but I had been playing for 12 years. I'd had enough. We played Wicklow in the Leinster quarter-final in 1981 and won by just two points.

John O'Leary was in goals by then and, at one stage, a Wicklow player came through the middle and took a shot… and John made a great save. I remember thinking to myself… *Well f**k you John, I'll have to go back out training on Tuesday night!*

When you start thinking like that, it's time to go.

TOMMY DRUMM
(& KIERAN DUFF)

DUBLIN 4-15 CORK 2-10
All-Ireland SFC Semi-Final Replay
Páirc Uí Chaoimh
AUGUST 28, 1983

Tommy Drumm and Cork captain Christy Ryan shake hands before Dublin's magnificent All-Ireland semi-final replay victory in Páirc Uí Chaoimh in 1983.

★ **DUBLIN:** J O'Leary; M Holden, G Hargan, R Hazley; P Canavan, **T Drumm**, PJ Buckley; J Ronayne (0-1), B Mullins (1-0); J Caffrey (0-1), T Conroy (0-2), **K Duff (1-3)**; B Rock (1-4), A O'Toole (0-1), J McNally (1-3). Sub: J Kearns for Caffrey.

★ **CORK:** M Creedon; M Healy, K Kehilly, J Evans; M Hannon, C Ryan, J Kerrigan (0-1); D Creedon, C Corrigan; T Murphy (0-1), E O'Mahony, D Barry (2-1); D Allen, J Allen, J Cleary (0-7). Subs: M Burns for Hannon, T O'Reilly for O'Mahony, E Fitzgerald for T Murphy.

THE ACTION

HAVING HAD VICTORY snatched away from them at Croke Park a week earlier, Cork welcomed Dublin – and their army of travelling fans – to the banks of the Lee for this All-Ireland semi-final replay. Nobody among the media experts seemed to be able to settle conclusively on a winner.

Some felt home advantage would tip things in Cork's favour, while others felt that the pressure of playing in front of their own fans would upset the Rebels. Whether or not the latter was true is hard to say, but what can be said for certain is that Dublin dished out an almighty hammering in the Páirc Uí Chaoimh sunshine.

It was clear from the off that Dublin were determined to make amends for their lacklustre performance in the drawn game, when they needed Barney Rock's late goal to rescue them. Kevin Heffernan and his backroom team obviously learned a lot about Cork in Croke Park, and they put that knowledge to good use, establishing an early lead which they never relinquished.

Kieran Duff opened the scoring after 30 seconds, and Dublin's early dominance paid further dividends inside three minutes. Barney Rock was hauled down by Cork 'keeper Michael Creedon, and Brian Mullins dispatched a low penalty to Creedon's right. Dublin were off! A free-flowing first-half saw Duff, John Caffrey and Joe McNally kick some beautiful scores to help their side to a five-point (1-7 to 0-5) interval lead.

When Dave Barry converted a Cork penalty early in the second-half to cut the gap to two, it looked like another epic tussle was in prospect, but that was as close as the hosts got. Moments later, Duff was allowed carry the ball unchallenged for 30 metres before slotting it low to the net. That made it 2-10 to 1-7, and the game was effectively over. Barry's second goal did cut the gap to four in the 63rd minute, but his muted celebration indicated that even he felt it was a mere consolation. Keeping their foot firmly on Cork's throat, Dublin again hit back immediately via Barney Rock's goal, before Joe McNally's soccer-style finish prompted a mini-pitch-invasion from the travelling Dubs' supporters. A happy away day for fans and players alike, and a first All-Ireland final since 1979.

★★★★★

66

THERE AREN'T MANY games where everything clicks, and that was a game where everything *clicked* for us. The atmosphere down in Cork was just incredible. Something that would seem unbelievable now is that the game wasn't televised. The GAA had a big debate about it and decided that they would just show highlights that night.

There was a big debate after the drawn game about where the replay would be staged. Cork wanted it in Páirc Uí Chaoimh, but there had only ever been one All-Ireland semi-final played outside of Croke Park, and that was in 1941 during the war. It was quite unusual in that regard, and it was quite unusual for us to stay overnight for a game, which we did on that occasion.

I'll never forget it… we went down and stayed in Blarney, so we had quite a good bonding session the afternoon and the evening before. A few of the lads went off and had a couple of pints. Kevin Heffernan was good that way, he wasn't overbearing. Most of us stayed around the hotel.

We had a team meeting in the evening, then got up the next morning and had breakfast together. So, the preparation was quite unusual… it was new to us.

I lived in Whitehall at the time, and going down to Croke Park was no big deal… you jumped on the bus to Drumcondra and walked in. It was all so ordinary. Travelling down on the bus to Cork, having the banter, staying overnight… that elevated it into a bit of an occasion.

The first game was interesting, because we had no right to draw it. We should have been beaten by Cork without a shadow of a doubt. They were the far superior team. The goal we got to level it was remarkable.

Brian Mullins played a ball to Ray Hazley on the left wing… he was up from corner-back. Barney Rock was waving furiously for the ball inside the square. Ray played the ball between two Cork defenders with the outside of his boot like he was threading a needle, and Barney stuck it away.

That was a really deflating outcome for Cork. We had played them twice that year in challenge matches… once in Páirc Uí Chaoimh and once in Parnell Park. They beat us by double scores in one of those games. I think it was 28 points to 14.

You have to remember also that this Cork team had beaten Kerry in the

Munster final. The Kerry team that had been going for five in-a-row the year before. On our end, we beat Offaly in the Leinster final, the team who stopped the five in-a-row!

When you put all those factors together, I could only really pick this game. It was such an enjoyable day. It wasn't even about how well or badly I played. I was busy chasing Dave Barry around the place, so it was a challenging game for me.

When we got down to ground before the game, I suggested to the lads that we'd walk the pitch just to get a feel for the place and see what the surface was like. It was a blistering hot day, and we walked out into the middle of Páirc Uí Chaoimh. I couldn't believe it. Standing in the middle of the field was none other than my uncle… Tom McSweeney. He was my late mother's oldest brother, and he was a founding member of Whitehall Colmcille… my club, who were called Whitehall Gaels initially.

Himself and my uncle Bill were involved in stewarding in Croke Park. Obviously, Croke Park was in charge of the stewarding that day, and they had to nominate a team to go down and make sure everything ran smoothly with the crowds and so on. *Who was nominated as the head honcho?* My uncle.

You couldn't make this stuff up. All of a sudden, I'm thinking… *God, this is wonderful.* My dad had died in 1969, and my mother had passed away in February of '83, so that memory was still fresh in my mind. Seeing my uncle there really resonated with me. The nearest thing I had to a father was my uncle Tom, who was a huge supporter… that memory is something I'll treasure for the rest of my days.

Then we went out on the field for real.

Christy Ryan was the Cork captain. I had great time for Christy, a great footballer. He passed away in the last year, which was extremely sad. Another reason for picking this game was Brian Mullins.

Brian had crashed his car before the 1980 Leinster final, when Offaly beat us by a couple of points. He really had to fight hard to get back. I don't think he was ever the same after that but, by God, he applied himself, and he was imperious that day.

My wife Rosemary got the bus down, as did my brother. Around 10,000 Dublin supporters travelled to the game, and the atmosphere was like a soccer match. People had been in the stands for a long time before the game started, and that bowl shape of the old Páirc Uí Chaoimh was really perfect for creating huge noise when it was full. I think CIE ran extra trains and everything, there was a massive buzz the whole week leading up to the game.

Given what had happened the first day, we had no right to think we'd put Cork away like we did, but the team was phenomenal. Mullins scored a penalty early on. As coincidence would have it, he also scored a penalty against Cork in the semi-final in 1974. To have the confidence to step up and stick it in the bottom corner was just typical of the man.

We never lost momentum from that moment on… and we went on to score three more goals. Joe McNally got the last with a little stepover and side-foot into the corner. We never looked like we were going to lose.

The All-Ireland final in 1983 was very controversial.

We had three men sent off, Galway had one. I'd consider a lot of those Galway lads good friends now, but we had to work on the *relationship* after that game. When I look back on '83, it was great to be captain of a side that won an All-Ireland, but the aftermath of that final was disappointing.

It should be the most wonderful feeling in the world to win an All-Ireland. I was lucky that I had won a few by then, but probably 11 of that team were winning it for the first time. For those lads to win and then have that legacy and all the controversy afterwards, it wasn't nice. For a whole host of reasons, when I look back on '83, the semi-final replay is the game that stands out for me.

There had been a bit of a turnover of players since the success of the 70s. Mick Kennedy had been playing in goal before John O'Leary got established, and we had a League of Ireland 'keeper in for a bit too, I think. We were experimenting with fellas all over the field.

Frank McGrath played centre-back for a while, and Con O'Callaghan's father Mossie was part of the panel at some stage. We were really trying to find new faces.

Two fellas who had come through were Barney Rock and Kieran Duff.

The thing with those two lads is that they always had that extra ingredient about them. They were big-game players, nothing phased them. They formed a backbone to that forward line at a very early stage in their careers… and then Tommy Conroy came along a bit later.

Tommy was a very fluid player, poetry in motion. He was the opposite to Anton O'Toole in many ways. I think someone once referred to the late Anton as… 'A one-man rush hour!' When he had the ball, he would move around all over the place. He had an uncanny way of juggling the ball, so you never knew which way he was going to turn. It was incredibly difficult to mark him.

Heffernan was always trying to do something different.

In the 70s he had Hanahoe moving out of the middle and creating this massive void in the centre of the opposing defence, so the ball could be played into Jimmy Keaveney. Once Jimmy got the ball, he was either going to score, or win a free which he'd put over.

Then in 1983, he picked John Caffrey. John had a great engine on him, so he'd start at corner-forward and come out into the middle of the field. That would create more space up front and it would give Brian and Jim Ronayne some extra support in midfield. That was something new and teams weren't used to seeing it, some didn't always know how to handle it.

While we had the makings of a good team, there was never a light-bulb moment where I thought… *This is a team that could win the All-Ireland.* We played Meath in Leinster and drew. The replay went to extra-time… it was touch-and-go in both of those games. There was nobody coming out of the dressing-room after that game thinking we were going places. We beat Louth easily in the Leinster semi-final, but we didn't play well.

The drawn game against Cork was described by some journalists as the best game since the 1977 semi-final. The pace was phenomenal. Jimmy Kerrigan was absolutely brilliant; he was all over Croke Park.

Dinny Allen scored two goals and was electric.

We were really lucky to draw it. The one thing I remember is that we never gave up. We kept believing, even though things weren't going for us. Joe McNally had a goal chance and missed it, but at least he was making the chances and he might get the next one. The replay was the game that defined us.

After the final we were the worst team in the world, but nobody goes out to play a game like that. We didn't. Galway didn't. As Mick Holden said afterwards, it was probably the worst game of football he'd ever played in, but it was the best game to win.

I was captain, but I would have been a fairly quiet fella both on the field and in the dressing-room. At the start of that year, Kevin Heffernan invited me into the little hut in Parnell Park where we had all of our meetings.

Tony Hanahoe, Donal Colfer and Lorcan Redmond were all there, and they asked me if I'd take on the captaincy. That didn't sit comfortably with me. I didn't see myself as captain material, and I wasn't sure why they asked me. It was probably because I had been fairly constant in the team for a number of years.

I made my debut against Longford in 1976. I started the next game, and then we were playing Meath in the Leinster final… and I was dropped. I remember Heffernan saying to me, 'Don't take it personally'.

I've never forgotten that, but I took it personally!

I was never dropped or taken off after that. I learned a lesson. I desperately wanted to play against Meath in 1976, but I made amends. I played against Galway in the semi-final, where Billy Joyce knocked me out with a box! Getting back into the team was the turning point.

I never wanted to lose my place again.

For all my doubts, being captain of Dublin isn't something that you'd ever turn down. When I was a young player in Whitehall, at under-12 or under-13, I was asked to be captain. My immediate reaction was to say… 'No, this fella over here should be captain, he'd be far better than me'. That said a lot about my character at the time.

We lost that competition and, afterwards, I thought… *Maybe I should have said yes.*

Oddly enough, when Kevin and the lads asked me to be captain all those years later, I remembered that moment. I said I'd do it.

Because I was fairly quiet, being captain put me outside of my comfort zone, and I found that I had to learn new things about myself. Preparing team-talks, knowing what to say, knowing what players to focus on…that was all new to me.

I had no idea whether the way I was doing it was the right way to do it, or what I was saying was the right thing to say… I was really out of my comfort zone. I suppose I was lucky that I had Brian Mullins, Anton O'Toole and Mick Holden there… seasoned players who I knew well and felt very comfortable around. That was an enormous help.

I seemed to get on with the players, and I found them very easy to communicate with. It was hard early on, and I could never say I found it easy. I was captain again in 1984 when we lost to Kerry in the final. Being the losing captain in the Centenary final was tough, especially so given Paul Clarke – a fellow Whitehall man – was captain of the minors that day, and they won.

For the two Dublin captains to be representing the same club, and the same school in St Aidan's, was very unusual. It would have been great if we both won, but it was still special.

So, while the captaincy wasn't something that sat comfortably on my shoulders, for the rest of my life I found that I was never short of a conversation with people. I've learned to be more open. It really helped me enormously in my ability to relate to people, and that's still true today.

I settled in at right half-back in the Dublin team once I got my place. I played midfield occasionally, and full-back an odd time.

I started full-back against Meath in 1983, but I hated it, and moved out to centre-back. I felt more comfortable there, so that half-back line of Pat Canavan, myself and PJ Buckley became a settled line.

We took control of the Cork game very early on. Mullins' passing that day was superb. I would find it hard to believe that Cork felt under pressure playing at home. I mean, it was a perfect day... they were playing in front of their own fans. Perhaps there was still a hangover for them having let it slip the first day.

That can sometimes have an impact. I don't think Dublin had ever been beaten by Cork in the championship at that time. I couldn't define what went so wrong for Cork, I just know that everything went perfectly for us.

As far as my own personal performance that day went, I remember being pulled out of position a lot. At wing-back, I was a man-marker, but at centre-back I'd let my man go a bit, certainly if he was drifting away from goal. I'd pick him up when he came back in. Maybe subconsciously, I had seen what happened to our opponents when Tony Hanahoe pulled their centre-back out of the middle and, somewhere in the back of my mind, I didn't want to let that happen to us.

It was a really fast game, and I didn't feel like I got on much ball... I was doing a lot of chasing and covering. It was just the occasion and the performance that made it special. I looked more on what the team did than what I did. There's an element of pressure to perform as captain, but I don't remember it being an outstanding performance from me.

My objective when I played was to win the ball and get it to someone in a better position as quickly as I possibly could. I wouldn't carry the ball if I could help it. If someone around me was having a bad day, I'd try to cover them a bit more, and vice-versa.

That was the trust we had, and that all good teams must have. In the 1983 final, Pat Canavan was brilliant… Man of the Match. Sometimes your teammates do amazing things. Some of the goals we scored that year were incredible.

We scored 15 in total in that championship. Barney Rock's ability to get goals, Kieran Duff's ability to get goals…that was key for us that year.

After the game, we travelled back to Dublin. It was euphoria the whole way back up, because we had 10,000 Dublin fans making their way back home, so no matter what town or village we went through… there was just this sea of blue. They would have all seen us on the bus and been cheering.

Rosemary was with us on the way back, which would have been unusual. It was a really special time. The fact that we'd won, and the fact that it was such a long journey back made it even better. If it was a normal game in Croke Park, lads would have gone for a few pints here or there, and gone their separate ways. Being on that bus journey home really added a whole other dimension to things.

The 1983 final was one of the proudest days of my life.

Being captain and getting to lift Sam Maguire, that was amazing. The game itself… we all know what happened and we know about the aftermath, but that sits outside of the fact that we won the All-Ireland, so I can separate those things. It doesn't diminish the feeling of being an All-Ireland winning captain at all for me.

Roll on 25 years, and about nine months before the jubilee celebration, we were trying to raise some money. I rang Mullins.

Back in '83, we didn't get a team holiday. *Nothing*.

So, I was determined to raise money for a trip. I said to Mullins, 'I've no desire to go abroad. What I'd love to do is go down west and meet some of the Galway lads and spend a few days with them'. Brian had been sent off that day, so I really wanted to get a steer from him as to whether he thought it was a good idea.

He said he'd ring Gay McManus and tell him we'd meet up with them.

We met Gay and Barry Brennan down in Naas, and we put it to them and told them what we wanted to do. They said they'd go off and put it to their lads. Word came back… 'Yeah, we're up for it!'

Ahead of the jubilee celebration in Croke Park, Mullins spoke to Nickey Brennan, who was president of the GAA at the time. He told him that if the GAA didn't invite Galway to the event, that we weren't going to turn up.

I think Galway were the only losing finalists to be invited to the jubilee lunch. We had been away playing golf with the Galway lads, we had a gala dinner with them, and Séamus McHugh presented us with a trophy to mark the occasion. We had a great time.

We turned up in Croke Park on the day of the 2008 All-Ireland final with the Galway team. What made it even more special was the 1958 Dublin team was being celebrated on the day too… 50 years since they won their All-Ireland.

We had three teams in this big suite sitting down for lunch. I brought my daughter Ciara along, and she couldn't believe it. There was such a good vibe in the room. That was our way of moving on from 1983.

KIERAN DUFF

The Dublin team, with Kieran Duff (far right in the back row), before the thrilling All-Ireland semi-final replay win over Cork in Páirc Uí Chaoimh.

"

THIS GAME STOOD out a mile for me because of the whole occasion and how it all came about. The unfortunate thing was it wasn't shown live, which would be unheard of now. The whole year was extraordinary, really. For a start, we weren't supposed to win Leinster, because Offaly were the All-Ireland champions.

Then Cork beat Kerry with a last-minute goal in the Munster final so, all of a sudden, Dublin and Cork are in an All-Ireland semi-final.

That was a bit of a surprise to people.

Before the Leinster final, it didn't really seem as though we were going anywhere. We beat Meath in a replay in the first round, but they gifted us two goals in the drawn game. I got a last-gasp free to get us the draw, but that was another game we really should have lost. Our team changed a bit after that.

We played Louth next, and if they had been able to score in the first-half, they'd have beaten us off the park. We ended up winning comfortably, but you wouldn't say we were impressive. On the basis of all of that, we weren't really given a chance against Offaly.

What stood to us in that Leinster final was that Eugene McGee was already looking past us to a semi-final. That's how I saw it anyway. I think we caught them on the hop a bit. Heffo made a few changes and had John Caffrey playing as a third midfielder and Joe McNally in at corner-forward.

Tommy Drumm was at centre-back at that stage having played on the wing earlier in the championship. Those changes all worked, and we put in a brilliant performance against Offaly. They were hot favourites, and it was revenge for the previous year when they had hammered us. I think their minds were elsewhere.

We then played Cork in Croke Park, and we were blessed to get out of it. Five points down with not that long to go, we get a late goal… and it ends in a draw. Blessed. The replay was just a brilliant occasion. Obviously, getting the win was massive, but the whole build-up to it was memorable as well. There hadn't been an All-Ireland semi-final played outside of Croke Park in over 40 years, and we didn't get to travel far to championship games.

Now we're faced with a trip to Cork. We thought… *Great!* The furthest we'd ever travelled before that was Newbridge or Navan.

The way it all unfolded was, after the drawn game Frank Murphy, who was top dog in the GAA at the time and was heavily involved in the administration side of things… straightaway he said that he wanted the replay in Páirc Uí Chaoimh, and he fought hard for it.

Early the following week it was announced that the replay was going to be down there. It didn't bother us in the slightest, we were actually looking forward to it. Also, the fact that we got out of jail in the drawn game… we felt that the pressure was on them a bit.

The whole thing was a novelty.

We were going down the day before, staying overnight in Cork.

That was something we'd never done before. We met on the Saturday afternoon, and I remember everyone was a bit giddy. There was no M50 in those days, no motorways… the journey probably took five hours because you're going through every small town along the way.

We arrived around 6pm and had a bite to eat… then a team meeting. A few of us went out for a walk around Blarney at around nine o'clock. Myself, Barney, Joe McNally and a few others. I stood out a bit at that time with the big mop of curly hair and the beard.

We walked into this pub for a pint, and there were a good few Dublin fans in there. We were just wearing our own clothes… we wouldn't have had polo shirts or tops with our initials on them back then!

We were getting our drinks, and a couple of the Dublin fans turned around to us, and asked… 'Howya lads… are ye down for the match?'

I looked at Barney and we said, 'Yeah…we're down for the game…just having a couple of pints'. They didn't recognise us at all!

Some fans they were!

But I thought this was great because we were left in peace. We had a pint or two, then we thought we better get out of there before someone did spot us! It was nothing too mad. Heffo wouldn't have been too far behind, so we didn't want to stay too long in case he came in and caught us!

Kevin always said to us that if having a pint or two the night before a game is something you normally do… then go and have a pint or two. Most of the lads wouldn't bother, but a few of us would. Mick Holden, God rest him, could never sleep the night before a game, so he'd always have a couple of pints.

It was just a nice way to relax.

It turned out to be an eventful night for me, in spite of the fact that we were all back in the hotel early. I was rooming with John O'Leary, and he had had trout or something for dinner. We were in bed about an hour and next thing… John's up puking.

He's in the bathroom sick as a dog, so that wakes me up.

I'm up with John, and we go down to Heffo's room to see what to do. Kevin decided that the only thing to settle the stomach was a brandy and port.

He wouldn't let me have any, unfortunately!

That wasn't ideal the night before a game. John was a little bit green around the gills the next morning, but by the time the game came around he was fine. I'd be a light sleeper, so I was up around 8am and down for breakfast.

As a group, we all then went to kiss the Blarney Stone and had a bit of craic there. We were so relaxed. When we played in Croke Park, we rambled up one-by-one and went in the gate. But here we were the morning of a game and we're all together. It was great.

We got the bus to Páirc Uí Chaoimh, and all we could see was blue everywhere. That was new for us... to be on a bus going into a ground and seeing all the Dublin fans waving up at us. We had been led to believe that not that many of our supporters would travel, so it was a great boost to see so many making their way in.

It was a glorious day... the sun was splitting the stones. When we got to the ground, we went down the tunnel to the side of the pitch. There was a game on before ours, if I recall correctly, so we went to have a look at what was going on. When we walked out onto the side of the pitch, we looked down to our right to see what we then called "Hill 17".

The Dubs on tour.

That end of the ground was full and the game wasn't starting for a while yet. Seeing that sea of blue was just fantastic. That terrace was a lot more compact than Hill 16, so everyone was packed in tight. It was brilliant to see. I'd nearly say the atmosphere that day was better than Croker. I felt like we outnumbered the Cork fans three to one.

From a personal point of view, and it has been said to me many times, it was probably my best game ever in a Dublin shirt. It was one of those days where everything went well. I got the first score of the game, and that set me up for the day. Everything ran for me.

I scored, I laid on scores, and I did a lot of work off the ball. If my man was taking a free, I'd ramble over to the far side away from him. We'd win it, and then I'd get the ball in space. Those things can work against you some days, but that day it all worked out.

I had come into the squad at the end of 1979.

Myself, Barney Rock and John O'Leary had just won the minor All-Ireland. Kerry had hammered Dublin in the senior final, and the likes of Jimmy Keaveney, Seán Doherty and Paddy Cullen stepped away around then. So that 70s team was starting to break up, and there was a new era coming in. My first Leinster Championship was 1980, when Offaly finally broke their hoodoo and beat us.

It wasn't until 1981 or '82 that I started to establish myself on the team, which was to be expected when I'd only come out of minor. As time went by, I would have gotten a reputation as being one of Dublin's dangermen, as would Barney.

I remember talking to the Meath lads some time ago, and they admitted they targeted me and Barney and one or two others in those games in the late-80s when they got on top. I always thought if we had beaten Meath in 1986 that we would have finished them, because they had a lot of lads who were on the go for a while. But we didn't, and we know what happened after that!

I was marking Mick Hannon in the replay in Cork, and he would have been niggling away at me throughout the first-half. If you look at our penalty, I'm running in after it and he took a bit of a kick at me, but I got the better of him and he was taken off at half-time. Michael Burns came on in his place and when I ran into my position at the start of the second-half, he starts digging and elbowing me.

Don't get me wrong, that was all part and parcel of the game, I was well able to handle that sort of stuff. Mullins came over all the same, just to make sure everything was okay!

We were five points ahead at half-time, and we would have been fairly confident at that stage because we had played very well for the entire half. One thing Heffo did in the replay was curb Jimmy Kerrigan's influence.

Jimmy had been Man of the Match the first day and had covered every blade of grass in Croke Park from wing-back. In the replay, Barney lined out at wing forward as selected, but then he went into the corner, and Jimmy followed him. So that really reduced his influence on the game.

Heffernan nullified the threat with that move. Jimmy moved out the field later in the second-half, but why he was left at corner-back for so long is another question. That was a mistake on their part.

The pressure was really on Cork to come out and respond at the start of the second-half, and they did for a while. Dave Barry got a penalty to bring them to within two points, but then I got my goal. I was given a bit of space, and when I was soloing through, I was planning on making a little angle for myself and kicking a point.

If you look back at it, I was veering slightly to the right of the goals. But when nobody came to me, I carried it another five yards and, all of a sudden, the goal was on.

I hit it low, didn't blast it… just placed it into the corner.

When the ball hit the net, I just made my way back to my position. Joe McNally gave me a big hug as I was on my way back out. Maybe if I was a more emotional guy, I would have run down in front of the Dublin fans at that end and given them the fist-pump, but that wasn't really my style.

I wouldn't even have done that in Croker.

The way I saw it was, that's what I was supposed to do… get scores! That really finished Cork off. We got two more goals after that, but they were add-ons really. The second goal was the one that really killed them.

My wife had come down with her father and brother, and we were booked in for the Sunday night too. It was one of those nights where I didn't see too much of them! A lot of the lads headed back, but a few of us stayed and made a night of it.

We went from pub to pub, and someone had a contact in the army, so we ended up drinking in Collins' Barracks until all hours of the morning! John Kearns was a good mate of mine and had no intention of staying overnight, but we managed to convince him. He ended up sleeping on the floor in the room with me and the missus, and whoever else was there!

It was just one of those mad evenings. Somewhere along the line, we bumped into Eamonn and Tony McManus from Roscommon, and they ended up joining us on the beer. It was a great night, and something we'd never experienced before.

The whole weekend really brought us closer together as a group. Teams these days would have weekends away fairly regularly, be that in pre-season training or before the championship. That wouldn't have been the case back then, but that Cork trip was almost a bonding weekend by default.

After a semi-final in Croker, there was no meal after the game. The southside lads would have gone south and had a few beers… the northsiders would have done the same, be it The Gravediggers or wherever.

Everyone went their own way after games.

We were probably the worst-treated squad in the country!

We used to speak to the Meath lads, and they'd have been getting a few bob for expenses, they'd get food after training. We were getting nothing unless it was an All-Ireland final or a league game down the country.

After the All-Ireland final, I was a bit down about what happened and getting the suspension and all of that. But then I started to think… *Hang on, an All-Ireland isn't just won on that day. It's about all the games that came before it too.*

People can have bad days and get sent off, and the media had us branded as thugs. In reality, there were just three incidents in that game that caused all the furore.

Both teams were just as bad as each other in my view, but we were the ones who ended up with more lads sent off! You look at the Meath-Mayo brawl in 1996. That was much more dangerous in my view. I appealed my ban, but to no avail.

The last hope was the 'Mercy Committee'. Three people sat on the committee on the Friday before Easter when Congress was on, and they looked at the incidents in question and could recommend the ban to be lifted.

I had done nearly seven months by then. The committee recommended that the suspension be lifted… and it went to Congress. Paddy Buggy, president of the GAA at the time, stood up at the top table and shot that recommendation down. It went to a vote from the floor, and nobody would vote against the president. So that was that… or so I thought.

The following Friday, I was down in the ESB Training Centre in Portlaoise on a course. Kevin Heffernan rang and left word to call him when I got back up to Dublin. He told me that there was one more avenue we could explore the next morning.

It turned out that Gerry Fagan from Armagh was looking for a challenge match against Dublin to open a pitch up there, and he was the head of the GAC (Games Administration Committee) at the time. Heffernan told him that we'd play the challenge on the condition that my suspension was lifted. He agreed to see what he could to.

I went into Croke Park on the Saturday morning in front of six or eight delegates and they asked me why I thought they should lift my suspension?

I told them what they wanted to hear, that I regretted what I did, and I'd done my time and all that. Arse-kissing, basically. All I was short of saying was… 'Please forgive me. I am sorry for my sins!'

One smart-arse on the committee said to me, 'What have you been doing to keep yourself fit these last six or seven months?' It was well-known I was training with the county team, but that's not what he was driving at.

'Have you been involved in playing any other sports?'

Again, it was well-known that I had been playing with Swords Celtic, and a couple of League of Ireland clubs wanted me to sign with them.

I had no interest in doing that, because I just wanted to get back playing gaelic football. Fair play to one of the other men on the panel, he stood up and said that whatever I was doing in my own time was my business, and had nothing to do with that hearing. But it's amazing that there was one fella who wanted to bring up 'The Ban'… and it long gone.

After all of that, the suspension was finally lifted.

That was the fallout from the 1983 final.

It wasn't what I would have wanted, but these things happen, and we wouldn't have had that All-Ireland without the replay win over Cork. It was an incredible weekend, and one that I never saw the likes of again.

TOMMY CONROY

DUBLIN 2-10 MEATH 1-9
Leinster SFC Final
Croke Park
JULY 22, 1984

Tommy Conroy won an All-Ireland medal in his debut season with Dublin in 1983, but for the remainder of his career he was ravaged by injuries.

★ **DUBLIN:** J O'Leary; M Holden, G Hargan, M Kennedy; P Canavan, T Drumm, PJ Buckley; J Ronayne, B Mullins; B Rock (1-4), **T Conroy**, K Duff (1-4); J Caffrey, A O'Toole (0-1), J McNally. Sub: C. Sutton (0-1) for Mullins.

★ **MEATH:** J Fay; B O'Malley, P Smith, P Lyons; P Finnerty, J Cassells, M O'Connell (0-1); L Hayes (0-1), G McEntee; C Coyle, M McCabe (0-2), L Smyth (0-3); F Murtagh, C O'Rourke (0-1), B Tansey (1-0). Sub: B Flynn (0-1) for Murtagh.

THE ACTION

HAVING WON AN All-Ireland title the previous September with a numerical disadvantage, Dublin again showed their resolve in the face of adversity with a hard-earned but deserved victory over Meath in this Leinster final meeting.

Meath should have taken a grip on the game three minutes in, after they were awarded a penalty for a foul on Colm O'Rourke. Somewhat surprisingly, it was corner-back Pádraig Lyons who stepped up to take the kick, and he drove it narrowly wide to let Dublin off the hook.

The reigning champions capitalised on their opponents' wastefulness, and had the ball in the net twice before the quarter-hour was up. On both occasions Meath 'keeper Jimmy Fay made brave saves, only to see the rebounds finished to the net by first Barney Rock, and then Kieran Duff four minutes later. Meath snatched a goal of their own through Ben Tansey almost immediately after Rock raised the green flag.

The real test of Dublin's character presented itself when John Caffrey, who had already been booked, was dismissed for a second offence. That left Dublin with 45 minutes to play with a man less, but they showed all their experience to navigate safely through choppy waters. Aided by those two goals, they led by two (2-3 to 1-4) at the break. Tommy Drumm and his charges would no doubt have been braced for a surge from Meath in the second period, but it never came.

The Royal County certainly felt the absence of full-back Mick Lyons, but it was at the other end where their problems lay. Seán Boylan's men dominated around the middle, with Gerry McEntee and Liam Hayes putting in strong performances, but they couldn't convert their supply into scores.

By contrast, Dublin were far more efficient with their limited possession. Much of the credit for that must go to Mick Holden and Gerry Hargan, both of whom excelled in defence. Hargan looked as if he might struggle on O'Rourke in the early stages, but he got to grips with the Skryne man and had a fine game. Meath made poor use of their extra man, opting to give Bob O'Malley the free role sweeping in front of his full-back line. Anton O'Toole, winning his eighth Leinster medal, fittingly had the last word, with the final point of the game.

★★★★★

❝

MY FIRST COMPETITIVE senior game for Dublin was against Derry up in Bellaghy in the league. That was some experience! We got the bus from Belvedere Place, and we were going up the north quays.

Kevin Heffernan gets off and goes into a shop and comes back with a pack of 40 Sweet Afton cigarettes.

We got to the border, and the RUC boys got on and had a look around the bus. That was something different to say the least. We came out onto the pitch, and what I remember very clearly is that there was a man playing a Lambeg drum in the field next to us. I played okay that day and got a point, I think.

Heffo took me off in the second-half, but I think that was more that he had seen enough from me to keep me around. That's what I told myself anyway!

Sometimes, I used to compare Kevin's eye for a player to someone watching a racehorse. A lot of very good players came and went from the panel. He would make decisions very quickly about fellas. There was one particular lad who came in and trained for a few weeks, but he never even got a game.

He would see lads in club games and bring them in for a few sessions, and I think he would just see one or two things and think… *No*. He just had an eye for a player, and he knew what he wanted from everyone that came in. It might have been harsh on some lads, but that's the way Kevin was, and it's hard to argue with his record.

He went with his gut feeling, I suppose you could say.

Coming back from Derry, the bus was stopped again.

This big RUC officer gets on with a couple of army guys behind him… all of them have machine guns too, by the way. It turned out that a few Dublin supporters had been left behind. I think their bus went without them. The RUC guy was basically telling us we'd have to take them.

I'll always remember Kevin standing up and saying… 'We'll look after our own, that's no problem'.

That whole situation of the RUC and British Army guys getting on… it's hard to put into words how I felt. I'm not saying it was intimidating, but you know you're somewhere different. You're still on the island of Ireland but, by God, you know things are *different* now. I remember talking to Ciarán Barr, who used to tell me about being stopped, having to open the boot... next thing they see the hurleys, and the player is stripping off at the side of the road. That was the day-to-day normality for GAA people up there.

What I will say is the welcome we got anytime we went up to play in the north was just fantastic. They love seeing teams coming up to play them... they're mad about their GAA.

I came through from the minors in 1981 with Joe McNally, who was in goals.

We beat a Meath team in the Leinster final that included Bob O'Malley, Martin O'Connell and Colm Coyle. Unfortunately, Dermot McNicholl and Derry got the better of us in the semi-final.

I was born in October, and the way the club scene was in Dublin at the time meant that I got to a point where I could play club minor, but I would have been considered overage for the county. I was playing hurling, playing football... just really enjoying my sport and not thinking too much about where it would take me.

When I came out of minor, I was brought into the senior set-up pretty quickly. I would love to have played under-21, but Kevin was having none of that! It's something that I wasn't too pleased about at the time, but I can see his point now.

He thought of me, and one or two others, as senior footballers, even though we were still eligible for under-21. He believed we were good enough to play senior, so his view was why would we be bothering with the '21s' when that was really just a development ground for players?

To come into the side in 1983 and win an All-Ireland in my first year was brilliant. But I remember how I felt in the dressing-room after that Galway game.

The conditions that day were awful, and I felt the game passed me by. Personally, I just felt I'd like to have done more.

We were after winning an All-Ireland and I was feeling bad about myself! Mickey Whelan came over and asked, 'What's bothering you?'

I said, 'Ah, I didn't play well Mickey'.

'What about it?' he told me. 'Didn't you play well the last day?'

Then I thought to myself... *He's right*. It wasn't about my performance; it was about the team.

I don't think any of us really enjoyed that win like we should have due to the circumstances and the fallout from the game. The following year was horrendous.

We went down to Division Two, and while we bounced back and got to the All-Ireland final, I think there was a huge hangover from 1983 which really affected the group. We were well-beaten by Kerry in that final. The one where we were right and ready to go was in 1985.

That was the one I always think back to. We gave Kerry a huge headstart, and we nearly pegged them back. Had we won that, history could have been different.

Kevin might have stayed around, and poor aul Seán Boylan might have got the sack in Meath if we'd beaten them in '86! But that's all ifs and buts. Sport doesn't always work out the way you want it to.

We opened the pitch in Naomh Barróg against Meath in 1984, and afterwards we all went over to the old Shieling Hotel in Raheny. I was sitting there with Brian Mullins on my left, and Joe Cassells on my right.

Joe says to me, 'Well Tom, how old are you?'

I was 20 or 21 at the time.

'And you've got your All-Ireland medal already. I'm playing 10 years… and I haven't even a f**king Leinster!'

Sometimes, when I look back, like losing to Meath in 1986, '87 and '88… I'm not saying it softens the blow, but when you look at lads like Joe, Gerry McEntee, Colm O'Rourke… fellas that had put their heart and soul into Meath football, sometimes you have to say, 'Fair dues lads'.

I had plenty of good days with Dublin and the club, and it's hard to begrudge those Meath lads the success they got after plugging away for years with no reward.

Kevin stepped down in the middle of the 1985-86 league, after we'd gone down to Mayo and taken a bit of a beating. *Were we really up for that one?* Probably not.

As a management team, Heffo and the lads might have looked at that and thought… *Hold on, where are these lads at?* Maybe that's why they decided to go at that stage.

I'd say if you got all the players together and they pleaded with Kevin not to go, he might well have stayed on. Who knows, but it was probably a slightly sad way for it to end. He knew all of the players so well, and it took a lot of time to build up that rapport with 25 or 30 lads.

When that's lost, it isn't easily regained. Kevin would have put a lot of time into getting to know what made lads tick.

I look back at the games from that time now and wonder what the tactics were? There was a time where I wanted to ask Kevin what the plan was?

As a half-forward, I could have been five yards off my man. *Was there a short ball given?* No, it was kicked as far as possible! Kerry in those days were far cuter. They'd be playing shorter passes, popping the ball in front of lads.

A lot of the Meath-Dublin games were frantic. It was more exciting to watch in many ways, but it was helter-skelter, and lads didn't hold onto the ball too long, probably for fear of getting nailed!

We had drawn with Meath in 1983… how we got by them, I don't know. We got a couple of bizarre goals across those two matches. But they were getting better every year and by the time '84 came, the crowds that were turning up for those games were huge. We even played them in the opening round of the league in '83 when we were All-Ireland champions.

That was another game I had trouble getting into on time! The interest was phenomenal. In some games, you had time to play a bit of football. In games against Meath, your only thought was winning the ball. After that, you saw what you could do with it, but winning the ball was the number one objective, because it was so frantic and so physical.

Offaly were the dominant team in the early-80s, and we had some great tussles with them too. They were a big, physical team. But with Meath, it was different. There was even more cut to it, if you want to call it that. I remember meeting Tony Nation from Cork once, and he was calling the Dubs 'dirty f**kers!'

I said, 'Tony, if you think we're bad… wait till you see what we have to deal with!'

The game has changed so much since then. For that Meath game in 1984 or any of the games around that time, there weren't really any great tactical plans. The management team got us ready, got us fit, and then it was really a case of… *Right, it's over to you guys now to go out and play.*

There was no real analysis of kickouts or anything like that.

We really just played what we saw. If I thought a pass was on, I'd hit it. If I thought I could take my man on and beat him, I'd do it. There were no prescriptive moves.

You got the ball and then you assessed your options, but we weren't walking into a dressing-room afterwards where someone was telling us how many possessions we had or how many balls we gave away.

I probably had a bit too much to say for myself on that front when I first joined the panel. Before the 1983 replay in Cork, we had a meeting in Parnell Park in that tiny little hut. Kevin was up the top smoking, and he said to us, 'Listen lads, the last thing I want to see down in Cork on Sunday is their half-backs soloing up the field'.

I don't even think the comment was directed at me necessarily, but I thought it was because Christy Ryan had caught a ball in the first game and gone on a run up the field, and they almost got a goal from it. Christy was centre-back, so was marking me.

I'm listening to Kevin and I'm getting really annoyed at this! The red mist descended a bit and I decided… *I can't let this go!*

Next thing, I put the hand up.

Heffo looks at me. 'Yes Tom, what's up?'

To this day, I don't know what I said, but it was a total and utter rant! When I was finally done, he looked at me and said, 'Okay!'

I was happy enough then that we'd sorted it.

I was walking out afterwards, and Anton O'Toole grabs me by the arm.

'C'mere, what the f**k was all that about inside there?'

I looked at him and said, 'What was what about?'

'The rant in there!' says Anton.

I suddenly realised that maybe it hadn't been the best idea! Anton went on, 'If any of us had spoken to that man like that in the 70s, we might not be around now!' Now, I didn't believe that for one second, because Kevin was well able to give it and take it, and not be too put out about it… but it made me think!

Kevin would have known what buttons to press with me, and he would have done so on several occasions. He'd come to me and say, 'Right Tom, I need you to do this for me'. Once I felt I was needed, I was only too happy to do whatever was required.

But if he was *telling* me to do something, I might not be as willing. He wasn't a dictator though, he treated the players like adults.

We had one session on a Saturday morning in 1984, in the height of the summer. It was a scorcher of a day, and it was one of the most gruelling training sessions we ever did. I used to tog out opposite Mick Holden... so I'm sitting down after trying to catch my breath.

I didn't even have the energy to get into the shower.

Mick comes in, gasping. The two of us are sitting there looking at each other, when in walks the bould Kevin smoking a cigarette. All he was doing was coming in to see how we were after the session.

He turns to Mick and asks how he's feeling? 'Jaysus, I'm wrecked Kevin. Give us a cigarette, would ya?' Kevin proceeds to hand him the cigarette, lights it for him... and Mick takes a big drag and sits back blowing the smoke towards the ceiling with this big sigh of relief!

We were preparing for an All-Ireland semi-final, and here's the manager giving one of his starters a cigarette. I was looking at this at the time thinking it wasn't the right thing to do, but looking back now, it was one hundred percent the right thing to do.

The session was done, and we'd all worked really hard, so whether Mick had a fag or not wasn't going to make any difference to his performance. That was how Kevin was; he knew when to crack the whip, but he also had a great human side to him and knew how to get the best out of the players.

My career was cut a bit shorter than I'd have liked.

When I look back, we were doing all the wrong stuff training-wise. We used to do these things where you lay on your back and raised your legs.

Up and down, open and close... it put massive pressure on the lower back.

When I was called in to train with Dublin, Mullins said to me, 'Listen, you'll find the training a little bit tougher. If you're asked to do 10 press-ups or whatever, just do them to the best of your ability'.

I remember doing these leg-raises, and I'm tall, long legs... they were the worst things I could have been doing.

I'd look down the line and lads would have their hands under their back to support themselves.

In 1984, about two weeks before the All-Ireland final, we did a tough session and I felt great after. We were warming down, and Pat Canavan kicked a ball to me. I went up, caught it and kicked it back. I didn't feel great then.

The next ball came… and I went down to pick it up.

Next thing, I'm in bits. I got an awful fright. Kevin came over and asked if I was okay? 'I can't move backwards or forwards.'

I managed to walk into the dressing-room eventually, and I went to a physio the next day who told me I'd pulled muscles in my back. That was on the Tuesday, so I was in my civvies on Thursday and Saturday. This is just over a week from the final.

Mullins came over and started grilling me about what was wrong, but sure I didn't really know myself.

He arranged for me to see Martin Walsh, the surgeon who had dealt with him after his crash. Martin told me that I'd torn all the muscles in my back. He told me I'd be grand, but that I'd have to mind myself and that I was always going to have a bad back, which I do to this day.

I did all the right stuff and minded it in 1985, but training changed a bit after that and I did some exercises that I really shouldn't have done… but I told myself I'd get through them. But then you'd play a game after, and you'd pay the price.

I tore both hamstrings before we played Meath in 1986. I ended up coming on in that game and had a chance to shoot. I knew I shouldn't, but I did anyway.

Liam Harnan blocked it and I tore the hamstring again. In 1987 I had a knee injury which again came because of my back.

I was flying in 1988, and Kevin came to me – he was managing the Vincent's hurling team at that stage – and asked me would I play a bit of hurling with the club?

'Ah, Kevin, please,' I told him. 'I'm flying with Dublin'.

But again, he said something to me like, 'C'mon, we won't win one without you. I need you to play!' He convinced me to go and play a couple of games with the intermediates, and of course I get my hand busted… I've a plate in it now.

I didn't realise at the time that it was broken, so I was down training with Dublin, and my hand was killing me. I was at the back of the line for sprints and Noel McCaffrey is next to me, so I asked him to have a quick look. He touched it in one place, and I nearly hit him with the pain!

'Tom, you need to get that seen to.'

It was madness really.

I made the decisions to all these things myself… I'm not blaming anyone.

I went to the Mater and was told it'd be okay in a few weeks. Of course, I had the Leinster final against Meath coming up, so I played that game with a support on my hand. I went up and caught one ball, and Gerry McEntee just whipped it out of my hands.

We could have won that, but we conceded a couple of softish goals and missed a penalty. In 1989 I had another injury which was also related to my back, and in '90 I broke my jaw. In 1991 I was back on the panel, going well, but got acute appendicitis so had to have my appendix removed.

That was really it for me with Dublin. I was only 28 or 29 at that stage. You could say I was unlucky, I suppose, but I had some great years with both the club and Dublin.

There were a few memorable games I could have chosen.

Obviously, the Cork replay in 1983 was one. Michael Keating, who was Lord Mayor of Dublin at the time, came into the dressing-room after that one and everyone went quiet, given the office he held. He spoke very well about how we had done the county proud and so on. Charlie Haughey was there too, he was chatting to Kevin Heffernan, who was listening intently and smoking a fag.

The Lord Mayor finished speaking and left the room… and then Charlie walked out soon after without saying a word. No speech, *nothing*.

So, we were all thinking… *Okay… Fair enough*. Then about five seconds later, he pops the head around the door and pumps the fist a few times.

'F**king great lads!'… and the place erupted! That was a great day.

The 1984 Leinster final was memorable for a slightly different reason. I was living in Raheny at the time with my now wife Doreen. I was driving a little two-door Toyota Starlet, and I can still remember the reg… 895 LSZH.

We left the house and collected Brian Mullins out in Sutton. Then we drove to my mother's house in Fairview, just to drop in and say hello. Pat Canavan grew up across the road from me, so the Canavans were there.

We got back in the car and drove up to Drumcondra, to Brian's father-in-law Barney Harris. Barney coached me in St Vincent's since I was under-11 all the way up through the grades. A gentleman. We're up there having a cup of tea and having the chat… then we thought we better get down to Croke Park.

Back into the car we got… you can just imagine Brian Mullins crammed into this little Starlet! We tried to get down Richmond Road, and the traffic was just bumper-to-bumper. We're nudging along, and I started to get a bit anxious.

I said to Brian that maybe we should get out and walk.

'No, no…relax Tom, we'll be fine,' says Mullins.

But we were crawling down Richmond. There was traffic, supporters everywhere… I had thought we'd be there in five minutes! A little bit of panic set in.

Eventually, we had to get out of the car and Doreen took over the driving. We had to break into a jog or at the very least a quick march to get down to Croke Park in time. The two of us with the gear bags over the shoulder trying to skip through the supporters without being noticed!

I thought I had a shortcut for us, but it turned out we couldn't get through there as I thought. We'd to come back… and all the way around by Meaghers, past all the Dublin and Meath supporters. By now, we're fairly hightailing it up Clonliffe Road.

The players' entrance was around on the Hogan Stand side, but on that particular day there was a bit of a problem with the crowd. Meath had won the Centenary Cup earlier that year, and a huge number of fans turned up. Now, whether people turned up late, or turned up without tickets, I don't know.

But there were a lot of people locked out. It was mayhem.

Here we were, trying to make our way through thousands of people, and we're getting slapped on the back and the whole lot.

Finally, we arrive into the dressing-room. The lads are togged out at this stage, ready to go. I think I was the first one in the door… and Kevin just looked at me. I looked over my shoulder and pointed to the senior man!

Heffo just said to the two of us, 'Get your gear on!'

We had planned the day so well and thought we were in great time, but then we hit the traffic and it all went out the window.

The game started and Joe Cassells was marking me.

First ball I get, I try to get around Joe.

BOOM! Free. That was Joe saying, 'You're not going any further, Tom!'

We got the two early goals, but I remember at one stage Brian flicked a ball on, and one of the Meath lads nearly took the head off him. Thanks be to God he had no teeth, because if he had had any, they'd have been gone!

Lorcan Redmond came out to check on him, and I'm there thinking Brian could be gone. He had a big cut on the inside of his lip. I asked him if he was alright? 'Once I keep going for balls like that Tom, we'll be alright.' He was immense that day.

That's just how those games were. When Joe Cassells rattled me, it wasn't a case of being surprised. We all knew that every challenge was going to be physical, and it was up to each one of us to stand up. Take the hits and give the hits.

This was senior inter-county football, and this was Meath. Even in the years when we were beating them, it was never easy.

The other thing that happened was that John Caffrey was sent off for nothing really. We were a man down for about 45 minutes. That wasn't ideal for us, and it was certainly extremely harsh. But there wasn't any great discussion about it at half-time.

Teams today would prepare for going a man down, or even having an extra man, and come up with contingency plans in training, but no teams would have done that back then. Every player would have known they needed to work even harder, and that was about the size of it. In the dressing-room in that '84 final, lads would have been looking at each other saying, 'Right, our backs are against the wall here fellas'. Every one of us would have known what was needed. There was nothing revolutionary about it.

My other main memory was Ciarán Sutton's contribution. The game was in the melting pot in the second-half when Ciarán came on. He caught this unbelievable ball from a Meath kickout and took off on a run. I was running alongside him calling for it but no, he kept going, bounced off a couple of Meath lads and kicked this incredible score.

I vividly remember that being a really important score for us. The 1974 lads would tell you the importance of Leslie Deegan's point against Offaly that year, and I felt this was something similar from Ciarán. That was a pivotal moment. Massive.

We went out in the second-half, and it was probably more comfortable than we expected. I thought Mullins was immense, because he shipped a few hits that day. You have to remember that Brian had come back from that very serious car accident a few years earlier. I had gone to Croke Park to see the 1982 Leinster final against Offaly. Brian was playing centre forward. Here's a guy who was a key player in the success of the 70s, a huge figure in the Dublin team, and the guy is nearly after being killed in an accident.

I'm sitting in the stand, and the abuse Brian got from Dublin supporters was horrendous. *Horrendous!* I wouldn't even repeat what was said. That upset me, not just because he was a clubmate, but also the fact that he had given so much to Dublin and had worked so hard to get back… and this was the thanks some people gave him.

What it also did for me was give me a huge determination to beat Offaly.

Twelve months later… that's what happened.

TOMMY CARR

KERRY 2-12 DUBLIN 2-8
All-Ireland SFC Final
Croke Park
SEPTEMBER 22, 1985

As Dublin captain in 1991, in the historic four game series against Meath, Tommy Carr collects the ball ahead of Brian Stafford..

★ **DUBLIN:** J O'Leary; M Kennedy, G Hargan, R Hazley; P Canavan, N McCaffrey, D Synnott; J Ronayne, B Mullins; B Rock (0-3), T Conroy (0-2), C Redmond; J Kearns (0-2), J McNally (2-0), K Duff. Subs: **T Carr (0-1)** for Redmond, PJ Buckley for Mullins.

★ **KERRY:** C Nelligan; P Ó Sé, S Walsh, M Spillane; T Doyle (0-1), T Spillane, G Lynch; J O'Shea (1-3), A O'Donovan; T Dowd (1-1), D Moran (0-1), P Spillane (0-2); M Sheehy (0-3), E Liston, G Power. Subs: J Kennedy (0-1) for Power.

THE ACTION

IN THE END, it turned out as most expected it would, with Kerry captain Páidí Ó Sé hoisting the Sam Maguire Cup above his head in front of his teammates and hoards of adoring Kingdom supporters. However, the manner in which this game was won was far from conventional. Dublin's race looked to be run by half-time. Kerry had come roaring out of the traps, with Jack O'Shea in particular looking imperious. The big midfielder got his side's opening two points, before stepping up to take a penalty in the 13th minute after Ger Power was deemed to have been fouled by Pat Canavan. It looked like a harsh call. O'Shea buried the ball high to John O'Leary's right to put Kerry 1-2 to 0-1 ahead.

Tommy Doyle, and O'Shea again, added points as the champions hit top gear and pulled away. Substitute Tommy Carr popped over only Dublin's second score just before half-time, and Kerry led by a whopping nine points (1-8 to 0-2) as the teams headed down the tunnel. Even allowing for the stiff breeze at Croke Park, the jig looked up for Dublin.

Nobody reckoned with the extraordinary second-half that was to come, however. Tommy Conroy followed O'Shea's lead by getting his side's first two scores of the second-half, before John Kearns landed one from distance to cut the gap to six. Dublin's comeback looked to have been nipped in the bud when Timmy Dowd found the net in the 48th minute, restoring the half-time margin. Again though, the Dubs hit back. Joe McNally awaited the break following Kearns' long delivery, hoping fortune would favour him. He got his reward and finished well off the crossbar when one-on-one with Nelligan, upending himself in the process. A Barney Rock free and another superb effort from Kearns from the left wing put just four between them with 10 minutes left.

Moments later, Kearns launched another missile into the square. Again, the Kerry full-back line was found wanting under the high ball, and McNally punched to the net. A point in it with five minutes to go! Kerry were on the ropes, but dug into their vast reserves to muster a knockout punch. Sheehy and Rock swapped frees before points from Spillane, Dowd and John Kennedy closed out the game for Mick O'Dwyer's men.

★★★★★

> 66

IT WAS MY first year with Dublin, my first time experiencing the man that was Kevin Heffernan. Up until then, I would just have heard the stories about him. The myth that was Heffo.

It was such an incredible time for me.

I almost picked another game. There was a challenge game in early 1985 on a wet evening in St Margaret's against Offaly or Laois. I think it was Offaly. The reason I almost went with that was because it was the first time I pulled a Dublin jersey over my head.

It was a big 'Wow' moment for me. If there was a mirror in the changing room, I would have stood in front of it forever!

But ultimately, I couldn't look past playing in an All-Ireland final in my first year with the Dubs. Donal Colfer and Lorcan Redmond and these fellas that had come through the 70s and 80s… and here I was landed into the middle of them. So many great names on the team too.

It was actually the toss of a coin as to whether myself or Charlie Redmond started that day. I was a bit of a utility player at that stage, which was really a drawback for me, because for the following 10 years I ended up going wherever there was a problem.

From wing-back to centre-back to corner-forward. I was everywhere.

I started 1985 in college in Galway with the army.

Heffo was onto me about joining the panel and I said, 'Well, I'm down in Galway'… to which the response was, 'If you want to be on this team, you'll be at training every night'. In other words… *I don't really care where you are!*

He said it in a nice way, and he made sure I knew *he thought* I was a good player. He actually called me over during training one night and said, 'Tell me about your culture, your history'. He wasn't sure if I was from Dublin or Tipperary. I had played with Tipperary for two year previous to that.

How I ended up playing with Tipperary was they saw me winning the Sigerson and contacted me to ask would I be interested in playing with them? I travelled down from college in 1983 and '84 to play with Tipp. To be honest, it was a depressing experience. There was such a lack of ambition.

Babs Keating was my manager one of the years. I was actually taken off in a McGrath Cup game... and two years later I was playing in an All-Ireland final.

I had a good start to that championship.

My first game was against Wexford, and I scored 1-3.

I remember toe-poking my goal in, and Anton McCaul trying to claim it! I was a bit shy so I wasn't going to say anything, but after the game Heffo told him, 'Anto, it was Tommy's goal, not yours!' I got a great mention in the *Herald* the following day, and this is not to sound big-headed in any way. I was just delighted to be there. It meant the world to me.

I was playing with Ballymun at the time. I had played all my underage football with Lucan, then I had come back from college in Galway and had wanted to play with the Dubs. I know about the club loyalty thing and all that sort of stuff, but Lucan were an intermediate club. What was more important to me, rightly or wrongly, was playing for Dublin.

There's a lot of talk we always hear about the club coming first. I have to be one hundred percent honest and say that it didn't come first for me. To represent my county was the ultimate. Even more than representing Ireland, because I went away to Australia for the International Rules.

It's probably heresy to say that, but that's what I felt. It was the Dublin football team. That was it for me. Though I was fortunate to be in the position to re-join Lucan in the mid-90s... myself and Jack Sheedy, who had also left the club to play with the Garda team. We were part of a Lucan team that won the Intermediate Championship and got up to senior! That Lucan team was also managed by Liam Hayes, who was living locally, and who was my rival as Meath captain in 1991.

That year in 1985, there were three of us who were newbies... myself, Noel McCaffrey and Dave Synnott. We were the new faces on the team. A lot of the famous 70s guys had gone, but Brian Mullins was still there, and he was the standout personality on the team.

Now, we all kinda knew Brian shouldn't have started that 1985 final. I think he struggled with the pace of the game. Brian was a God to me, but he had been on the go a long time at that stage and had been in a fairly bad car accident a few years before that which would have impacted him.

He was very good to me when I joined the panel. He was a great mentor and would always have a word of encouragement for me. People might have thought he was a tough, uncaring guy, but he was brilliant to me when I came in first, which meant a lot.

Things were going well for me in my first season with Dublin, and we got to the Leinster final where we beat Laois on an awful wet day. I kicked a point with my right foot, probably the only time I ever did that. So, we're through to an All-Ireland semi-final against Mayo. I ended up marking my good friend, and the fella who went on to be my Best Man at my wedding, John Maughan.

I wasn't going great, so I was moved in corner-forward. Looking back on it, I was a little bit lost on the day. I didn't really get into the game and was taken off. In fairness to the management, they told me I had played well, and I was doing fine.

Coming up to the All-Ireland final, Lorcan called me aside and told me that they weren't going to start me. They were going to go with Charlie.

'No problem,' I said.

I was the shy, new guy on the panel, and I was delighted to be there. The game comes around, and after about 15 minutes... I was brought on. It was actually a great way to come into such a big game, because I had no nerves at all. Plus, I had the little bit of disappointment from not starting to drive me on.

I hopped up off the bench, and I just had a great sense of freedom. Tommy Doyle, who had a big reputation at the time, was marking me, but I got on plenty of ball and things seemed to be breaking my way. Every time I turned around, he wasn't there. I thought to myself... *This is great!*

I scored my point near the end of the first-half. All these mythological characters were on the pitch. You had Páidí Ó Sé, Mikey Sheehy, Bomber Liston... all these great names, and here I was running around like a little boy! I really remember that feeling very well, that I almost couldn't believe that I was on the same field as these lads. I also felt during the game that I was doing a lot of hard work and making a lot of good runs, but the ball wasn't coming to me that often. Now, the football was quite wild, it was get the ball and kick it.

In some ways I remember it quite well, but in other ways, it went by in a bit of a blur. I was floating on air. I didn't know where I was... *and I knew exactly where I was,* if you know what I mean.

It was all too good to be true. And it wasn't that I was star-gazing, because I never did that, I always felt like I could compete with anyone… whether I could or not was another thing! I remember the roar that hit us when we went out. I'd never experienced anything like that. The pounding in your ears for that 10 or 15 seconds!

Maybe it was the acoustics within Croke Park at the time, but I'm not sure it's as loud now as it was. It was one of the greatest highs of my life to be able to run out with the Dublin football team on All-Ireland final day.

After the game, your family would wait outside the tunnel under the stand outside the changing room. Now, I wouldn't be the best in the world to take defeats… I would get very down about them and didn't handle that side of things very well. But I remember my dad, who has since passed, saying to me, 'Ah sure don't worry, you'll have lots more of these. You've loads of time!'

So, I kinda thought then… *D'ya know, he's right. It's not so bad. I'll have loads more of these.*

It had been Dublin and Kerry for the previous 10 years, so of course I thought it'd continue that way. Instantly, I was nearly looking forward to the league starting that winter, because I was just mad for road, mad for action.

Had I been starting, I wouldn't have been nervous, but looking back on my state of mind at the time, I'd say I would have been taken off again. The two or three-week build-up to the game… knowing you're starting?

I think I would have found it difficult to get into the game. The reason I say that is because when I think back to how I felt when we came out, the noise, the excitement… it was nearly too much to take in. To then have to go and try to perform and win the game, I think too many things would have been going on in my head. It was nearly like an out-of-body experience!

As well as all of that, if I had been starting, I think Kerry would have paid more attention to me. When I ran on after 15 minutes as a sub, maybe Tommy Doyle wasn't paying much heed to me. I wouldn't have had the same sense of freedom starting versus coming off the bench. There was nothing to lose either, because Kerry were running away with it at that point.

I would never have been a person overcome with nerves, but my family used to take me to Croke Park all the time to watch the Dubs, being lifted over turnstiles and fighting with stile men and so on.

When you've spent 15 years of your life watching these fellas in Croke Park, and you've this big idea of the Dubs and Jimmy Keaveney, to then suddenly be out there yourself… it's an awful lot to cope with. I would have been good at managing any nerves, and the challenge of what was ahead of me always superseded any anxiety I might have had about a game. Everyone has emotions, and some emotions are stronger than others. My need to prove myself was my biggest emotion.

We were being beaten out the gate at half-time. 1-8 to 0-2. In we all came, very dejected. Heffo was very cool about it. There wouldn't have been any shouting and roaring, but he was very direct. He would pick fellas out and tell them that they weren't doing their job. It was much more direct than it is now.

You've got to be a bit more diplomatic about it these days!

Back then, it was either you do your job or if you can't… we'll bring someone on who can. Subsequently, in 1991, I got a bit of a roasting off Tommy Dowd and Pat O'Neill said to me, 'Can you mark him, or can't you?'

I replied, 'I can!'

'Well f**king mark him then!' There was no beating around the bush.

We were down in ourselves, but we put up a great fight it in the second-half. When we got it back to a point, I remember thinking… *Jesus, are we going to win this?* That was an unbelievable thought, and I wonder did some of the other lads think that too. I don't think we had the smartness to realise that we *had* Kerry.

We had the momentum… they had let a nine-point lead slip.

To be honest, I'm not sure we had the leadership and experience on the pitch to see it out. Brian Mullins had gone off at that stage. We had shot our bolt, and we got a bit of luck along the way. Kerry had gone to sleep a little bit, but then found their fifth gear and pulled away. They were an aging team at that stage, and we would have been told to run them I'm sure, but we didn't do that.

While they were getting on in years, Kerry were still a very strong team physically. We kicked a lot of ball, and they would have won a lot of the 50-50 battles. We didn't use our athleticism as much as we could have, and maybe part of the reason that we went so far behind was that the likes of myself, Noel and Dave didn't have the experience that the Kerry lads had.

When they were brought back to a point, they were able to do the right things to go and get the insurance scores.

After the game, we went to the pub for a few drinks with our families, then we had the function out in a hotel in Clondalkin. I met Kevin Heffernan in the car park on the way in and he said, 'You did really well today. You'll have plenty of opportunities, so don't be too down about it'. That was a bit of a lift to get from the great man, but that was his last championship game in charge of Dublin.

Obviously losing was disappointing, but Kerry were favourites and I think there was a feeling afterwards… *Well, thank God we weren't beaten by 15 points.*

We had made a go of it.

Did I get a feeling in the dressing-room that lads thought we had let it slip? I don't think so. I'm not sure it was ever ours to let slip. It never felt like it was, and it would have been more a case of stealing it. You'll always know from the atmosphere in a dressing-room whether a team is disappointed that they lost, or disappointed that they were shite, relieved they escaped… whatever it is, you can almost smell it.

I don't remember getting a sense from anyone that we left it behind. But that's only my recollection. Some of the lads might tell you differently. It certainly wasn't absolute devastation. I remember when I was manager and we lost the replay to Kerry in 2001… now *THAT* was devastation!

In 1985, I think there was a huge amount of pride in Kevin Heffernan that he sent out a team in the second-half that put up a fight. What was as important to him as anything is that the players would try, that they'd give everything they had. He hated bluffers or pretenders. Even that night at the function, there was a reasonably good atmosphere around the place.

I didn't come off the pitch thinking… *Wow, what a team Kerry are!*

I always tried to fight being in awe of any player or any team, because it won't help your performance. I would have been thinking… *F**k sake, we're every bit as good as these guys, but too many of us don't believe it.* That would have been my sentiment, and I would have carried that through my career.

I think too many teams are beaten by the aura of their opponents, including teams playing Dublin in the last few years. Dublin haven't had to do half as much in recent seasons as they did 10 years ago, because they're about eight points up before the ball is thrown in. Okay, Mayo got them this year (2021), but in general terms, I believe a lot of teams are beaten before the game has started. I didn't feed into the Kerry myth, though of course I knew they were fantastic players. I actually marked Jack O'Shea in a Munster Championship match in 1982 or '83 when I played for Tipperary… and I thought I did okay.

My parents were both from Tipperary, and in 1960 they moved up to Dublin out of economic necessity. My two sisters were born down there, and me and my two brothers – one of them being Declan – were born in Dublin.

In 1980, I went into cadet school, and my family moved back down to Tipperary at that time. That's how Declan ended up back there. He did his last two years of school in Thurles CBS. I was in college in Galway for three years, and when I came back I didn't go back to Lucan Sarsfields.

In fact, I looked to get into St Vincent's.

I met Buster Leaney, who played for Dublin for a while and was a big Vincent's man. He was also an army officer… a commandant or a colonel. I met him and basically said, 'Sir, I'd like to join St Vincent's'.

I wouldn't really have been known at the time. I had won two Sigerson Cups with UCG in 1983 and '84, but that would have been low enough on the national radar. The answer I got back from Buster was, 'We don't take country lads'.

I was thinking… *I'm not a f**king country lad!*

But I said, 'Fine'. In that kinda thick way people say it. I wasn't too pleased.

Another army officer then contacted me… Des O'Donnell. He had heard I was looking to join a team, and he was involved with Ballymun Kickhams. Out I went to Ballymun, and we nearly had a county team out there. The McCauls, Gerry Hargan, Barney Rock, Declan Sheehan… we had a heap of Dublin lads.

We won the county championship in my first year, which was a big help to me getting on the Dublin team. Everything happened that year in 1985.

It was Heffo's last year. Every person gets to a stage where they get tired, and it doesn't mean as much as it used to. I think Kevin probably realised that at the end of '85. I felt the same when I stepped away as a player at the end of 1994. I got tired of losing.

You'll have plenty of opportunities.

Sometimes you don't get as many opportunities as you think.

GERRY HARGAN

DUBLIN 1-11 KERRY 0-11
NFL Final
Croke Park
APRIL 26, 1987

Gerry Hargan and Meath captain Mick Lyons, who later became the best of friends after playing for Ireland together, await the 1987 Leinster final.

★ **DUBLIN:** J O'Leary; D Carroll, **G Hargan**, M Kennedy; D Synnott, G O'Neill, N McCaffrey; J Ronayne (0-2), D Bolger (0-1); B Rock (0-3), J McNally, K Duff (1-3); D Delappe, M Galvin (0-1), A McCaul. Sub: D Sheehan (0-1) for Delappe.

★ **KERRY:** C Nelligan; P Ó Sé, T Spillane, M Spillane; S Stack, T Doyle, G Lynch; J O'Shea (0-1), T Dowd (0-1); J Kennedy (0-1), D Moran, P Spillane (0-2); W Maher, M Sheehy (0-4), G Power. Subs: J Higgins for Stack, E Liston (0-2) for Maher.

THE ACTION

AFTER SUFFERING HEARTBREAK at the hands of Kerry on more than one occasion in previous seasons, Dublin finally got one over on their great rivals in this National Football League final.

In what was an epic climax to the league season, Kerry were heavily fancied coming into the game, but they were on the back foot from the off. With just 75 seconds gone, Charlie Nelligan was picking the ball out of his net. Joe McNally played an exquisite ball from under the Hogan Stand into the arms of Kieran Duff, who buried a low shot.

That goal laid the foundations for a lightning start from the underdogs, who found themselves 1-5 to 0-1 up after 20 minutes.

It was clear that Dublin had more work done on the training field than Kerry, which was understandable given new manager Gerry McCaul targeted a good league campaign in his first season in charge. However, the Kingdom rallied coming up to half-time, and had cut the gap to just four points (1-6 to 0-5) by the time Séamus Prior brought the opening period to an end.

With McCaul's promptings no doubt ringing in their ears, Dublin started the second-half brightly, but were let down by their shooting. Duff, Barney Rock and David Delappe contributed to six wides in the opening 10 minutes, and those misses looked costly as Kerry landed three in-a-row to cut the gap to one. Rock, Declan Sheehan and Mick Galvin then steadied the ship to restore Dublin's four-point cushion. Kerry's golden opportunity to swing the game back their way came soon after.

Eoin Liston – who came on at half-time – was on the end of a passing move involving Pat Spillane and Jack O'Shea. 'The Bomber' laid the ball off to Mikey Sheehy who, for once, couldn't apply the finish... his shot was deflected over the bar by Mick Kennedy. With that went Kerry's last real opportunity to threaten the scoreboard in any significant way. They simply never looked like winning the game with points alone.

Duff's goal ultimately proved decisive, and captain Gerry Hargan lifted Dublin's first league trophy since 1978, and just their sixth in all.

★★★★★

66

THERE'S A BIT of a history to this league campaign. We played Cork in the quarter-final, and it went to extra-time. They refused to come out because they said they had to get the train home. I presume it was a ploy to do something similar to what happened in 1983 and get a replay down in Páirc Uí Chaoimh, but the schedule was so tight that there was no time for replays in the calendar.

We ended up with this bizarre situation where the ref threw the ball in for extra-time… but with only one team on the pitch. Barney Rock soloed down to the Canal End and stuck the ball in the net, and we won the game.

We beat Galway in the semi-final in Portlaoise, which put us through to a final against Kerry. I had played in All-Ireland finals against Kerry in 1984 and '85 and they beat us well, particularly in '84. That's why this game is special for me… it was my first time to beat Kerry in a national final.

Gerry McCaul was in his first year in charge, and he was a Ballymun clubman like myself. Gerry had a big background with Sigerson Cup teams in UCD. He did very well with Ballymun Kickhams, and we won the Dublin championship in 1982 and '85 under his management. It was a bit of a choice out of the blue to give him the Dublin job in a way. He got Seán Doherty and Tony Hempenstall in as his selectors, but Gerry was the main man; he did a huge amount of work.

He was the most unfortunate Dublin manager ever! He got no luck at all.

When he came into the job, he tried to move things forward. His organisational skills were first-class, and he was very detailed in everything that he did. He used to bring in one of those boards with the little pieces on them that you could move around, and we did video work with him too.

Gerry would go around and talk to each individual. He was very thorough in how he went about his business. He was the first guy to bring in weight training, especially upper-body stuff.

Something that he also introduced which never happened before was, we started getting food down at Parnell Park. We started getting fruit and milk and other stuff after training. That was all Gerry's doing.

We never got anything before that.

We were lucky to get a shower sometimes! Now you see how players are looked after with meals and so on – and so they should be – but back then there was nothing for us. Gerry changed that.

We trained harder than normal for that first league campaign, because he wanted to do well in his first season. He really pushed us hard, and it was tougher than Kevin Heffernan's training would have been at that time of the year. He knew his stuff, Gerry.

A few new lads were brought in and given a run, the likes of Timmy O'Driscoll from Kilmacud, Declan Sheehan, Glen O'Neill... so Gerry took a chance with a few new faces and was trying to integrate some of the promising minors into the side. Gerry's brother Anto was on the team too, so that added another layer of pressure. Anto had been there under Heffo, but was in and out of the team, even though he was going really well with Ballymun and was one of the best forwards in the county at the time.

Gerry was really good at what he did, but he was so unlucky. Running into that great Meath team, losing games by a couple of points, missed penalties... he couldn't get a break! It was a pity because he wanted to prove that he could bring Dublin back to the top table, and worked so hard to do so.

I started my Dublin career properly in November 1982. I had been in with a panel of about 36 lads in 1981. I was 22 then and I was basically brought in as a greyhound to run around Parnell Park and keep the more experienced lads on their toes.

We'd start with about six laps, and I'd be breaking my backside to be up the front. I got a couple of games in the O'Byrne Cup and didn't do particularly well. We played Meath out in Kilmacud, and I got a bit of a roasting.

In the Leinster Championship in 1982, we played Offaly in the final and got an awful hiding. I was sitting on the bench with No 26 or something on my back. It wasn't a great day for any of us. Afterwards, we were all brought to the Ashling Hotel... and Heffo came in.

There were about 36 lads in the room.

He sent maybe five lads away. Gone... off the panel.

He was ruthless. Then he went through the rest of us one by one. A lot of lads were playing with junior clubs at the time, and he said they'd have to move to a senior club if they wanted to progress their careers.

He came to me and said, 'You'll have to learn to kick with your right foot, because you're only left-footed'. That was it, and we were sent back to our clubs to work on whatever it was that we were told.

Soon after the All-Ireland of that year was played, a guy I know called to the house on a Thursday evening. He told me Dublin were playing Kerry in the National League on the Sunday, and Kevin wanted me to come in to training on the Saturday morning.

'You know what you can tell Kevin Heffernan!' I replied.

He wasn't my favourite person in the world at that time! But yer man tried to talk me around, and I eventually said I'd have a think about it. I went to my father and told him what the story was. I told him I didn't want to go.

He thought that I should, so that's what I did.

I went training on the Saturday morning, went down to Tralee on the Sunday morning, and we beat Kerry… and I was full-back for Dublin for the next 11 years! The moral of the story is, if you get a chance… take it!

We won the All-Ireland in my first full year in the team, and then lost to Kerry in 1984 and '85. So, beating them in the league final in 1987, even if it was a *league* final, was special for me.

Gerry McCaul asked me if I'd be captain at the start of that season, which I was only too happy to do. The league started in the winter at that time, so that campaign would have commenced at the back end of 1986. I was captain all the way through to 1989.

By the time 1990 came, I said to Gerry that I didn't want to be captain anymore. Tommy Carr had come along, and I thought it was time for a different voice in the dressing-room. Things were becoming a little bit stale with the lads listening to me all the time, and I thought Tommy would be an ideal man to replace me, which he was.

Tommy was a great leader during his time with Dublin.

What I remember most from that league final game is that Eoin Liston wasn't playing. He'd usually have been full-forward, but he wasn't starting that day. To be honest, I found it very difficult to mark him. It was next to impossible.

He was so broad… so big, so strong.

If we weren't winning midfield and they were dominating, then it was goodnight. One year… it could have been the 1985 All-Ireland final, Jack O'Shea and Ambrose O'Donovan absolutely lorded it around the middle.

They were able to pick out their passes and we were trying to wrap up Ger Power, Mikey Sheehy, Liston, Pat Spillane… it was very difficult. Liston was quick over 10 or 15 yards, and he was physical. In terms of toughness, Colm O'Rourke was the toughest guy I ever marked.

But Liston's sheer size made him really hard to handle.

Like Kieran Donaghy after him, he had that basketball background which meant he had great hands, but also knew how to use his body to shield the ball. If he got in front of you, it was like trying to get around a bus. It just wasn't going to happen.

So, I had to try to read the game. I knew that once their midfielders got the ball, it was going to be coming in my direction. Sometimes you had to take a chance and hope you got a break, because once he got the ball in his hands, it was pretty much impossible to get it off him. But the risk then was that you could end up looking like a complete gobshite if you read it wrong!

I didn't have to worry about Liston from the start that day, but Mikey Sheehy was there instead, which wasn't much better from my point of view! Mikey was an unbelievable footballer, but he obviously wasn't as big or physical as the Bomber, so I had more of a chance of matching him.

They had Tommy Doyle, the Spillanes, Jacko… they had a strong team out, so we were expecting a tough game. Anytime you play Kerry in a final of any kind, you'd always look forward to it.

Kieran Duff got us the early goal and that ended up being the difference. Dully had a fantastic game, one of his best in a Dublin shirt. We got a good lead, but they gradually got back into it. My old friend Eoin Liston came on at half-time and, although he wasn't one hundred percent fit, he still caused us a lot of problems.

They got on top for a bit in the second-half, but we managed to hold on… Declan Sheehan came on as a sub and got a point for us at a vital time. As captain, I got to lift the trophy, which was a huge honour for me.

Things were looking up at that point, and we were really looking forward to the Leinster Championship. The league wasn't taken too seriously at the time, but it was a great boost for us to beat Kerry.

For the younger lads like Declan Bolger, Declan Sheehan, Mick Galvin… it was brilliant for them, because they wouldn't have had any baggage from the 1984 or '85 finals. A lot of that Kerry team was coming to the end of their careers too, so there was a great opportunity for Dublin to drive on and win a couple of All-Irelands.

The only problem was that Meath were coming strong then and beat us in 1987 and '88 on their way to winning two All-Irelands.

We got past them in 1989, and lost to Cork in the semi-final, which is the game that I still think about to this day. We were cruising, but we had nobody to blame but ourselves. Maybe it was a bit of inexperience from some of our guys on the day. Keith Barr got the line… in fairness to him, I think he was drawn into something by Dinny Allen and reacted! But you'd be having heart attacks playing behind Keith, because he was liable to do anything!

He hasn't changed a bit either… I'd meet him occasionally. What a servant to Dublin though, and what a character.

I felt if we'd beaten Cork, we'd have won the All-Ireland.

We could always beat Mayo. It was psychological, but we would always beat them. So '89 felt like a big miss.

1992 was my last year. We got to the All-Ireland final against Donegal. We were training in Parnell Park. This was in the days when crowds were allowed in to watch the sessions. I found out years later that Donegal had a few spies there.

I got injured on the Tuesday before the final and I said to Pat O'Neill, 'I won't be able to play'. I had pulled something in my calf for the first time ever, and I went to Fran Ryder too and told him what happened. He told me not to worry, that I'd be playing on Sunday. Of course, the Donegal lads in the crowd would have seen me pulling up.

I was marking Tony Boyle in that game and the first ball I went for… I felt a twinge up the back of my leg.

Over I went to the sideline to tell them I couldn't play on.

I was told… 'You have to stay on!'

The next morning, I had to be carried down the road to Doheny and Nesbitt's for a pint. That's how bad it was. I played the whole game, but I really should have been taken off. I continued on the best I could, but I was disappointed with how it ended.

I was called back in for the league the following season, but I went to Pat and said I'd had enough. It was time to go. He said, 'Fair enough'.

That was it. Retirement creeps up on you.

You lose a little bit of speed, reactions slow down, and your body just starts to feel the effects of years of playing and training. Nobody wants to let their teammates down. I could have stayed on and been No 25 or 26 on the bench, but that wasn't something that interested me. That said, when they won in 1995, I was thinking maybe I should have hung on for two more years!

We felt like we were building something after 1985.

We had pushed Kerry close in that final, and we were doing well in Leinster again after seeing off that Offaly team that won the All-Ireland in '82. They had some great players, especially Matt Connor.

I used to have to mark Matt… or try to.

He was a genius. Left foot, right foot… no problem.

He'd sell you a dummy and turn on a sixpence. Getting over them was a big thing, because we knew we were going places then. We were doing well in the league, even if we didn't take it that seriously. It's not like it is now. There were seven teams in the division at that time so you could afford to lose a couple and still stay up.

It was a young enough team that Heffo was starting to put together. I suppose it'd be called 'rebuilding' now. But we certainly felt like we were going in the right direction.

We had beaten Meath in a Leinster quarter-final in 1983 after a replay. I got a terrible time in *The Meath Chronicle* after those games. I dunno who the writer was, but he said I could have put a saddle on Colm O'Rourke and rode him around Croke Park!

My mother is from Trim, so that's how I saw it.

She used to get the *Chronicle* every week. They weren't impressed with me, but you could only laugh at it. I got a terrible going over in the press after those games… O'Rourke gave me a bit of a roasting. I was inexperienced at that stage, whereas Colm was a lot cuter, and I really thought I was gone after that.

I thought there was no chance I'd be kept in the team, but Heffo stuck with me. I owe him a lot. He could have easily put someone else in there. To this day I'm grateful for that, because my Dublin career could have been over before it started only for Kevin Heffernan.

When he stepped down in January 1986, it was a big shock to me.

He was a God. If he walked into the room, there'd be complete silence. He used to put us under terrible pressure at team meetings though.

My God, *terrible*! For example, if we were playing Meath tomorrow, we'd be sitting in this little box room in Parnell Park, and he'd go to each individual and say, 'What are you going to do to improve the team?'

And you had to give an answer straight away!

Then he'd go to the next man, and you couldn't give the same answer as the lad before you. You'd be sitting there pissing yourself thinking… *Jesus, what am I gonna say here?*

I'd say whoever was No 15 was absolutely bricking it!

The six backs would all talk about being out in front, being aggressive… win the ball. But he'd put you under fierce pressure! You'd really be sweating it.

Heffo was one of the first to bring in the video analysis too. If you went training on a Thursday night, you mightn't get home until half twelve. We'd be in watching footage of games and going through things off the back of that. It was Kevin's life. He was a huge figure and what he said went.

If he said to do A, B and C… and you did A and B, but not C… you were gone. But I'll say this… if he saw you were giving him one hundred percent, he'd give you one hundred percent.

It was a big surprise when he went.

We were in shock. Tony Hanahoe, Lorcan Redmond and Donal Colfer, who had been with Kevin all the way along, had a good few miles on the clock. It was so time-consuming and took a lot of work even then.

They were such a tight group so, once one of them was going, they were all going to go. But they left in the middle of a league campaign, so there was probably huge shock at the timing of it, not to mention the void that was left by such a legendary management team departing. Robbie Kelleher and Brian

Mullins came in, and there was a different dynamic then, which was only natural. Training changed. Lots of things changed.

Succession is always difficult; we've seen that time and again in many sports.

I played in four All-Irelands, and I only won one.

We weren't expected to win in 1983, but you have to take your chance when you get it. You'd think that I would pick the game where I won my only All-Ireland medal, but that game was so controversial. The whole aftermath of it, the years that followed… I met up with a few of the Galway lads years later, and there was no real animosity, but the whole thing left a bad taste.

I remember going to The Burlington Hotel the day after the game, and the referee John Gough was there with his officials. There was just a really bad atmosphere. We won the All-Ireland, but that's really all there is to say about it.

You always look back on your time playing and think you could have done better, you could have won more, but I was lucky… I had a great career. Football was very good to me. I went to Australia in 1986 for the International Rules when Heffo was manager. *Do you know what he did?* I could have killed him.

He put me rooming with Mick Lyons! I wouldn't have known Mick at all before then. I wouldn't cross the road in front of Mick at that time in case he'd run me over!

So, the two of us are in the room… and at first it was a bit awkward.

'How's it going?'

We became great friends, but I couldn't believe it at the time. Pádraig Lyons was on the trip too, Colm O'Rourke… we had a great time. We had to get on because se were representing our country.

Heffo used to say… *'One in, all in'*… so we had to have that tightness as a group. They were all great lads. When they were playing for Meath, they did what they had to do. And I did what I had to do for Dublin.

VINNIE MURPHY

DUBLIN 2-12 MEATH 1-10
Leinster SFC Final
Croke Park
JULY 30, 1989

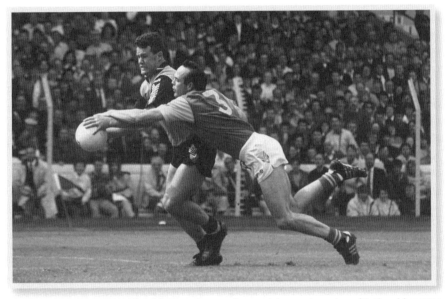

Vinnie Murphy beats Meath's Mick Lyons in one of many intense struggles with the old enemy.

★ **DUBLIN:** J O'Leary; D Synnott, G Hargan, M Kennedy; K Barr, T Carr, E Heery; D Foran, P Clarke; **V Murphy (1-2)**, K Duff (1-2), B Rock (0-5); P Curran (0-1), J McNally (0-1), M Galvin (0-1). Sub: M Deegan for Synnott.

★ **MEATH:** M McQuillan; B O'Malley, L Harnan, P Lyons; K Foley, T Ferguson, M O'Connell; L Hayes, G McEntee; D Beggy, PJ Gillic, C Coyle; C O'Rourke (0-1), B Stafford (0-5), B Flynn (0-4). Subs: M McCabe (1-0) for McEntee, J Cassells for Beggy.

THE ACTION

HAVING HAD THINGS all their own way in Leinster for the best part of a decade, Dublin had lost the last three provincial finals in-a-row – and a league final – to a resurgent Meath. Seán Boylan's men had made good on their emergence from the Dubs' shadow to win back-to-back All-Irelands in 1987 and '88. However, they went into this game without the imposing presence of Mick Lyons, and Dublin – playing in front of a newly-refurbished and packed Hill 16 – sniffed blood.

Meath went into an early lead through Colm O'Rourke, but Dublin replied emphatically. From John O'Leary's kick-out, the ball cleared midfield and found its way to Kieran Duff. The Fingallians man was a late call-up to the starting line-up after Charlie Redmond was deemed unfit, but his first contribution was a memorable one. Duff eased Terry Ferguson out of the way before carrying the ball through the heart of the Meath defence, and burying it into the top corner of the net.

Bernard Flynn was causing Dave Synnott considerable problems and had clipped over three points by the time Mick Deegan was sprung from the bench after 22 minutes to curb his influence. At the half-time whistle, Dublin led by the bare minimum. Colm Coyle's running battle with Keith Barr had been simmering since the start of the game, and the Meath man picked up a booking before half-time. With nine minutes gone in the second-half, Coyle snapped and received his marching orders for a late challenge on the Erin's Isle half-back.

Flynn levelled things up moments after Coyle's dismissal, but three unanswered scores from Rock, Paul Curran and Vinnie Murphy gave Dublin a three-point buffer. However, Meath's dependable doggedness raised its head once again. Stafford took a point when a goal looked on to leave the score at 1-9 to 0-10 with just 10 minutes to go. Moments later, Liam Hayes scrambled along the end-line like, in the words of the late great Jimmy Magee... 'an All Black forward' before popping the ball back to the edge of the square for substitute Mattie McCabe to punch emphatically to the net in front of a stunned Hill.

Dublin were in no mood to roll over on this occasion, and rallied to finish the game in spectacular fashion. First, Murphy grabbed a goal.... 2-8 to 1-10... followed by insurance points from Mick Galvin, Paul Curran, Joe McNally and Murphy again.

★★★★★

66

THE REASON I picked this game is that it was my first Leinster title and Meath were our biggest rivals. Dublin hadn't beaten Meath in the championship since 1985, so they had the whip hand over us. They beat us fairly well in 1987, and in '88 they won by two points but we put a penalty over the bar in the last minute.

There were a few new faces coming through at the time. I had come into the team in 1988, and Keith Barr and Paul Curran were there in '89. So there was a new generation of Dublin footballers coming along… but Meath were still the big bogeymen for us.

There was a feeling that they had bullied Dublin and pushed us around a bit from 1986 to '88. We weren't as physical or as seasoned as they were… they were the older team. So 1989 was a watershed for the younger lads, but also for the guys who had been around for a number of years and had had some success at the start of the decade, but had suffered at Meath's hands for a few years.

Some of the older lads probably saw this as a last-chance saloon, so winning that game was huge. Aside from Leinster finals, we lost the National League final to Meath in 1988 after a replay, and Cork beat us in the '89 league final. We had a really bad record in finals and that was something we needed to change in order to make the breakthrough.

I was only 18 in 1988, so I was still playing minor club after I'd made my senior inter-county debut, which was a bit strange. I played in a league final for Dublin one week and the next I was playing minor club… and lads were looking for my birth cert! I was playing for a junior club too, Trinity Gaels… so going from playing minor and junior club football to playing senior inter-county… that was a big deal.

I was lucky enough in that first year. I was finding my feet and Barney Rock was out with a shoulder injury at the beginning of the league, so that allowed me to get a few games. Barney was one of the biggest stars in the game, and when he came back it was like… *Okay, Barney's back, Vinnie's gone!*

But then Kieran Duff got injured, and I got back in and had a couple of decent games. When you look at it, I got a run of four games because two of the legends of Dublin football were injured. Kieran came back in and again I thought I'd be getting the hook, only for Tommy Conroy to pick up a knock. So I ended up getting a start in the championship in 1988 due to a little bit of luck, though I must have been doing okay to keep getting the call to cover these lads.

1989 was a bit different because I had established myself in the team and those new lads who came in – the younger lads – they added a new freshness to things, and there was a real spark to training throughout that year.

Playing against Meath, while it was obviously very tough and they were a physical team, it wasn't something that I found difficult to handle really, because I was playing junior football for my club and, back then, it was open season on Dublin footballers. Referees seemed to have the attitude… *Well, you're a superstar so you should be able to handle this!* There were certain places you'd go where…let's just say, you'd have to keep your wits about you.

What I found about stepping up to playing Meath wasn't necessarily how hard you were getting hit, but how clever they were with what they did and how they did it. The pulling and dragging, the little pull or nudge at just the right time… I wasn't used to that. Meath were a fantastic football team, and they don't get enough credit for that, but they were definitely masters at the dark arts.

Most of my playing time against Meath around then would have been at wing-forward, marking Martin O'Connell, who was one of the cleanest players on that Meath team, so I got a softer time than a lot of the other lads!

I was centre-forward in 1988, however, and I was marking Liam Harnan. Now, most fellas if I hit them… they'd go down. They might get straight back up, but they'd go down first. I remember hitting Harnan with everything I had – I was about 13 stone at the time – and he dropped to his knees… and he was growling.

Growling!

I thought to myself… *That's him gone for a few minutes.* About 10 seconds later I hear this new growl in my ear. It was Harnan back up, and on my shoulder. After that I just thought I'd stay away from the physical stuff and keep moving! That was different. To come up against really strong men like that who could take whatever you could hit them with… that was probably the biggest difference I noticed when I started playing senior. But the physicality wasn't a big shock, it was the cuteness and the trash-talk… that was new!

There was a fair bit of animosity between the sides at that time. The older Dublin players wouldn't have liked what they saw as underhanded tactics from Meath. They wouldn't have liked the way Meath went about their business… with the targeting of Dublin players and so on. I remember talking to Bernard Flynn and a few of the other Meath lads in more recent years, and their attitude from 1986 on was basically that they weren't going to let any new Dublin player grow and develop into a player that might do Meath damage.

They were going to hit us and niggle us and do whatever it took, physically or mentally, to run any new faces out of the Dublin team. If you made a mistake, there'd be a comment here or a comment there.

It never went to the levels that we sometimes read about now. It was never anything nasty or personal, but they seemed to sense if your confidence was down… and they'd play on that.

They also knew if you were fiery and how to push the buttons to get a reaction. They were going to test any new Dublin players and ask questions of them. *Do they have the physicality? Are they going to be able to take whatever is coming?*

There was a big row in the league final replay in 1988.

Kevin Foley hit Kieran Duff and I came in briefly and got involved, but I thought I'd be sent off, so I tried to meander away. Then, I got sandwiched between Mick Lyons, Harnan and Colm O'Rourke. You couldn't have picked three harder lads if you tried. I ended up on the deck.

The blood was boiling at that stage, and I won the next ball that came out and got around O'Connell and let it into the full-forward line. With that, O'Rourke hit me a shoulder and to this day I've never been hit as hard. My soul left my body for a moment and came back to me when I hit the ground.

The thought did cross my mind… *Is this where you really want to be?!*

I was after being pole-axed twice. But as Liam Hayes once said about me… 'He got two of the finest belts ever seen in Croke Park… and both of them were deserved!' I'm not sure I'd fully agree with Liam on that one, but that was the way those games were. When I got involved with Foley they probably saw that as reason enough to defend their man and, look, what goes around comes around. If you were getting involved, you had to expect some form of retribution. You just had to get up and get on with it… or exit stage left.

We ended up losing badly, but I was then playing for the Dublin hurlers later that day… against Meath. I was that sick from the belt, I wasn't in much shape to play hurling. Now if you think the Meath footballers were tough… try the Meath hurlers. *And when they saw a Dublin footballer coming?* I might as well have been on the Bull Run in Pamplona!

In 1989, the cards were put on the table and there was an admission that maybe Meath had pushed us around a fair bit, but also that we had allowed them to play and get a lead and get on top of us. Then yeah, we'd come roaring back into the game when it was too late. So we felt that we were giving them a good start every time and then basically running out of time.

The training was tough that year compared to other years. It was savage enough in 1988, but in '89 we trained 28 nights out of 30 at one stage. Two and a half hours of pure savagery. I think I was about 13st 4lbs at that stage – I'd have to lose a leg to get anywhere near that now!

We trained really hard, but we would always have talked about Meath because they were the best at the time, and they had been in the top two teams in the country for the previous three or four years. We played them in the league that year in Navan, and it was decided that we were going to set our stall out in that game.

There always seemed to be a flashpoint in those games where something kicked off. Gerry McCaul said that to us, that Meath used those incidents as a rallying call to get together… that there was a bit of tribalism or whatever you want to call it. You grabbed the nearest man to you and got stuck in. So it was decided that we were going to stand our ground.

Another thing Gerry said to us was that if we were going well, someone usually got a belt from a Meath lad just to slow the game down and to disrupt us… and turn the whole game into a war. So we were prepared for that.

We started well in that league game in Navan. Then Tommy Carr got a ball and one of the Meath lads came in and gave him a box. Tommy put the ball under his arm, and jumped up and threw a punch back. PJ Gillic came in and all hell broke loose. At the same time over on the other side of the pitch, Eamonn Heery and Bernard Flynn were going at it.

So there were pockets of rows breaking out all over the place. It was ugly and it made a few headlines the next day, but it was the first time where we really got stuck in and said… *No more… This isn't happening again. You can throw what you like at us but we're not gonna take it lying down.*

We ended up winning that game comfortably, and that was a platform for winning the Leinster in '89.

The 1989 Leinster final came around and it's Meath again. Kieran Duff wasn't due to start that game but Charlie Redmond had an injury… so Kieran started at centre-forward. Very early on, a kick out from John O'Leary cleared everyone and Kieran got the better of Terry Ferguson just outside the '45'. After that it was a foot-race. Dully was a great ball carrier and he took off and buried it in the roof of the net from about 20 yards. That got us off to a great start and gave us a huge lift.

It was a scorching day, and we always felt we were better on a dry day than a wet one. The other thing was that Mick Lyons was missing for Meath and that was a big plus for us for the simple reason that Joe McNally was a huge influence in our team at full-forward. A lot of ball went through him, and Lyons would always have done quite well on Joe. But with him out, Liam Harnan had to move from centre-back, so Meath lost that physical presence at No 6 as well. Joe won a lot of ball and set up a few scores. He was able to do something which not many lads before or since were able to do – that was the ability to knock a ball 10 or 15 yards left or right with his hands as it came in. He had great peripheral vision to be able to see what was on.

Joe set up a score for Barney in the first-half, where the ball bounced up in front of him and he slapped it about 20 yards to his right, straight into Barney's hands… and he popped it over. He was a brilliant man to bring other players into the game, which is something I'm not sure he got credit for.

We got off to the perfect start, but it was early days and we would have been aware that there was a sucker-punch coming. It was a cracking game of football… end-to-end.

I always felt Meath were a bit slicker in their link play in the forwards, it almost felt like they had pre-set plays, whereas we didn't have anything like that. We'd knock it into Joe and work off him. With Meath, if PJ Gillic got the ball, Flynn would be in a certain position or O'Rourke would be in a certain position… and it wouldn't be in an orthodox position, they could be 35 yards out on the far side. And the defender might think… *They're not in the play…* but they'd end up with the ball and stick it over.

We got a boost early in the second-half when Colm Coyle got sent off for a second booking. Himself and Keith Barr were having a bit of a ding-dong all game, and Colm caught Keith with a bit of a late hit and the ref gave him the line. Colm Coyle… he was definitely a man that people would have different opinions on, but he was the sort of guy every team needed. He'd die for the cause. We had our own lads like him in Heery and Keith himself… they were our Colm Coyles! We probably thought we had it at that stage and we'd win fairly comfortably. We should have known better.

Liam Hayes was always amazing against Dublin. We talk about underrated, and we talk about John McDermott as being one of Meath's greatest midfielders but, to me, I don't think they ever replaced Hayes. He was a colossus for Meath against us, and the amount of times he dragged them back into games by the scruff of the neck against Dublin… and he did it again in this game when he set up their goal. Watching it, I couldn't believe what I was seeing. He clean-picked it, he over-carried it… he's barging… he got fouled about 20 different ways… and how he got through I'll never know. I think he crawled over John O'Leary at one stage! Anyway, he popped the ball across to Mattie McCabe, who had become a bit of a super-sub for Meath, and he punched it into the net and that put them a point up.

We had planned for this, because we knew there'd be a sucker-punch from Meath and it was about responding to that.

We knew from previous years that we'd recover, but sometimes the recovery was too slow or came too late, so we had to get a score quickly to get back on track and kill the Meath revival as quickly as possible. We had tried to get into the mind-set of not making a drama into a crisis and try to respond. Thankfully we did.

Barney put a long ball in, I caught it and I stuck it in the net. When I caught the ball, I saw a bit of a gap and I went for it. It took a bit of a deflection but it didn't go left or right, it just made the ball go slightly lower so it dropped into the middle of the net. If it wasn't deflected it would have gone into the top corner so it would have been an even better goal!

A lot of Meath people say that it wouldn't have happened if Lyons had been there, but I say that it would have been a penalty because I would have had the ball and he'd have fouled me! I'd have the craic with them about that.

That was the thing we had learned… we had to stop the comeback in its tracks. We hadn't done that in the past. We actually took our foot off their neck two years later in 1991, but on that day in '89 we didn't. Mick Galvin got a great score, Joe Mc got an unbelievable point from under the Cusack Stand and we tacked on a couple more to win by five points in the end. I know that five points doesn't sound like an awful lot, but there were an awful lot of two-point 'hammerings' between Meath and Dublin.

Two or three points was considered a bad beating back then.

Having someone like Keith Barr coming in – that was his first year on the team – was huge. It's amazing the difference even one guy can make. The training that year had an awful lot more spice and pep to it than previous years and the amount of times Keith and Dully would have clashed in training… it was a weekly occurrence!

They were two fiery characters, but Keith trained the same way that he played. He didn't offer apologies and he didn't ask for any either – and Colm Coyle was the same. So the entrance fee to watch those two alone was worth it, because they'd be up to all sorts. They were similar players too, they could talk to you, they could pull and drag you, but if they wanted to play they could do that too. Eamonn Heery was like that too, but he wouldn't have been as vocal – Keith would let you know what he was going to do, then do it… then tell you, 'I told you I was gonna do that!' Eamonn would just do it.

Different characters, but those lads brought a tougher edge to things. Paul Curran was similar– he wasn't the biggest man but he was so tough. He was like a ping-pong ball… when he hit something he bounced straight back up. So those few new faces definitely added something different in 1989.

There was probably more 'honesty' back then, if you want to call it that. Lads would jump for a ball and the best man would win it. Now lads are probably more inclined to try to punch it away rather than trying to catch it. In Mick Lyons' era, you'd see him catch the ball a lot. It'd be rare that he'd try to punch it. Back then it was a case of putting the ball in and let the best man win it. We certainly didn't make any changes to our game just because Mick Lyons wasn't there.

Meath pulled off some amazing comebacks during that period, but that day they just didn't have it and the heads dropped a little. We had gone to another level and the confidence was up. The sun was shining, the Hill was back after being closed in 1988… everything just went perfectly for us.

Unfortunately, things didn't work out in the semi-final against Cork. From that period from 1987-'95, we felt we were always the second-best team in Ireland. Rightly or wrongly, we felt that if we had won Leinster in 1987 or '88, we'd have beaten Cork. We got our chance against them in '89 but I always felt we played better in the sun than the rain.

In that Cork game, we got off to a great start… we were 1-2 to no score up after 10 minutes or so. I got the goal from close range. But then Mickey Kearins sent off Keith Barr, which was a joke. It was just one of those things for Keith… you live by the sword and you die by the sword, and he came out on the wrong side of it that day. They got two goals from penalties. If they didn't go in, I firmly believe we'd have blown Cork out of it in the second-half.

It wasn't to be, but when I look back and I think of the years where I think we could have won an All-Ireland, 1989 was definitely the one!

JACK SHEEDY

DUBLIN 1-10 MEATH 0-12
Leinster SFC Semi-Final
Croke Park
JULY 4, 1993

Jack Sheedy competes high against Meath's Liam Hayes in the epic four-game drama in the 1991 Leinster Championship.

★ **DUBLIN:** J O'Leary; C Walsh, D Deasy, P Moran; E Heery, P Curran, D Harrington; P Gilroy, **J Sheedy (0-1)**; J Gavin, K Barr, N Guiden (0-1); D Farrell, V Murphy (0-1), C Redmond (1-7). Subs: P Bealin for Harrington, M Galvin for Gavin.

★ **MEATH:** M McQuillan; B O'Malley, E McManus, K Foley; G Geraghty, M O'Connell, C Murphy; C Brady, J McDermott (0-1); D Beggy, PJ Gillic, (0-2), J Devine; C O'Rourke (0-5), B Stafford (0-3), T Dowd (0-1). Sub: L Harnan for Foley.

THE ACTION

IN THEIR FIRST championship meeting since the epic four-game saga of 1991, Dublin and Meath served up another memorable encounter in Croke Park in this Leinster semi-final. The game began in tentative fashion with both sides sizing each other up. A low-scoring first-half saw Dublin lead by just a point – 0-5 to 0-4 – at the break.

That first-half was not without controversy though, as Graham Geraghty's goal was ruled out for over-carrying by referee Tommy Howard. It looked to be a harsh call but the Dublin support in the crowd weren't complaining. For their part, Dublin also had a goal chalked off, but this was more clear-cut, with Vinnie Murphy inside the small square when he punched Jack Sheedy's high ball to the net. The game had been smouldering nicely, but it would catch fire in a pulsating second-half.

Meath midfielder John McDermott had the sides level within a minute of the restart, but moments later Man of the Match Charlie Redmond made a crucial intervention. First, he edged Dublin back in front with a point, before burying the ball to the net after good work from Paul Bealin and Jack Sheedy. With the Hill in full voice, it looked as though Dublin would win the game with a bit to spare.

Once again however, Meath showed all their grit and determination to edge back into the game bit by bit. They still trailed by one with the game ticking into added time. It was then that two of the wisest heads on the field combined, it seemed, to set up a replay. Brian Stafford's short free found Colm O'Rourke, and the Skryne man lofted over a trademark point from 40 metres to level the game.

Most observers felt that the final whistle would go from the resultant kick-out, thus earning the GAA yet another valuable pay-day. Tommy Howard had other ideas, however, and Dublin swept downfield. The ball was worked to Redmond who let fly for the winning score. Bob O'Malley made a wonderful full-length block on the Erin's Isle man, but Redmond was quick to chip the loose ball up to the unmarked Sheedy, who drove over the winning score from 45 metres.

★★★★★

66

I DON'T REMEMBER the game massively well, but there are bits and pieces I recall. It wasn't a game that stood out for fantastic passages of play or anything like that, but for me personally and for the team as a whole, I felt it helped our development. I know we didn't end up winning an All-Ireland that year, but the likes of Barney Rock and Kieran Duff had finished up in 1991, so in '93 we had a lot of new faces.

Meath were the same… a lot of the side that played us in '91 had walked away. Liam Hayes, Gerry McEntee, Mick Lyons, Joe Cassells, Terry Ferguson… they were all gone. Lads who were the backbone of those great Meath teams of the 80s and after.

We were missing Tommy Carr due to suspension, and Tommy was a big part of everything for us. You had the likes of Jim Gavin coming in, and Dermot Harrington made his debut that day for us. Meath had Jody Devine, Graham Geraghty, Cormac Murphy, John McDermott and Enda McManus, who were new to their set-up.

But, despite that… the build-up, the atmosphere, the tension in the game… those things were exactly the same. And the colours of the jerseys were the same… and the intensity that everyone brought to it was the same.

It was a given – an absolute given – that whatever 15 lads Seán Boylan sent onto the pitch, it was going to be a battle and there wasn't going to be a whole lot in it at the end. There were still a few of the old guard there… Bob O'Malley, PJ Gillic, Brian Stafford, Colm O'Rourke… lads who were part of what Meath had been doing for the last 12 years or so. The core Meath values were there too.

You expected nothing less than a ferocious game and the fact that it was the first meeting since 1991, that meant it was built up a little bit more. We had won a Leinster in 1992 and lost the All-Ireland final that year, but we didn't beat Meath along the way. Leinster titles back then always meant more when you beat them.

Meath had beaten us fairly consistently in the late-80s and won two All-Irelands along the way. They'd been in four All-Irelands in total. That's how you measured yourself as a Dublin footballer. The performances you put in against Meath were what people made note of. That's absolutely no disrespect to the other teams, because I remember going down to Wexford and getting hammered around the place and coming up against lads from other counties who were really good footballers.

But Meath were the kingpins and you measured everything against them. So yeah, winning a Leinster having beaten Meath along the way would be considered a solid foundation for what we were trying to achieve.

I had been on the panel in 1984 when I was 21, but I never played a championship game. I came in after the end of the league and played in a few challenge matches and was part of the squad for that championship season. We lost the All-Ireland final to Kerry that year and, a few weeks after that, I was to play in a challenge match for the opening of Naomh Barróg's pitch in Kilbarrack, against Meath ironically.

I had a league match with Lucan that morning. We were intermediate at the time, and I was captain. Then that afternoon, we were playing in a tournament final out in Maynooth. Bodies were fairly thin on the ground, so I played both games with the club and I didn't go to the Dublin challenge match. This was in the days before mobile phones, so I had no way of getting word through to Kevin Heffernan that I wouldn't be at the game in Barróg.

I tried making contact with someone, but with no success. A few weeks later there was another challenge match against Longford. My dad was down in Lucan village that night and someone said to him, 'I see Jack's name in the paper for a challenge match against Longford tomorrow'. *This was on the Saturday night.* There had been a storm all over Dublin and the phones were out all around Lucan.

I couldn't make contact with anyone in the County Board or the management, so I just jumped in the car on the Sunday morning and headed for Longford. When I got there, I jumped out of the car and went up to Kevin and said, 'I'm sorry I haven't been able to contact you'. Himself and Tony Hanahoe, who was actually the manager at the time, were standing there looking at me. I explained the situation to them, but I don't think Kevin was too enamoured with my reasoning!

He just said, 'Go in there and tog out, and get your jersey'. So I togged out, got the boots on, and went out onto the field.

I sat in the dugout for the whole game... didn't get a kick of a ball except maybe at half-time. That was it, I never got another call after that! I was desperately disappointed. I understood after the game in Barróg how they felt, but I'd no way of contacting them. I made the decision to go with the club, which was probably the wrong decision in hindsight. For the Longford game, there was nothing I could do about that.

My dad told me on the Sunday morning about it, so I borrowed his car to drive down. As I was driving in the gate of Pearse Park, the Dublin bus was right in front of me. I spoke to the two lads, they weren't impressed, and I didn't hear from them again. They had their way of doing things, I can understand that.

They probably thought I had no interest, but I didn't drive to Longford for the fun of it. It was everything to me to play for Dublin, especially coming from a small club as Lucan was at the time. But look, that's the way things go.

I played with the Dublin juniors in 1985 and we got to an All-Ireland semi-final, and again in '87 when Cork beat us in the final. I had been called into the senior panel in 1986, but I pulled my hamstring playing with the club the week before. I went along to the session just to watch, and they said they'd call me back when I was fit... but I never heard anything. When Paddy Cullen and Pat O'Neill came in, they held trials and I was called in to them. I was playing with the Garda club at that stage – I had transferred – so the trials went well, and I got the call to come onto the panel.

I was 27 at that stage, and I was probably starting to think my chance was gone. It would be fairly unusual for a lad to start his inter-county career at that age. I was playing good football with the club, playing anywhere around the middle eight, so when the trials came up I was delighted. I was actually down in Cork with a group of lads when I got word that they wanted to take a look at me.

I knew a good few of the Dublin panel at that stage from club games and the Dublin juniors. But it was certainly a late calling. I was probably in awe of the whole set-up. When I was on the panel in 1984, Dublin were coming off the back of winning an All-Ireland in '83 and you were looking at the likes of Brian Mullins, Tommy Drumm, Barney Rock... talk about being in awe. I was probably star-struck for the entire year I was there.

In 1990, it wasn't quite the same because Dublin hadn't had success in a while, but it was still daunting because having not made it the first time and having not played minor or under-21, you're asking yourself if you belong there? I felt like I was playing catch-up all the time. I wouldn't have been massively over-confident in my ability, or comfortable in the surroundings, but the one thing I said was that I'd leave no stone unturned, and I'd sacrifice whatever I had to in order to be successful.

I put my head down and I think with every game I became a little bit better, a little bit stronger. I was playing centre-forward, wing-forward and midfield, positions where you'll always be involved in the game. If I had been in the corner and relying on ball coming in, it might have been a different story... and I probably became that little bit more influential in the team by virtue of the fact I was playing in those central positions.

That's why I picked this game, because it was a game where I thought... *Yeah, I'm good enough to be here.* 1991 was fantastic in so many ways. I made my championship debut and played in those big games against Meath. Then in 1992, because we were beaten in the All-Ireland final and because of the manner of the defeat, I felt I could have done more, and I felt the team could have done more.

Therefore, the league final and replay against Donegal in 1993 was another stepping-stone and confidence-booster. I was learning all the time. Learning what to do, when to get involved, when to hang back, when to do things differently.

In the lead-up to that game against Meath at the beginning of July, it just felt like we'd taken a lot of knocks. We had learned a lot along the way, and I was starting to feel comfortable in my surroundings. The intensity of the game was phenomenal. There were no massive hits but there were a fair few sturdy hits, as always. I think the youthful influx on the Meath team, in particular, added a lot to it. You didn't bounce off the likes of John McDermott and not feel it.

They worked very hard and the speed that players like Jody Devine and Graham Geraghty brought to it meant it was always going to be a tight game. The time you got on the ball was split-second stuff, and if you did the right thing then great, but time on the ball was so scarce that you could be a hero one minute and a villain the next because of the pace of the game. There were a lot of very direct balls played in... we were looking for the key guys inside. When you weren't, you were busy harrying and hassling lads.

We got into the lead early, but Meath pegged us back, and we went in just a point ahead. Thinking back to the games in 1991, they were fast, but I felt that game in '93 was another level up again. I always had a good level of fitness, so I probably adapted to inter-county football quick enough in that regard.

I was midfield with Pat Gilroy and marking Colm Brady that day. Colm was a great footballer. He was your typical Meath midfielder really. A big, rangy guy… strong, quick, good hands, probably not dissimilar to Liam Hayes, but I think overall on the day a lot of things went slightly better for me than they did for him.

With the way the 1991 series of games against Meath ended, with me missing the free, I was gutted after it – now, it was about 70 metres out, so I didn't really have a huge expectation that I'd kick it.

I always had plenty of distance from frees; accuracy might have been an issue sometimes though! I had kicked frees of that distance before and since, but because it was so far out, nobody ever brought it up. But I wouldn't have stepped up if I didn't think there was a chance that I would kick it. I had strained my hamstring earlier in the game, so I was trying to kick the free and not tear my hamstring at the same time. It would have been fantastic, but it wasn't to be, and you move on.

So, it was ironic then that I was the one who kicked the winner in 1993. When Colm O'Rourke kicked an equaliser right at the end, all the memories of 1991 came flooding back. Even though I was still in the middle of a game, I was getting little flashbacks. Pat Gilroy won possession from the restart – Pat had a great football brain – and we worked it up the Hogan Stand side of the pitch and got it to Charlie, who would have been our go-to guy for getting a score nine times out of 10.

We did everything right in terms of how it would be judged in today's game. We held possession, we were patient… and got it to the shooter. Charlie wound up for the shot and Bob O'Malley got a fantastic block on it. I was up supporting the play, and it just so happened that when Charlie got blocked down, he chipped it up to me and I took a swing at it and fortunately, it went in the right place.

As I took the shot, I still had Charlie's voice in my ear… he was shouting at me to give it to Paul Curran, who had gone outside me. Thankfully, I ignored Charlie's advice. It was a sweet strike. I always believed that things work much better in football when you do them on instinct.

It was natural, it was being in the right place at the right time… it was making a decision – that's probably what stands out from that score. A year or two before that, I probably would have given it to Paul Curran. I got myself into the right position and I took the shot on. It was a very sweet moment to watch it sailing over into the Hill end and to see the reaction of the crowd.

But I remember immediately thinking… *This is Meath. F**k. We can't lose the next kickout.* I actually came out from the score in reverse, to make sure I was completely aware of what was going on; so that we didn't get hit with a sucker-punch once again.

Mickey McQuillan put the ball down and Tommy Howard blew it up as soon as he kicked it out. It was a very special moment for me having got the winning score but, more importantly, it was a special moment for the team because we had put 1991 to bed.

After the game, I shook hands with a few of the Meath boys and then back in the dressing-room I had a couple of small cuts and bruises to get looked at – which was the norm after those games! Good, bad or indifferent, I always emptied the tank, so I was always one of the last to leave the dressing-room… I'd be so drained.

Mentally that was a tough game by virtue of the fact that the scoreline was bouncing back and forward all the way through.

We scored a goal early in the second-half which was key. Paul Bealin came on at half-time and went to No 11. He had been carrying a bit of a knee injury. Keith went to No 6, Curraner went to wing-back and Dermot Harrington went off. Bealo won a kick-out, laid it off to me and I took it on and laid it off to Charlie, who stuck it in the back of the net. That put us 1-7 to 0-5 up, and we were playing really well. Typically, though, Meath clawed their way back into it and chipped away.

Brian Stafford kicked a couple of points, Jody Devine and John McDermott got a score each… Rourkey kicked a few as well. So, having been five points up and looking like we're coasting, it's back – again – to being one of those tight Dublin-Meath games where you could cut the atmosphere with a knife. Having lost in similar circumstances two years previously, the throat gets a bit dry in those situations, and the brain starts to go into overdrive. You just keep telling yourself… *Next ball, next ball*… but when Colm kicked that equaliser, I thought that maybe it was time up at that stage.

I'd have to say that's my favourite score in a Dublin shirt, because of the significance of it. Thinking about the free in 1991, thinking about all the doubts I had about myself as a player… the way I was out of the county set-up for so long. That score justified all the work that had gone in in the years before, and it justified – to me – my place in the Dublin team. To win a game against Meath with the defining score… it doesn't get much better than that as a Dublin footballer.

My last championship game for Dublin was the 1994 All-Ireland final. I did my cruciate at the back end of '94 in a challenge match against Meath in Moynalvey. I just went up for a ball on my own and I landed badly. I can say for sure it was nothing to do with Liam Harnan! I think Liam was farming that day!

I got into the gym and worked away on it, and I was almost back for the 1995 Leinster final, but it went on me again in the week of that game. When Mickey Whelan took over in 1996, I was in the squad, and I felt like I was in good shape and good form, but management didn't agree and I was sitting in the stand for the Leinster final that year along with Kieran Walsh, Vinnie, Paul Clarke and one or two more. I didn't get called back in for 1997.

My Dublin career was a lot shorter than I'd have liked or hoped for, but if you'd have asked me in 1987, '88 or '89, would I get back in, I'd probably have said that I wouldn't. I was trying hard, playing well with the club… and pulling on the Dublin jersey was all I ever wanted. I was very lucky in some ways to get back in and it was a fantastic four years.

I went from being a complete unknown in 1990 to being nominated for All Stars – picking up one – and doing what I always wanted to do. Playing for Dublin.

CHARLIE REDMOND
(& JOHN O'LEARY)

DUBLIN 1-18 MEATH 1-8
Leinster SFC Final
Croke Park
JULY 30, 1995

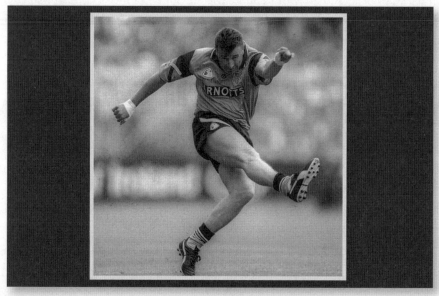

Charlie Redmond hits one of his trademark free-kicks against Meath in Dublin's historic 10-point win in the Leinster final that propelled them to the All-Ireland title.

★ **DUBLIN: J O'Leary**; K Galvin, D Deasy, P Moran; P Curran (0-2), K Barr, M Deegan; P Bealin, B Stynes; J Gavin (0-1), D Farrell (0-3), P Clarke (1-2); **C Redmond (0-7)**, J Sherlock (0-2), M. Galvin (0-1). Sub: V Murphy for Galvin

★ **MEATH:** C Martin; B O'Malley, M O'Connell, C Coyle; G Geraghty (0-1), C Murphy, B Reilly; PJ Gillic, J McDermott; J Devine (0-1), T Giles (0-3), E Kelly (1-0); C O'Rourke (0-2), B Stafford (0-1), T Dowd. Subs: C Brady for Stafford, E McManus for O'Malley, O Murphy for Kelly.

THE ACTION

THERE WAS NEVER much between Meath and Dublin. A kick of a ball here, a controversial goal there. Nobody expected that to change when the familiar foes met in the 1995 Leinster final. Since suffering the ultimate heartbreak at the end of the four-game saga in 1991, Dublin had gained the upper-hand on their rivals and neighbours. Narrow wins over the Royals in 1993 and '94 had banished the memories of Kevin Foley's goal to a large degree and, four years later, the Dubs' eyes were firmly focussed on claiming an elusive All-Ireland crown.

Meath, in spite of losing some of their All-Ireland winning stalwarts in the previous seasons, had looked impressive in their Leinster campaign, running up huge scores against Longford and Wicklow. Some new faces had arrived on the scene, but old hands like Colm O'Rourke, Bob O'Malley and Brian Stafford gave Seán Boylan's side an experienced look. It would, however, be the last appearance in a Meath shirt for all three. The challengers started brightly with Jody Devine opening the scoring inside 15 seconds, but Dublin quickly got to grips with things and, with Dessie Farrell tormenting Cormac Murphy, they led 0-6 to 0-2 after 25 minutes. Brian Stafford and Colm O'Rourke replied with two points for Meath before the half-time whistle, but Dublin maintained their four-point advantage – 0-8 to 0-4.

Meath, famous for their comebacks, looked set to be on course for another one when Evan Kelly palmed the ball to the net six minutes after the restart to level the game. When Graham Geraghty sent over a point from distance to give them the lead minutes later, another famous Royal win looked on the cards. Nobody could have predicted what would happen next. Dublin outscored their opponents by 1-9 to 0-1 in the final 20 minutes of the game to blow the shell-shocked Royals out of the water.

Charlie Redmond was at the centre of everything good for the boys in blue, scoring a wonder-point from play, knocking over his frees with trademark accuracy, and setting up a score for Paul Clarke with a brilliant cross-field pass. Clarke himself provided the killer blow with 12 minutes remaining. Jason Sherlock's effort at a point dropped into the square and Clarke rose highest to fist it to the net.

★★★★★

“

I WAS ALWAYS a creature of habit. The week of a championship game I'd always do the same thing, whether it was the preliminary round or the final. Get my hair cut, cut the fingernails... all the silly stuff! But I'd keep exactly the same routine every week ahead of a game.

We trained in Parnell Park on the Thursday night and had our team meeting. When we were leaving, management always had a bag of balls waiting for me to bring home. I'd go and hit a few frees on the Friday. We got into a habit either that year or the year before, where we'd train on the Saturday at the same time that the game was throwing in at on Sunday.

So, we'd train at half three on the Saturday, let's say. Training took place out in Santry in Trinity sports grounds, and I'd always call in to see my mother and father on the way out to training to make sure they were okay, that everyone was sorted for tickets and that the money was there for them so John Costello wouldn't be sending the sheriff around to me!

I called in that Saturday as usual and, as I walked in, my father was having a stroke. Everything went up in the air very quickly, as you can imagine. I called the ambulance, I ended up missing training... and I spent the rest of the day in the Mater Hospital. We were told quite quickly that he was going to survive, but we didn't know how badly he'd be affected. Thankfully, in the end, he was grand, though of course we didn't know that when we were sitting in the Mater that day.

I had to make contact with Pat O'Neill to let him know why I was going to miss training, and I knew Pat would be a little bit scared and maybe wouldn't play me. But I spoke to him and told him I was ready to play.

'Are you sure?'

'Yes... one hundred percent!' I know it's a real cliché, but there was no way in the world my father would have wanted me to miss the match. Games of any kind against Meath back then – particularly Leinster finals against Meath – were the reason we played gaelic football.

The morning of the game was as normal as it could have been under the circumstances. Your thoughts are with your father in hospital and your family, but I got on with things as I usually would. My father-in-law came down from

Cavan with his buddy, and I made them breakfast. That was one of the things that happened before every game. The two lads would arrive to the house at about a quarter past twelve and I'd have The Full Irish waiting for them. I promise you, I wouldn't touch a bit of it!

I'd have a boiled egg and a bit of toast around half nine, but that'd be it.

When the father-in-law was done with the fry-up, he'd drop me up to Mick Deegan's house in Finglas. Then myself and Deego would go from there to pick up Robbie Boyle… then it'd be on to Croke Park and the usual battle trying to get a parking spot, and get the Gardaí to let us through the cordon. We'd always get through… eventually!

The game itself? I don't remember a huge amount about the first-half. I remember it was tight enough, but we went in with a bit of a lead. Then around 10 minutes into the second-half we got a free, and it was in this little spot in Croke Park that always gave me trouble. It was just the angle… even in training I used to struggle with it.

I put the ball down and I looked up at the posts, and I thought… *F**k it, it's this angle again.* It's maybe a hard one to explain, but I was always someone who liked to curl the ball in on an arc. This angle felt like hitting it straight down the throat of the goals, if I can put it that way.

It was on the left hand side, about 20 metres out and maybe half-way between the sideline and the centre of the pitch. I always felt as though the ball wasn't travelling far enough for the arc to bring it in, and I never liked hitting the ball straight. I hated missing a free at the near post. If you missed on the far post, you've generally hit the ball well. But if you missed at the near post, then that usually means it's a badly-struck free. I had all this stuff going through my head as I stepped up… and of course I missed. Next thing, Meath went on a drive down the field and scored a goal, and very soon after that got a point. They were one up. I was up the other end giving out to myself for missing the free and I kind of said to myself… *You better do something here!*

We got a sideline ball not long after that and I came almost beyond the '45' under the Cusack for it. Deego took it short to me… I felt like I needed to do something special. I turned Enda McManus, but he was at me all the way… pulling and dragging, but I was strong enough at the time to be able to hold him off and keep going. Before I knew it I was after dodging a few tackles… I was only 30 metres or so out.

At that stage I thought I better let fly here! I put the ball a mile into the air… it seemed to hang for about five seconds before it dropped over the bar. I would say it was probably the best point I ever scored for Dublin. That was about 20 minutes into the second-half. It put us two points up.

That point seemed to set us on our way and it really got me going again after having missed the free. I got another ball a minute or two later under the Hogan, down in the corner and drove it across to Clarkey… one of the best passes I ever hit, and he put it over. We were flying at that stage.

This was Jayo's first year in the team, of course – everyone who was around back then will remember 'Boom Boom Jayo' that summer on the radio ads – and he was brilliant for us. But I think he was quiet enough that day. He had a shot which went straight up into the air and Clarkey… to this day, I don't know how he did it, because I wasn't a million miles away from him and I was thinking… *What the f**k is he up to now… Trying to flick the ball into the net.*

Next thing, I see the ball in the net. I was sort of to the right of the goal, and I could see Jack Sheedy. Jack was injured at the time and was handing out water bottles. I saw Jack jump and the water went everywhere!

That goal put us six up and we were cruising it at that stage. Meath just seemed to die. With time almost up, I got another free about 35 yards out on the right hand side. I put the ball down and looked up at the goals. And I genuinely didn't realise what the score was at that stage, I just knew we had it won. I saw the scoreboard behind the goal and copped that we were nine points up.

Back then, if you beat Meath by two points, or you lost by two, that was a 'hammering'. Before that game, one journalist had added up the scores over the last 10 years between the two of us in the championship and it was absolutely level. That was how tight the games were in those days. When you beat Meath, you earned it.

So, when I looked up and saw the scoreboard, I thought… *Jesus, this is to put us 10 points up!* I placed the ball, but when I was walking back, the ball fell off the spot I had it on. It just moved slightly. I knew that if I went to try and replace it, the referee would call me for it and throw the ball in, and I'd miss the opportunity of beating Meath by 10 points.

Just step up and hit it.

I didn't kick it that well, but it went over.

I think straight from the next kick-out, the referee blew it up. It was a glorious summer's day, we'd won a Leinster final against Meath, and we'd beaten them by 10 points. It didn't get much better than that... the sweetest of the sweet. The thing was, it was a new Meath team in a lot of ways. They had beaten us in 1991, then Laois beat them in '92, and we beat them in '93. Then we beat them again in 1994 on a horrible wet day, when Mickey McQuillan made the only mistake he ever made in a Meath jersey when he let my free squirm through his hands into the net. We knew things would be tight.

You were never sure where you'd be going training on the Tuesday after a Meath game. *Would I be going back to Erin's Isle, or would I be back to Santry?* It was a different time. I know we have the backdoor system now, but in those days, there was an awful lot more capital invested in the championship... one shot and you were gone.

I was marking Bob O'Malley in that game and Meath took him off early in the second-half. I don't know was there a bit of trouble in the Meath camp – I kind of got that sense when he was going off that maybe there was something not quite right. It surprised me, because he wasn't having a bad game. Enda McManus came on and I knew a bit about him, but he wouldn't have had Bob's experience. I have to say seeing Bobby go off was a huge tonic for me.

Not playing in the game never entered my head because my father would have been really annoyed if I didn't play. There was never any question about it – I was playing, and that was it. One thing that happened after the game was, one of my sisters ran onto the pitch and gave me a big hug, and that was the only time any of my family came onto the field after a game. Obviously, her emotions got the better of her and she ran on, but it was a lovely moment too. It probably caught me a bit by surprise at the time.

I got very emotional myself because everything that had happened in the previous 24 hours just hit me when I saw her. To be honest though, I didn't want people to see me like that on the field, so I gathered myself after she went back into the stand.

Everything seemed to happen so quickly in that game. We were behind, then I got the point on the run, Clarkey's goal… and then I'm standing over a free at the end to put us 10 points up. I was very surprised when I saw the scoreboard. It was a very strange game in that regard and I felt that, for the one and only time ever, Meath threw in the towel. I don't say that easily, because we had huge respect for Meath, but that was how it felt.

They seemed to have given up the ghost.

One of the fans ran on after the game – I knew his face because he was at all the Dublin games – and he's shouting at me… "WE BEAT MEATH BY 10 POINTS!"… and the smile on his face. It was just…it was everything you wanted from a game. For us, having had 10 years of battle after battle against Meath.

Hard games. Every game that was won, truly won.

The pain… you hit and you got hit, some of it legal, some of it not!

But when every game was over, it was over. Nobody ever said anything, nobody complained. That morning, I remember saying to my late wife, 'I think we're going to beat them well today… I think we'll win by four points!' Because four points was a big win over Meath then.

'DON'T SAY THAT!' Gráinne warned me. 'YOU'LL JINX YOURSELVES! DON'T SAY THAT AGAIN!' When I came out of the dressing-room that day I said, 'I was wrong, wasn't I? We beat them by 10!'

But, while I say it was hard, you never wanted to miss those games. If you don't want to play against Meath then you shouldn't be playing for Dublin, and if you didn't want to play against Dublin, then you shouldn't be playing for Meath. It was an annual event, and you didn't want to be anywhere else other than on the field in Croke Park when those games got underway.

After that game in 1995, we thought we had put Meath away for a while. Someone said to me in Hanlon's, and it wasn't one of the players, I might add… 'We won't be seeing them for a while!' There probably was a perception that it might take Meath a couple of years to recover. It took them a couple of months! I only realised last year, when I was talking to Colm (O'Rourke) that it was his last game, as it was for Staff and Bob O'Malley.

There was something different about that year, and that Leinster final definitely added to the feeling. Colm told me after the All-Ireland final in 1995 that he knew after the Leinster final that we'd go all the way. He said to me that when we started to get on top (in the Leinster final) and went three or four points up, that he felt like he had to do something. So, he gave Paddy Moran a bit of a belt, and Paddy hit the deck.

Colm was getting on with the game... 10 seconds later he gets a tap on the shoulder, and there's Paddy smiling back at him. Colm said that was the moment he knew we'd win the All-Ireland that year. He had come up against Dublin countless times, so he obviously felt there was a harder edge to us that year. Paddy was a tough nut. We were training in Parnell Park one night in 1994, and Paddy put Niall Guiden over the wall with a shoulder.

The day before the All-Ireland final in 1995, we had a team meeting. Pat O'Neill was going through the team and giving some instructions. 'Now John (O'Leary), keep communication clear, make sure you're talking to the lads... Ciarán (Walsh), stay close to your man, don't give away any soft frees...' All the usual stuff. Then he comes to Paddy.

'Paddy... Paddy... *Paddy* (exasperated)... I don't know what to say to you! You've broken up half of this team, now go out and break up half of theirs, will ya!' I always maintained that if I'm putting out a Dublin team that I want to go into battle with – Paddy Moran is my No 4 every day of the week.

In the aftermath of the game, a few reporters were in the dressing-room. I didn't mind doing media stuff, but I wasn't too keen on it that day because I wanted to get out and get up to my dad. I left Croke Park pretty much straight after the game to go up to the hospital, only for him to tell me that Gerry McEntee had stuck his head in that morning to make sure everything was okay.

Gerry had heard what had happened. It just shows you that the tentacles of the GAA reach into every sector of life. There was a fella... we were beating lumps out of one another for years, but there he was checking that my father was okay. It says it all really. My father was an awful lot better at that stage. We didn't stay too long because he was a bit tired. He got out a couple of days after and he was a bit shook, but he was okay.

From a very early age when I was taking the frees, a fella called Pat Timmons out in Erin's Isle always told me to point the pip as he called it – the valve –

towards the goal. Then as the years went by, I would hit a few for the club. I wasn't a particularly good free-taker, and I wasn't taking them for Dublin because obviously Barney (Rock) was the man.

For one of the Leinster finals though, Barney was injured and I ended up taking a few frees. I think I hit the post with one, and dropped another one short. I wouldn't have considered myself a free-taker and I didn't practice frees at that stage. Barney getting injured made me realise... *Well, someone is going to have to step up, so it might as well be me.* I started practicing probably around 1991, and I hit a few frees during the four games with Meath. I hadn't really developed a style at that stage though. I had a strong leg, and I could get plenty of distance. I wasn't always that accurate, but I became accurate because I worked at it.

When I started practicing and I had the valve pointing at the goal, I realised that the two O'Neill's logos were on either side, and so the way I looked at it was there were six panels on the ball. Four going around it as a square, and the one on the top and bottom. I looked at it like there were corners on the ball, which probably sounds strange, but that was the way I thought about it... and the ball was always placed in the same way from that point on.

Once I had settled on the position of the ball, I then had to think about my position in relation to the ball and the posts. So over time, I figured out what I felt comfortable with and what worked best in terms of getting a good contact on the ball... that was the seven steps back, three to the left, and then of course there was the little shimmy on the way up to get the bend on the ball.

The other stuff came over time.

Pulling at the nicks came from Peter Dods, who was a Scottish rugby player, who used to take their penalties and he would pull at his shorts as part of his kicking routine, so I picked that up from him.

The licking of the fingers? I've no idea where that came from! People used to say to me I'd lick both hands, but it was only my right hand... I've only realised that in recent years when I saw some old footage. I thought I used to lick both hands too! I don't know where it came from... it was just one of those things that became a routine and I didn't even think about it, it just became muscle memory.

The practice sessions were the same. I'd have eight balls.

Always eight balls. Wayne (McCarthy) would be behind the goals, and I'd hit eight from the one spot and he wouldn't kick them back out until I'd hit all eight.

Then I'd move to another spot and he'd kick the balls back out to me. We'd do that for 50 minutes three times a week, and we'd work on different things – like kicking into the wind, bending the ball from left to right, keeping it low… just to try to cover all eventualities.

I was always tinkering a little bit.

My style was different to Barney's in that he was quite a straight-on kicker. The way he kicked it had much less margin for error than me, but that's a testament to how good he was, because he was so accurate and rarely missed. With Barney's technique, if you didn't hit it perfectly, then it could go wrong. For me, I gave myself as big a margin for error as I could! I could kick it badly and I might still get away with it and it'd go over. It's interesting then to look at Jimmy Keaveney's style. He was kind of in between me and Barney. He was more straight-on than me, but not as straight-on as Barney.

The interesting thing at that time was that pretty much every team had one man who was the recognised free-taker. Brian Stafford for Meath, Mikey Sheehy for Kerry… Larry Tompkins for Cork. It's the same now in some cases, but not to the same extent. You might see two or three different lads hitting frees in a game, depending on the distance or whatever. Some people felt back then that certain lads would suffer in open play if the frees weren't going well for them. I generally was able to keep the two things separate. I would take consolation from the fact that I might not get the ball into my hands for 15 minutes, but if we got a free, I'd score it. That happened many times.

A lot of people thought that 10-point win over Meath would give us the springboard to go on and win the All-Ireland, but that definitely wasn't the case. We got to the final in 1992 and '94, and lost both. What's more important than a Leinster final is who you play in the semi-final. We played Clare in 1992 and Leitrim in '94. With all due respect, they were both comfortable wins for us, so we were going into an All-Ireland final having not had a testing game in maybe seven weeks or however long it had been since the Leinster final.

But in 1995, we had Cork in the semi-final and we knew that would be a tough game. The Meath game stood to us going into the Cork game, but the Cork game really stood to us in the final.

JOHN O'LEARY

John O'Leary leads the Dublin team during the parade before the 1995 All-Ireland final, but the successful year was built on a massive 10-point win over Meath in the Leinster final.

"

THIS GAME HAS always stuck out for me because of the margin of the victory. It was 10 points. Not three goals and a point... 10 physical scores. Going back over my history playing against Meath from 1983 onwards, all the way up to '96 and '97, the most that was ever between us was a goal, I'd say.

We really just beat them well. It was an era where we were playing really good football.

We had progressed from the 1991 saga, made a final in '92, semi-final in '93, final in '94, and here we were again in our fourth Leinster final in-a-row. We were in a tough place because we were there or thereabouts, and there was no backdoor, so every June it was all clocks back to zero... you were starting from scratch in that relentless pursuit of the All-Ireland title.

The provincial final was a very big step along the way. It's Meath!

That brought the usual anxiety and tension that went hand-in-hand with games against Meath at that time. It was always exciting playing against them. Croke Park was jam-packed and the games were always ferocious.

It felt like a really significant achievement to beat Meath at any time, but to beat them by so much was special. It was just another step on the road in one sense, but we were a team who could have been quite tired by then without knowing it.

I always talk about the 1995 team starting in '91… we were on a long, long journey and we could have become jaded. It didn't feel that way, but if we had only beaten Meath by a point, how would we have felt going into the Cork game the next day?

Nobody can answer that now, but the fact that we beat them by 10 gave us a great bounce, and it really helped us rebound from the disappointment of 1994, which was probably still in the back of our minds.

The day after the 1994 All-Ireland final, I remember saying to one of the lads that we've got to come back again next year. Then I was chatting to Paul Curran at the start of 1995, and I said the same to him… 'We're going to go after this again'.

Paul said, 'Yeah, but I'm going to trip you up when you're going up to collect the cup!' We made this agreement that we'd lift the cup together. I went over to him after the All-Ireland final… 'C'mon, remember the deal?'

He looked at me. 'No!'

I reminded him… 'We said we'd lift the cup together!' That's why that happened. That reflects the resilience that we had at the start of that championship in 1995. I think some of the media and maybe some fans thought we were going to crumble and give up, but that was never going to happen because we knew how close we were. We weren't going to leave it behind.

People might have thought we had a soft underbelly, but that probably only surfaced late in the championship when we came up against new teams. Donegal exposed us a little bit in 1992 in terms of our preparation. We walked into a bit of a sucker-punch in that one, which was partly our own fault. After that, in 1993, '94 and '95, we played really good football. Good, fast, attacking football. We played well enough in the Derry and Down games, but we just got pipped. But there was a huge amount of inner strength in that team.

Take, for example, the four games against Meath in 1991. Those games would have knocked the stuffing out of most teams. A lot of observers would have said… 'You'll never come back from that'. We had at least two of those games in the bag and managed to give them back. That would have knocked the heart out of most teams, but we came back in 1992 and got to an All-Ireland final.

We had a great bunch of guys, and the freshness in 1995 came in the shape of Jayo and Keith Galvin. Personnel-wise, everything else was the same.

In spite of the resilience and all that, the pressure was building. One thing which I found happened was that people were starting to like us! There was a bit of sympathy building because we had been so close on a few occasions. It's hard to imagine anyone feeling sorry for Dublin nowadays!

It's hard to pinpoint anything specific that changed in 1995. It was just a really good group of players. Pat O'Neill took over in 1993 and he instilled a bit of his character into the team, I would say. He didn't make any dramatic changes, but some of his DNA and his lumpy elbows maybe came into our play a little! Pat left at the end of '95 and all that momentum was lost. We fell away really quickly.

We were four up at half-time in that 1995 Leinster final, but that really wasn't much of a lead in those Meath games. We had been in too many battles with them over the years to be sitting too comfortably in the dressing-room. We would have reiterated what was said before the game about keeping the foot down and not taking any chances. Typically, at half-time against Meath – if we were leading – we were ready for the charge.

It came quite quickly that day. They got a goal early in the second-half. Tommy Dowd got in behind and I had to go and close him down. He passed it off to Evan Kelly, who palmed it in. A few minutes later, Graham Geraghty landed a point from about 30 metres which put them in front. Our lead was gone in around 15 minutes. A bit like in 1989 though, we were able to bounce back pretty quickly with a point from Paul Curran. It was always important with Meath that you didn't allow them to get a run on you, because their fans were always at their loudest when they had come from behind.

We got back in front, and Clarkey's goal more-or-less finished the game. It was a bit lucky in that it was a Hail Mary shot from Jayo that dropped short, and Paul punched it to the net. We were all slagging him that he just threw his fist at it, and it could have ended up anywhere. Mick O'Dwyer was on commentary that day and he let a yelp out of him like Gary Neville when the ball hit the net! Jack Sheedy was behind the goal, and he jumped up in the air.

In the last 10 minutes, we were almost showboating. I've a clear memory of enjoying the closing stages of the game, because I knew we had them. We'd got them by the throat. *This is it. This is what real enjoyment feels like. We have them. We have them.* It was point after point. We were killing them. Every score felt like another nail in the coffin. We were in full flow. It didn't get any better than that.

It was a weird feeling, because I'd never played in a game at that stage of the championship where it was so comfortable. Leinster finals, All-Ireland semi-finals and finals… they were always tight. Even if you won, you could never sit back and enjoy the last few minutes because there was always just a kick of a ball in it. What happened that day, it didn't normally happen, so that made it very special. It was also a mark of our respect for Meath that it meant so much.

Beating a lesser county by that margin would be expected, it'd be no big deal. But this was *Meath*. I didn't feel they went out of the game, they kept going, but we snuffed them out totally in defence and our forwards were running riot. Carrying the ball, playing one-twos, kicking great scores from all over the place.

I'm not sure we would have been thinking too much about finishing Meath off for a few years. Nobody knew at the time that it would be Colm O'Rourke's last game, or Stafford's and O'Malley's last game. That would have been a bit too clever on our part. I certainly wasn't thinking about that, I was just focused on winning the game and winning it by such a margin was more than enough for me. I wasn't dwelling on whether Meath lads were going to retire.

I was playing behind Keith Galvin, Dermot Deasy and Paddy Moran. I would have been fairly vocal and there was a huge amount of trust between us. If I shouted at one of them to go, then they knew I had them covered behind. I liked lads to play hip-to-hip with their man. Stand alongside them.

Don't be playing from behind and trying to take a ball off a lad once he wins it. You have to take chances, and back yourself to win the ball. I would have played a lot of games 10 or 15 yards off the goal-line and swept up behind the lads. We had a great understanding and, to my mind, the risk of playing alongside your man was worth it. If you're playing behind your man all the time, then you're at a disadvantage straightaway.

I played sweeper-keeper a lot. Laochra Gael was on recently with Bernard Flynn and they showed a clip of me miles off my line. I must have been 30 yards from goal, but I made sure Bernard didn't get by me! I don't think he was too thrilled with that, but I had to take one for the team there.

Kickouts have evolved a lot since then, and there's a perception that we used to just kick it as far as we could back then. While it certainly wasn't as complex as it is now, we did have a strategy. The two corner backs would push out really wide toward the sideline… Paul Curran would walk in towards me. If his man didn't follow him, I'd chip it to Paul. If his man did follow him, I'd put it into the space behind Paul, and Clarkey would drop back deep, or one of the midfielders would slide over.

The same would apply for Deego on the other side. If the half-forwards didn't follow Curraner or Deego and I chipped it short, their manager would be on their case. So, on the next kick, they'd follow back, and I'd put it into the space. It worked fairly well. There wouldn't have been lads keeping track of the stats, but I think we were fairly successful at retaining possession on our own kickouts.

If you look at the All-Ireland final that year, the very first kickout I had, I went short to Keith Galvin. I keep telling lads that I was the Dublin keeper who started the short kick… Stephen Cluxton is getting way too much credit for that! There were plenty of corner-backs who walked out with their back to me… they didn't want it!

But I had a simple view. If I could pass to someone who was closer and it would guarantee possession, then I would try to do that. Long kicks to midfield were 50/50 at best. I'm sure Pat O'Neill's heart was in his mouth at times, but he would have trusted me to make the right decision and play what was in front of me rather than just doing the same thing over and over regardless of who was free.

Paddy Moran was a bit agricultural; we'd give him a bit of slagging. There wouldn't be much finesse about his style of football, but he gave you everything and he added a seriously hard edge. He was quick too, which people might not realise. Keith Galvin was the young lad with the hair gelled and the collar up… he looked a bit more like a soccer player maybe! But he had pace and he was a tight marker. Wally (Ciaran Walsh) and Dermot Deasy were solid, steady lads. We'd train six-vs-six, and we'd go ballistic if we let a goal in. We worked really hard on communication, and we were fairly tight and aggressive.

Going into any of those Meath games, we wouldn't have been doing loads of video analysis or anything like that. There would have been a little bit of that, but nothing like the extent of what's done today. But we knew those Meath lads so well. Even in 1995, they had a few new faces, but most of them had been around for at least a couple of years.

It was simple enough; we'd focus on ourselves and our strengths. It was man-to-man, so that made it fairly straightforward. If more lads won their battles than lost them, then we'd be in good shape.

When you look at some of the games against Meath from the late-80s, there was an awful lot of messing going on. A lot of rows, a lot of sendings-off.

It takes two to tango, but I think Meath were trying to set down a marker that they were the top dogs. They were better at that than we were! By the time we were into the mid-90s, that had all pretty much gone. There were two reasons for that, I think. Firstly, I would say both sides realised it was fairly pointless. Secondly, the game had evolved.

The frees and sideline balls from the hand had come in and the game had gotten much quicker. There were fewer stoppages and fellas didn't have time to get involved in rows as much as in the past. We were focused on playing football and we realised we didn't need to get drawn into unnecessary distractions.

As great as 1995 was, I would have regrets that it fell apart so quickly. Especially when you see Meath going on to win the All-Ireland the next year. They aren't easily won, but it felt like it was there for the taking. There were no really outstanding teams around. But to be fair to Meath, they went and won it. I would have been looking at it thinking… *There's the team we beat by 10 points. How can they go from that to winning an All-Ireland? And how can we go from winning an All-Ireland to this?*

I know they had some new faces, but that's how I looked at it. The fact that Pat left, for whatever reason, meant we lost a lot of momentum. That's nothing against Mickey Whelan who replaced Pat, but to get to 1995 we had started in '91. Pat had been there throughout that period, so that link was broken in 1996 and the new management team had to start from scratch. A few players walked away, a few faces didn't fit, and things fell apart a bit. It's hard to believe it would be 16 years before we'd get to another final.

The fact that we beat our greatest opponent from the previous 15 years to such an extent, it felt at the time, and even more so since, as one of the most satisfying victories of my 18 years playing championship football.

It was a great honour to beat them by so much, because it just hadn't happened, and in the two years after that it was back to being really close again.

The way we finished that 1995 Leinster final, that's probably the closest we ever got to the current Dublin team. We weren't content to sit on a three- or four-point lead. We were ruthless and kept putting more scores on the board.

That's how the current Dublin team operates. I was standing in the goals and had a great view of everything. The sun was shining, and we were giving an exhibition. I remember thinking to myself… *This is magic.*

PAUL CURRAN

DUBLIN 1-10 TYRONE 0-12
All-Ireland SFC Final
CROKE PARK
SEPTEMBER 17, 1995

The Dublin team that defeated Tyrone in the 1995 All-Ireland final, with Paul Curran (fourth from left in the front row) sitting next to team captain John O'Leary. They would also be on the Hogan Stand together, lifting the Sam Maguire Cup as captain and vice-captain.

★ **DUBLIN:** J O'Leary; P Moran, C Walsh, K Galvin; **P Curran (0-1)**, K Barr (0-1), M Deegan; P Bealin, B Stynes; J Gavin (0-1), D Farrell (0-4), P Clarke (0-2); C Redmond (1-1), J Sherlock, M Galvin. Subs: P Gilroy for K Galvin, R Boyle for M Galvin, V Murphy for Farrell.

★ **TYRONE:** F McConnell, P Devlin, C Lawn, F Devlin, R McGarrity, S McCallan, S McLoughlin, F Logan, J Gormley (0-1), C Corr, Pascal Canavan, C Loughran, C McBride, Peter Canavan (0-11), S Lawn. Subs: M McGleenan for Loughran, B Gormley for S Lawn, P Donnelly for McCallan.

THE ACTION

HAVING SUFFERED AT the hands of Donegal, Derry and Down in previous seasons, Dublin finally broke their Ulster hoodoo to claim their first All-Ireland crown in 12 years. The game was not a classic by any means, and was marred by several controversial incidents, but that didn't matter one bit to the Dublin team or their adoring fans. Having come so close in 1992 and '94, it was simply a matter of getting over the line for this group of Dublin players.

Appearing in just their second All-Ireland final ever, Tyrone made light work of their inexperience at this level and raced into a 0-3 to 0-0 lead after just five minutes. Dublin settled however, and landed three consecutive frees – curiously from three different players in Keith Barr, Charlie Redmond and Paul Clarke – to level things up. Redmond had been an injury doubt before the game but took up his position in the starting 15. It was nip and tuck for a period, and Dublin held a narrow 0-6 to 0-5 lead when the crucial score of the game arrived on 25 minutes. Jason Sherlock showed his bravery in beating the imposing figure of Finbarr McConnell to a loose ball, and toe-poked it towards Redmond, who finished from close range. That goal helped the Dubs to a 1-8 to 0-6 half-time lead.

Tyrone ate into Dublin's advantage after the break and had the gap back to three (1-9 to 0-9) with 45 minutes gone. Incredibly, neither side would score for the next 22 minutes. During that barren spell came the biggest talking point in many a season. Paddy Russell gave Redmond his marching orders, but the Dublin forward remained on the pitch for a further two minutes before eventually being ordered off again.

This time, he departed the scene. Canavan ended the scoreless period when he made it a two-point game with five minutes remaining. Paul Clarke popped over only Dublin's second score of the half on 67 minutes, and it would prove to be crucial. Canavan tapped over two further frees to leave just one between them as the game entered added time. Tyrone then thought they had levelled it when Sean McLaughlin slotted over a late, late point, but referee Russell adjudged that Canavan had played the ball on the ground when setting up the Tyrone wing back.

★★★★★

66

YOU REMEMBER THE one that crowns it. We were an unfortunate team in many ways, so I was just lucky that we got over the line eventually. When you look at how things are now with all the success Dublin has had, we were the opposite – we were getting to finals and losing.

When you look back at the 90s, eight different teams won All-Irelands in that decade, which is extraordinary. That will never happen again, ever. I think there were four different winners in the noughties, but the 90s was just an incredible time in terms of the number of strong teams in the country. The competition was huge, and to even win a match in your province was hard enough, so to win a provincial medal and then try to go on and win an All-Ireland was very difficult.

I made my championship debut in 1989 and I was all over the place in that first season. I started at corner-back in our first game against Kildare in Newbridge, then we went back to Newbridge for our next game, a Leinster semi-final against a very good Wicklow team and I was centre-back. For the Leinster final I was wearing No 13, but I was playing at left half-forward on Kevin Foley. So basically, I was everywhere that first season, and that continued for a few years after that.

In 1992 I nailed down that wing-back spot. I got the jersey for the first round game against Offaly in Tullamore, and I never looked back for the rest of my career. They were tough days. I remember Dublin going down to Wexford Park for a championship game and coming out of it by the skin of our teeth. Lads put everything into those games because it was do or die. There were no second chances.

That first year (1989) was great, even though we lost to Cork in the All-Ireland semi-final. Beating Meath – who were going for four Leinsters and three All-Irelands in-a-row, which was unheard of in their history – was very special. Not many people gave us a chance. Things were very different back then – there was no such thing as driving the coach in under the stand and not having any interaction with the fans.

Dave Foran and I parked up on Dorset Street, walked down Jones' Road, and in under the stand where the guy on the gate let us in. A couple of Meath supporters saw us and one of them shouted over… 'Ye'll be going home with no medals today lads!' That's something that has stuck with me to this day because he was probably saying something that most people believed. It turned out to be a cracking game on a scorching day. There was smoke from the Hill, we got a fantastic goal from Kieran Duff who was a late replacement for Charlie Redmond… then there was Mattie McCabe's goal which looked like flipping it back Meath's way. But then Vinnie got a deflected goal in past Michael McQuillan, and we got a few late scores.

That was a very special day for me making my first appearance in a Leinster final and coming away with the Delaney Cup, especially when you factor in that my father won an All-Ireland medal with Meath in 1967. Sadly, he's no longer with us. I won't say he turned into a Dublin supporter, but on the days that Dublin played Meath, I think he was quite happy if Dublin won.

Looking at the 1995 campaign, we'd been through the wringer in the years before that… 1991 and losing the four-game saga against Meath; '92 and losing the All-Ireland final, unexpectedly in most people's eyes, to Donegal; '93 and losing a semi-final to Derry; '94 and losing the final to Down. There always seemed to be some drama along the way too.

We missed penalties in 1992 and '94. *But did we ever get to the stage where we started to think it would never happen for us?* No, that was never something that came into our heads. It's probably something similar to the feeling the Mayo players have had in recent years. Once you're competing on the second-last or the last day of the season, then players always believe that they can get over the line.

I remember coming back in January 1995 and we were just as determined as ever. We trained as hard as we did the year before – possibly harder – and even though we were getting a little bit older, we did have an injection of youth in the shape of Keith Galvin and Jason Sherlock. Brian Stynes had started in 1994 but he was still relatively new and was definitely a better player in '95. We just seemed to be more determined, more experienced, and maybe the little bit of luck that we didn't get in the previous years came our way in '95 on a couple of occasions. I won't say that the rest of the country was feeling sorry for us at that stage, but it did feel like they wouldn't be unhappy to see us winning an All-Ireland.

I haven't watched the game back in a few years, but there would be certain parts of the game that will never leave me. We started poorly… Tyrone went three points to no score ahead. Ulster teams were going for five All-Irelands in-a-row at that stage, and I think a lot of people thought it was going to be Tyrone's time to win after Down twice, Donegal and Derry had their day. We couldn't have got off to a worse start, but Keith Barr's free-kick stands out to this day. I played half-back with Keith and that free-kick was just inside the 65-metre line. It was a massive kick and it had plenty of room going over the bar… that was a real settler for us. The next two scores we got were also dead balls from two different players. I'm not sure that has even happened before or since – that your first three scores in an All-Ireland final are three dead balls from three different players.

We'd got ourselves back into it fairly quickly and for the rest of the half we took over. We dominated midfield and started to get well on top. Charlie's goal stands out too as it put a bit of daylight between the teams for the first time, and we went in with a five-point lead. It was a good first-half and we were confident coming back out, but we were a team that had taken plenty of hits and we were vulnerable, obviously.

Tyrone started coming back and, in the end, we were lucky to get over the line. I think every Dublin player will admit to that.

There was the disputed moment right at the death where Peter Canavan allegedly touched the ball on the ground. That would have been an equaliser and we would have had to come back another day. I wasn't too far away from that incident and all I can say is there would have been no argument from any Dublin player if that had been allowed. We would have had to dust ourselves down and get ready for a replay.

I think that the advantage would have been with Tyrone if that had happened. They would have gathered a lot more belief that they could win what would have been their first-ever All-Ireland at that time. The overriding emotion when Paddy Russell blew the final whistle was relief.

On the Wednesday night we had the GOAL challenge, and after that night I'd had enough of the celebrating. Along with all the other Dublin lads, I had a club match the following Sunday. We were playing St Mark's and I ended up busting my shoulder because I was all over the place after the week we had. So that kept me quiet for four or five weeks!

In terms of the year as a whole, I wouldn't say we did anything hugely different. We had the same group pretty much, the same management team, so we just rolled on. We were definitely that bit more determined as I mentioned, and we ploughed through the hard training. It didn't all go well for us that year.

We were relegated from Division One in the league. Later on in 1995 we played Leitrim – as All-Ireland champions – in the first round of the league and we were beaten. That was a big back down to earth moment for us and, unfortunately, we stayed there for a good few years after!

I was due to be marking Adrian Cush, but he got injured before the final so I was marking Ciarán Loughran. He was a tough little character and a strong runner. That Tyrone team in general actually, they wouldn't have been the biggest in stature, but they were a tough, physical bunch.

I didn't have much to do for the first 15 minutes. The ball just didn't come my way. Like all defenders back then, my first job was to look after my man. It's totally different to football these days. If I was playing now, I wouldn't have to mark too many lads because they'd be back in their own back line. I got a few touches and was involved in a few scores.

I started to get on top of Ciarán and he was replaced by Mattie McGleenan after half-an-hour. Stephen Lawn came out from the corner, and I picked him up until half-time, then he was taken off and Brian Gormley came in… and I was on him.

I don't know if I'd say I saw off two different lads, but it was man-to-man, and it was very easy for a manager to see who was doing well. No 5 marked No 12, and if No 12 got a point, then it was obvious that it was his marker who was to blame. That's how I looked at it anyway. If my man kicked a point, I'd be getting worried. If he scored two, I'd be looking towards the line.

If he scored three, I'd be walking myself before I was hauled off! That's the way it was, it was much easier to see who was playing well or badly. I find now that it's hard to keep track of where lads start, where they finish, who they're marking and so on. It was easier to hold someone accountable when it was straight man-to-man.

I would have been considered a fairly attacking half-back by the standards of the time. My best game was attacking at the right time, but it wasn't all-out attack by any means. That said, if our midfield was dominating kickouts, you'd be on the front foot all the time. I would always take a chance in the first minute or two, and take off up the wing. If a fella followed me then I wouldn't quite think that I had him for the day, but I knew he was worried about me.

The odd player, when I'd make that run, I'd look back and he'd be over the far side of the field! So, I'd be thinking... *Feck this anyway, I'm going to have to look after him today and I won't be able to play the game I want.* That happened quite a lot towards the end of my career when I couldn't get back as easily, and I was burning oil a bit!

I wouldn't say that the management was too pleased with my style of play back then though. Particularly if you went on a run and lost possession or kicked a bad wide. You would always be picked on for those kind of things at the team meetings on Tuesday or Thursday. It wasn't always plain-sailing, but I think in the end I probably won them over and was able to make the decisions myself.

It was a game of cat-and-mouse really... there was an element of gambling in it. But if I'm coaching a team, I like my forwards to dictate the game to their man. I don't like my forwards – particularly my very good ones – to be chasing defenders back down the field. That's one of the things I don't like about the game nowadays. Even our best forwards are back defending or making blocks, when they'd be better served up the field in front of goal where a fella like me wouldn't want to be dragged.

I think there's still a bit of cat and mouse today, but too much mouse... and not enough cat!

The atmosphere in those games against the Ulster teams was different. To be fair, when we were playing Meath in those games in 1989 and into the 90s when Croke Park was jammed and both teams were good enough to go on to win an All-Ireland, the noise was incredible. But there was something different about the northern teams.

There was an explosion of Ulster football from 1991 to '94 when they went on that run of winning All-Irelands, and it was like every person who was supporting those teams had a flag. The sea of opposition colours in the crowd in those games against Donegal, Derry, Down and Tyrone was just unreal. More so than our own supporters or the Meath supporters. Every fan from Ulster seemed to have a flag. They really seemed to have the attitude of... *Let's make as much noise as possible, and let's make it visual.*

I remember for the parades in 1992, '94 and '95, it was very, very noisy. Especially that section in front of the Canal End. Extremely noisy. Extremely visual. But it was something that we got used to. Maybe it had an effect the first couple of times we saw it, but we had learned to block it out by the time 1995 came around.

I wouldn't necessarily be waving and smiling during the parade, like Jack McCaffrey seemed to be able to do, but you don't always know what's going on inside someone's head just by looking at them. I wouldn't have been a nervous person before matches. I always looked forward to them. I always enjoyed them.

I always knew my role and what was expected of me, and I went about my business in a quiet way. Towards the end of my career, I became a bit more nervous, for a variety of reasons. You're coming up against young lads, you're a bit older yourself, you're still playing in the same position, and you're probably still expected to be doing the same things that you were doing five or six years earlier.

I was at my peak in and around 1995. I was in my mid-twenties at that stage which would have been considered your prime years at that time. Nowadays, with the way lads look after themselves, the peak years are probably pushed out a bit to maybe 28 or 29.

We were five points up at half-time so the dressing-room was fairly calm. I don't remember exactly what was said, but the entire management team had licence to say a few words. Pat was the manager, but Fran Ryder, Jim Brogan and Bobby Doyle would all have made their way around the dressing-room talking to players and offering words of encouragement.

Pat had the final say before we went back out. It wouldn't have been Jim Gavin-type stuff discussing stats and that kind of thing… there might have been a bit of bad language and asking us if we were going to let this slip again, more that sort of thing. It would have been a bit of a rallying cry.

We had a few injuries going into that game. Charlie was obviously a doubt, but Dermot Deasy missed out on an All-Ireland that year. He would have been full-back, which would have allowed Ciarán Walsh to move into the corner, his more natural position. I think Dermot would have been a lot cuter on Peter Canavan. He wouldn't have panicked when Peter got the ball, and he maybe wouldn't have fouled him as easily.

When we discovered that Dermot wouldn't be playing, Ciarán was given the job to mark Peter and I actually think he did quite well. Peter only got one point from play. Now, I know he kicked 10 frees, but that kind of tells you the story of the game. We're talking about a fairly young Peter Canavan too, of course; I think he would only have been 24 at the time. He was going to get a lot better.

Our main concern that day was to not concede a goal. The last thing you want in an All-Ireland final against a northern team is for a goal to go in. Their fans are noisy enough anyway, and if you give them an opportunity to get out of their seats, it can have a negative effect on the team.

We would have discussed that a lot – not conceding a goal – and maybe that led to a bit of panic fouling from Ciarán, who just didn't want to let Peter inside him and give them the confidence-boost of a goal. We got that in other finals. Down got a goal in 1994 that lifted the roof off. So, giving away a goal might have been a big blow.

The big controversy in the game was Charlie's sending off. The ball was played over to him in front of the Cusack and it went over his head, but he was fouled. I remember being happy that we got the free because we might get a very valuable score, which we needed. Then I saw Charlie reacting.

You'll see on the tape that I ran down to have a word with Charlie. Now, I don't know if Charlie heard what I said… I don't even remember what I said, but I was very annoyed that he'd reacted that way because I knew that firstly… the ball was going to be thrown up and also… we could be down a man here. It felt like the All-Ireland was on the line at that moment.

He got his marching orders, the Tyrone crowd went crazy, Charlie protested and somehow – don't ask me – he just decided to stay on the field. He actually got on the ball a few minutes later. If he had scored, maybe Tyrone might have got their replay! The linesman spotted it, called Russell over, and Paddy then made sure Charlie made his way off. We had to reorganise and dig in.

I hadn't realised that he was still on the field until he got sent off for the second time. It didn't even twig with me when he got the ball that he was still on. I just saw a player kicking the ball.

Jason came out of the full-forward line, and we got a little bit more defensive. We were taking on water at that time because it was just wave after wave of Tyrone attacks. They didn't get the scores that they should have got during that spell, which would have killed us off. But it was certainly a difficult time for us.

We only scored two points in the second-half, but it seemed to go fairly quickly. There wasn't a real burst of scoring from Tyrone that got them back into it. It was more a drip, drip of scores that cut the gap down to four points… three points. It never felt to me like they were going to get anything out of the game until they got their last point to make it a one-point contest.

It never felt like there was any need to panic from our perspective. Tyrone got three points at the beginning of the second-half, but then there was a spell of over 20 minutes where neither side scored. I think if Tyrone had kept the scoreboard ticking over a bit more then we might have been in trouble, but it never felt to me like we were going to lose the game… until they got that last score.

I did get a bit of a familiar feeling at that stage. It was a one-point game, John had the kickout and I was thinking that if we win it, we're home and dry… but if they win the ball, then we're under pressure. They won it and came forward down the Hogan Stand side and Ciarán Corr played the ball in, probably going for a score. It fell short and John came out to clear the ball and anything else that was in his way.

It fell to Canavan, and if it had come straight to him he would certainly have popped it over himself, but it went behind him and he had to readjust, lost his footing a bit and scooped it out to Seán McLaughlin. He popped it over, but Paddy Russell decided that Peter touched the ball on the ground.

We were lucky, there's no doubt about. Someone was looking down on us at that moment – for once!

Seán went running off thinking he'd scored the equaliser. I was very close to Peter when he played the ball, so I knew straightaway that the free had been given. *Relief.* That's the only word I can use. Keith Barr took the free and that was the last kick of the game. The fans went mad and started coming onto the field.

I was shaking hands with one or two of the Tyrone fellas and, next thing, I got this tap on the shoulder from John O'Leary. He said, 'Let's go… We had a deal!' I didn't know what he was talking about, but at the start of year – I was vice-captain that year – he said to me, 'If we win the All-Ireland, we'll pick up the cup together'.

A couple of seconds after the final whistle goes, he had the wherewithal to seek me out and bring me across to the Hogan Stand. I'm sure people were wondering what I was doing lifting the cup with John, because that didn't happen at that time. It has happened a few times since, but it wouldn't have been common at all. It said a lot about John that he remembered our little agreement at a moment like that, because I had certainly forgotten it.

I got Man of the Match in the 1995 final, though I wouldn't think that it was necessarily one of my best-ever games for Dublin. It was solid more than spectacular. There was no 'wow' factor, I was just executing the basic skills. Probably when we got on top in the first-half, the launch-pad for that was the half-back line of myself, Keith and Mick Deegan. I set up a few scores, including the goal, which came from an interception in the half-back line.

If Pat O'Neill had stayed on as manager, we would have been just as organised in 1996 and I think we would have had the confidence that being champions brings. We also would have had Ciarán Whelan to add into the mix. For whatever reason, Pat and the entire management stepped down, and Mickey Whelan came in.

Mickey is a great coach and a great manager, and his contribution to Dublin football over many, many years is well-documented. But he just wasn't the right man at that time, for whatever reason. Fellas took liberties in training from the very beginning… missing training sessions because they were playing golf and that sort of nonsense. We got what we deserved in 1996 and ended up with a 16-year gap between All-Irelands. That's why the present group are so impressive. They understand that nothing is given to you.

You have to go and earn it. That's what they do, they forget about the last one and move on to the next one. We were unable to do that.

COLLIE MORAN

DUBLIN 2-11 MEATH 0-10
Leinster SFC Semi-Final
Croke Park
JUNE 23, 2002

Beating Meath in the Championship in 2002 was the game of Collie Moran's life, when victory and the appearance of new players (like Alan Brogan, above, offering Moran support in the Leinster final that summer against Kildare) gave everyone hope of a successful decade ahead for Dublin.

★ **DUBLIN:** S Cluxton; B Cahill, P Christie, C Goggins; P Casey, J Magee, P Andrews; C Whelan, D Homan (0-1); **C Moran (0-4)**, S Ryan, S Connell; A Brogan (0-3), J McNally, R Cosgrove (2-3). Subs: D Magee for Homan, D Farrell for McNally, D Henry for Andrews, J Sherlock for Moran.

★ **MEATH:** C Sullivan; M O'Reilly, D Fay, C Murphy; P Shankey, H Traynor, P Reynolds; N Crawford (0-1), J Cullinane; E Kelly (0-2), T Giles (0-1), N Nestor (0-1); R Magee (0-2), G Geraghty (0-2), D Curtis. Subs: A Moyles for Cullinane, R Kealy for Curtis, O Murphy (0-1) for Moyles, A Kenny for Kealy.

THE ACTION

DUBLIN WENT INTO this game looking for their first victory over Meath since dishing out a 10-point hammering in the 1995 Leinster final. 65,978 fans welcomed the sides to the redeveloped Croke Park and, by the end of the 70 minutes, the signs were that Tommy Lyons' own redevelopment job was coming along quite nicely indeed.

This was another Dublin vs Meath game which provided huge entertainment for the gathered masses. The Boys in Blue had much the better of the opening period and got their first big break when Ray Cosgrove – one of Lyons' impressive new faces – capitalised on John McNally's free which was drifting wide. The Kilmacud man seized on the opportunity and fisted the ball to the net as the Meath defence dithered. At the other end, Stephen Cluxton produced a fantastic double save from Donal Curtis and buoyed by that, the Dubs continued their dominance and led by 1-7 to 0-5 at the interval, with the impressive Collie Moran contributing three from play.

They started the second-half in similarly impressive fashion and had opened up an eight-point lead shortly after the restart, with Meath looking in total disarray. However, as they have done so often in the past, Seán Boylan's charges rallied. Dublin's shooting disintegrated and they failed to land a score for 22 minutes. Meath chipped away at the deficit and got five points of their own during that time to cut the gap to just three with a little over five minutes remaining.

Were the Dubs to suffer more heartbreak at the Royals' hands?

A tense finale looked in prospect as, once again, it looked as though Dublin's tendency to hit the self-destruct button would come back to bite them, but Cosgrove again popped up at a vital time to steady the ship. Alan Brogan's attempt for a point dropped short, and Cosgrove punched the ball from the hands of Meath keeper Cormac Sullivan and into the net to put the game to bed.

Meath complained that their keeper was inside the small square when he was challenged, but Pat McEneaney waved away their complaints as the Royals waved goodbye to their Leinster crown. Cosgrove capped a fine personal performance by landing the final point of the game from a free to give the Dubs a seven-point winning margin.

★★★★★

"

IT WAS TOMMY Lyons' first year in charge and the league results had been a bit up and down. Then we went down to Wexford in the first round of the Leinster Championship and Tommy had introduced a lot of new players… Barry Cahill, Paul Casey, Alan Brogan… and Cossie (Ray Cosgrove) was back in and a mainstay of the team.

There was a lot of change that year and we scraped past Wexford in Dr. Cullen Park and could easily have been beaten. I think Paul Casey cleared a ball off the line at the end. It would have been a huge upset.

As a result, the expectations around the county coming into the Meath game were pretty low. I'll always remember that Wexford game because it was the same day Ireland played Cameroon in the 2002 World Cup. If anyone remembers the kick-off times, the Ireland game was at 7am or something like that, and then our game was that evening. It was obvious that a lot of the Dublin supporters had been up early for the soccer and celebrating all day!

It's obviously different to Croke Park down there – it's a smaller venue. We were warming up in front of the terraces and you could hear the jokes and the banter from the crowd. It was gas craic, but we just about got out of there alive.

That was the Saturday night of the June Bank Holiday weekend, and you'd usually go for a few pints after a championship match back in those days, and it'd be back to training on the Tuesday night. But I don't think we did that night, because we knew what was coming. As punishment I suppose for just about scraping past Wexford, Tommy had us out in Leopardstown racecourse, and it was brutal. Just pure running.

This was the day after a championship match when you'd normally be going to the pool. He ran the hell out of us and when it got to the stage that we thought we were finished, he brought us in and said, 'One more lap of the course to finish!'

When *that* was done, next thing Tommy says, 'See you here again tomorrow at five o'clock for more of the same!' We'll all remember that! None of us went out on the beer on the Saturday because we knew Tommy was gonna run us on Sunday. But I'd say a few lads had an eye on the Sunday night pints… but that went out the window when Tommy said we were training on the Monday too.

That was a total surprise! We had a championship match followed by two absolutely bruising sessions. It wasn't much of a long weekend, that's for sure!

That was the backdrop to the Meath game. You couldn't say we were coming into that game flying by any means. Then you add in the fact that they had won All-Irelands in 1996 and '99, and lost one in 2001 having hammered Kerry in a semi-final… at that stage Meath still had many of the best players in the country. Darren Fay, Trevor Giles, Graham Geraghty, Ollie Murphy, Evan Kelly… so we were certainly underdogs.

There was a bit of a buzz around the place because it was the new-looking Croke Park… the new Hogan Stand was complete. I think the previous year when Meath beat us, only the lower tier was built.

Maybe we came into the game as an unknown quantity and maybe Meath took us a bit for granted. We got a dream start to the match… Cossie got a goal early on. It was slightly fortuitous in that it was a free from about 50 metres that Johnny McNally dropped short. Ray got there ahead of Cormac Sullivan and fisted it to the net.

Then you had Alan Brogan who was class that day, and Meath probably wouldn't have known too much about him.

I was a minor in 1998. We were beaten in the Leinster final that year and there was no backdoor at that stage. That was Tommy Carr's first summer in charge as Dublin senior manager when we were beaten by Kildare in a replay in the Leinster quarter-final. Again, no backdoor. Tommy had taken over from Mickey Whelan, but he was still operating with a lot of the 1995 All-Ireland winning team and I think he decided that he was going to put his own stamp on things.

A lot of guys were let go and I was brought in from the minors, and I got a run as a sub in the league of 1998/99. I wasn't in the team for the Leinster final in 1999, but I was in it from that winter's league, and it went from there.

It was a difficult time for Dublin football with the lack of success, the transition in the team after that All-Ireland win, and also the managerial changes. Tommy Carr was ousted in the winter of 2001. I would have been a supporter of Tommy's and we certainly felt we were heading in the right direction. The camp was very unified and highly-motivated.

Looking back on it now, if you were trying to explain to Brian Fenton or Brian

Howard that players were standing up defending a manager who hadn't won a Leinster title in four years, they might find it hard to fathom! But times were different then. Meath were the top dogs, and Kildare had Micko and they had dreams of an All-Ireland, especially after losing in 1998.

With there being no backdoor until 2001, there was no margin for error or bad luck at all. We felt if we got out of Leinster – which usually meant beating either or both of Meath and Kildare – that we were as good as anything that was out there. A bit different to the landscape today.

The players were disappointed when Tommy Carr went, but I think it's fair to say that that team didn't have anywhere near the amount of scoring forwards to make an impact. Worse than that, we didn't have a reliable free-taker. There were games where we'd have had several different lads taking frees.

A manager can't do a huge amount if he hasn't got a solid free-taker and scoring forwards. If you look at that team that played Kerry in Thurles for example, you had the likes of Enda Sheehy and Ken Darcy – who were midfielders by trade – playing in the forwards. I was probably naturally a half-back, but I was playing in the forwards! There was a much better range of scoring forwards coming through under Tommy Lyons and Pillar.

We felt that Tommy Carr was taking the fall for this and there wasn't a huge amount more that he could have done with the resources he had, so I think that's where the support from the players was coming from.

When Tommy Lyons came in, he was very media-friendly, but don't let that fool you. The training was very tough. It was probably a step back from Tommy Carr because the longer he was there, it was less about the long-distance running and more about speed training and weights.

Tommy Lyons came in and it was back to Cathal Brugha barracks with poor floodlights and no footballs. Running in circles. It was a tough regime, but that was just his way. While 2002 was a wonderful high, when things started to go wrong in 2003 and '04, that media relationship goes against you. You can't have it both ways.

If you open your doors in the good times, you've got to be ready for the bad times too. But certainly in 2002, it was what Dublin and the supporters needed after being in the doldrums for a few years. We were all riding on the crest of a wave that summer.

With Tommy's training, I'd say there was a large element of weeding lads out who maybe didn't want it enough, for the want of a better expression. He was strict when it came to training and, in fairness to him, it was clear from very early on that he would drop anyone regardless of who they were. After 2003, there was probably a lot of disquiet in the camp because that was a bad year and we felt like we were falling behind in the training methods. He did change some things in 2004, but the first two years were particularly hard. We weren't doing weights in 2002 and '03 at all, but that changed a little bit in '04. It must be said that when we got out to St David's in the summertime, there was a lot of ball work and matches and that kind of stuff which was enjoyable.

But Tommy was psychologically tough on players. There were a lot of mind-games going on, probably trying to make lads feel uncomfortable. It's hard to describe, but I think he would have tried to make lads question their place on the team or even on the panel. The older guys who were more established… he was calling them out. But that was just the way Tommy managed, that was his nature.

Going into the Meath game in 2002, okay, we'd had a bad few years… but Tommy always had great belief in himself and in us. I don't remember too much about the specifics of the build-up, but I know that not too much was expected of us and the hype before the match wouldn't have been the same as before other Dublin-Meath games. In a funny way, because Tommy Carr was gone, a lot of the pressure was gone too.

In Tommy Carr's last couple of years, we felt like it was do-or-die, that we had to win. Whether it was Kildare in 2000 or Meath in 2001… Tommy was several years into his term and we knew we had to deliver, or he'd probably be out of a job. It was a tight-knit squad, and we weren't as successful as we'd have liked.

So, there was a mentality that we were all – players, coaches, manager – in it together and we were building towards something. When that didn't happen, it was disappointing.

With 2002 being Tommy Lyons' first year, it felt like there wasn't as much pressure on. If you look back at that game, that's really how we played. That was exemplified best by Alan Brogan. He was making his big-time debut in Croke Park and he was throwing dummy solos and kicking scores. He gave Mark O'Reilly, who was known as a tight marker, a torrid time.

We had developed such a lead that it was hard for Meath to get back into it.

They made a bit of a run at us, but the second goal killed them off. It would actually have been interesting to see how we would have handled it psychologically if the game had been a bit tighter, but we had a big buffer.

There was a real desperation to win a Leinster title at that stage. I had played two years at minor, three years at under-21, and then four seasons in the senior squad, and 2002 was my first Leinster title. I didn't win any at underage. It was a huge deal.

The game went very well for me personally. I got three points in the first-half and another one in the second. I hit the post at one stage, and I got fouled for a tap-over free in front of the goal. Thinking about those games before that and the ones that came after, for a wing-forward in Croke Park – in those days at least – to get six scoring chances was unusual in a Dublin-Meath game. It was usually about the battle and 13 or 14 points would win you the game. It'd be a scrap and the odd moment of skill might be the deciding of the game, so from my perspective there was a lot more space and it was a more open game than some of the others where you'd win a break… and you'd be swamped and hit.

I got a score early on and things went well for me after that. Cossie's second goal was key. Alan Brogan took a shot for a point, but it went way up in the air and dropped short. Cossie went up for it with Cormac Sullivan and punched it into the net. That kind of goal made it feel like we were finally starting to get a bit of luck that we hadn't been getting in the previous years. When it went in, I was thinking… *Finally, we're getting a lucky break.* That goal was the score that quelled the Meath comeback really and sent us on our way.

The difference between that game and the Leinster final in 2001 was huge in terms of the nature of it. In 2001 you had Ian Robertson wrestling with Darren Fay and the defenders were on top. I don't know if the new pitch was bigger, but in 2002 scoring opportunities seemed so much easier to come by. It just felt like a more open game, I can't put my finger on it. In the second-half, I don't remember getting my hands on much ball. Meath got on top around the middle and were getting back into it and we went a long period without scoring.

We were surprised by how far ahead we were at half-time. Generally, in those Meath-Dublin games, even if one side or the other was playing badly, it would still be tight. To be five up at half-time was something we wouldn't have expected.

That team wasn't used to success, and we had let a big half-time lead go against Kildare a couple of years before when they came out and got two goals.

That was the crucial thing in that Meath game… that we didn't let in a goal. If they had come out and got a goal it might have rocked us a bit. Stephen Cluxton was in his first proper season in the team – which is unbelievable really, it's a lifetime ago – and he made a few brilliant saves that day. *Would we have had the mental strength to prevail over a team as good and as experienced as that Meath team if they'd gotten an early goal in the second-half?* I'm not so sure.

When you look at the fact that we were able to bring on the likes of Dessie and Jayo, that shows the experience that we had on the bench, which was the result of throwing in the younger lads. But that allowed us to bring on some older heads to finish out the game. Once we won that game, even though I had no medals up to that point with Dublin, I never felt like we were going to lose the Leinster final.

That might sound like a surprising thing to say given our record at the time, what had happened against Kildare in 2000, and the fact that we still had propensity to push the self-destruct button, but I felt like once we got over Meath, we'd win the Leinster. We did, albeit we made hard work of it.

Looking at the six forwards that day, you basically had a new full-forward line with Alan, Ray and Johnny McNally. That reinvigorates things. When a new manager comes in and lads who were maybe thought to be undroppable are suddenly not getting a start and some newer faces are in, it gives a bit of a boost to lads who were on the fringes… you know that every position is genuinely up for grabs.

That win ignited the interest in the team and the expectation basically overnight. The Dublin media were drumming up interest in the lead-up to that Kildare game, which had a record attendance at that time for a Leinster final. The hype was huge, the weather was great, we had a young team… there was just lots of excitement around.

It was a great summer. We trained in St David's, which was never fully opened to the public, but there'd be a few regulars who'd be at all the sessions. But the media interest really shot up. There'd be profile pieces which wouldn't have happened before. You had Cossie getting all the goals, you had Alan who was so young and exciting and of course there was the history with his dad playing with Dublin in the 70s… so there was a lot for the media to latch onto. Then, of course, you had Tommy (Lyons) being so media-friendly and drumming it all up.

It's a lot different now in terms of how slick the media stuff is. Back then, the journalists would have rung directly through to players, and you'd know a lot of them. I found it easier to just do the interviews, to be honest. A few years after that, the media ban started to come in and I nearly found that more stressful than actually doing the interview. You'd be getting messages on your phone from lads that you'd know, and you were under orders not to respond.

I found that more difficult than just taking a call for 10 minutes and chatting about the game. That was just the way it was back then. It probably could have been handled better.

By the same token, in 2003 and '04, we lost to Laois and Westmeath respectively. Now, whatever about losing to Meath and Kildare, who were perceived to be traditionally stronger counties, to lose to Laois and Westmeath was a different thing altogether.

I remember listening to the phone-in shows and people going nuts! After we lost to Westmeath in 2004, we drew London in the qualifiers in Parnell Park. We'd usually meet an hour and a half before games in Parnell because we all knew our way there, knew where to park and everything was very familiar. We'd get there, tog out and do our warm-ups. That day against London, Tommy had us meet up an hour earlier than usual, because he was afraid there'd be protests at the gate.

We haven't seen that kind of stuff since then.

It was bizarre that we were playing London, and we were nervous. The confidence was so low because we'd been getting such criticism. You're thinking… *What if these lads get a run on us at the start and we get dragged into a dogfight!* It didn't work out that way, but it just shows you where the headspace was at that time.

I missed the rest of that summer because I broke my arm after the London game. Kerry beat us well in the quarter-final. They got a goal that was a shot for a point which came back off the post and Dara Ó Cinnéide stuck it in the net. I was watching and we had been doing okay, but you could just see the confidence go. It was like sticking a pin in a balloon.

We had no belief and again it just felt like we were back to a place where things weren't going our way. That was a low point. To go from the highs of 2002 to what followed in '03 and '04 was strange.

In 2003 we had Armagh in the qualifiers and again we were doing okay… then Clucko got sent off and it all went through the floor! But that was the story of that decade, there were always these bizarre moments when things went *wrong*. The current team couldn't be more different in terms of personality and character.

That's the beauty of those guys – they always make the right decision and stick to that plan. Back then it was just the opposite.

ALAN BROGAN
(& PADDY CHRISTIE)

DUBLIN 2-13 KILDARE 2-11
Leinster SFC Final
Croke Park
JULY 14, 2002

In his breakthrough season in blue, Alan Brogan bursts past Ken Doyle and Ronan Sweeney as Dublin finally got their hands on the Leinster title in 2002.

★ **DUBLIN:** S Cluxton; B Cahill, **P Christie (0-1)**, C Goggins; P Casey, P Curran, P Andrews; C Whelan (0-1), D Homan; C Moran, S Ryan, S Connell (0-2); **A Brogan (1-2)**, R Cosgrove (1-4), J McNally (0-3). Subs: D Magee for Curran, J Sherlock for Connell, D Farrell for McNally, D Henry for Homan.

★ **KILDARE:** E Murphy; B Lacey, P Mullarkey, K Doyle; K Duane, D Hendy, A Rainbow; K Brennan, D Earley; E McCormack, K O'Dwyer (0-1), R Sweeney; T Fennin (2-2), M Lynch, J Doyle (0-7). Subs: G Ryan for Hendy, P Murray (0-1) for O'Dwyer, S McKenzie-Smith for Lynch, T Harris for Duane

THE ACTION

TOMMY LYONS' BLUE revolution continued in Croke Park as Dublin's seven-year wait for a Leinster title ended in a gripping final against Kildare. The Lilywhites will feel hard-done by after contributing to a hugely enjoyable contest, but Dublin did just enough to get over the line, and perhaps had the rub of the green which had abandoned them in the years since 1995.

Kildare had their own share of luck too it must be said, notably in the 45th minute when Darren Magee's loose pass in front of his own goal presented a gift to Tadhg Fennin, who gleefully finished to the net. That helped Kildare to a two-point lead with a little over 15 minutes to go, and it was the kind of score that could have caused Dublin to collapse. On this occasion, however, they turned the tide with a mix of determination and flair.

Two goals in as many minutes ultimately decided the game. Alan Brogan got the first when he latched onto a breaking ball from John McNally's '45' and cutely dodged a tackle before finishing off the far post. It was a real poacher's goal, and the perfect illustration of what Brogan has added to Dublin's forward line. Speaking of poachers, seconds later the man of the moment popped up with another goal to add to his summer tally. Kildare were caught woefully short at the back, and Ray Cosgrove side-footed the ball casually to the net past a totally exposed Enda Murphy. Cue huge celebrations from the newest darling of the Hill. The swagger that Dublin have lacked for so long was back.

Kildare battled manfully to rescue the game, and the tension in the air was notable as the time ticked away. The scar tissue that Dublin have accumulated over the years couldn't but be felt, and it was a nervous ending to the game for them. Fennin almost got his hat-trick in the 71st minute, but Stephen Cluxton pulled off a magnificent save as the Dublin supporters reached for the oxygen masks. Moments later, Michael Collins blew for full-time, and the Dublin players made their way to Hill 16 and climbed the fence to share the win with their supporters. As Coman Goggins lifted the trophy, manager Tommy Lyons looked on with tears in his eyes. He was hardly alone.

★★★★★

66

I PLAYED MINOR in 1999. We won Leinster but were beaten by Down after a replay in the All-Ireland semi-final. They went on to win it. Benny Coulter was on that team and was the best player in the championship that year. The following year I was minor again, but I broke my wrist and only got back for a bit of the Leinster campaign, where Westmeath beat us.

That was a big disappointment, because we looked like we had a strong team coming off the previous year. I came through the development squad system, so I would have been involved with Dublin since around under-15.

I took each year as it came along really, I don't ever remember thinking… *I'm definitely going to play senior for Dublin.* Obviously, I wanted to, because I was a huge Dublin fan, but I never made any assumptions about it.

When I look back on my career, there are a few games that stand out. The All-Ireland wins were obviously very special, but that first Leinster title in 2002 just about edges it. We had had a barren run where we hadn't won a provincial final since 1995, and it was my first year playing senior with Dublin.

People might see us winning Leinster titles now and think celebrations are a bit muted, but that's like winning anything a number of times, the celebrations become a little less wild the more you win.

I was only out of minor when I was brought onto the league panel in Tommy Carr's last season in charge. I came on against Tyrone in the league that year, and then I went to America for the summer. When I came back, Tommy Lyons had come in and things went from there. I was 20 at that stage.

The beauty of that team was the mix we had.

Some of the older lads wanted Tommy Carr to stay on, and maybe that played into a little bit of dissatisfaction with Tommy Lyons as time went on. I can honestly say I never noticed that around the place, it was only after Tommy Lyons went that it came to light. He came in with his own ideas, he made some big changes in terms of putting some of the older guys on the bench. That probably didn't go down well with certain fellas, but it's hard to look past the results Tommy achieved in 2002.

There was a group of players who had lost multiple Leinster finals and had a bit of baggage, but for the new lads coming in… it was a shot to nothing. Ray Cosgrove had a fantastic year, and you could see that by the way he played, he was full of confidence and playing with freedom. He certainly wasn't carrying any pressure into those games.

You also had Johnny McNally, Barry Cahill, Darren Magee and Stephen Cluxton coming in. There was a real freshness to the team. I played all the league that year and I started fairly well. I think we played Donegal in our first league game in Parnell Park, and I got 1-3. We had Roscommon next, and I got a goal there too.

I felt it was really important to get off to a good start. Getting scores in those early games gave me huge confidence and got rid of any doubts I might have had in the back of my mind. I knew from that point on that I could compete at that level.

That Leinster in 2002 was like winning an All-Ireland for that group. We had a great first year under Tommy and could easily have won the All-Ireland with the momentum we got off the back of that Leinster final win.

We played Wexford in the quarter-final and we just about got out of there. I got a point but was fairly quiet. In fairness, the preparations weren't ideal! Myself and Barry Cahill had to do an exam that morning in Maynooth and we got a Garda escort to the game, so it was messy enough for us. The exam was set for the afternoon from 2pm to 5pm, so we might have missed the game, which was at half six.

We got permission to do the exam early, just the two of us, but we had to be in the company of a Garda at all times until the exam started in the afternoon. In other words, they wanted to make sure that we weren't in communication with anyone who was sitting the exam at 2pm. We did the exam from 9am to 12 noon, so there was a two-hour period where we had to have someone with us and make sure we weren't doing something we shouldn't have been doing! To be fair to the college, they did us a huge favour, but it was a messy enough day.

The win against Meath in the semi-final was massive for us. They had lost the All-Ireland final to Galway the year before, and most people fancied them to beat us given our performance against Wexford.

I got three from play that day. I was marking Mark O'Reilly, who had been around a while, but was still regarded as one of the best corner-backs out there.

To get a few scores off him in Croke Park gave me a huge boost going into the Leinster final. All of those things added up for me… the good start to the league, the performance against Meath, so I was going into the Kildare game in great form and full of confidence.

The crowd for the Leinster final in the new Croke Park was incredible. The place was packed. Kildare might not quite have been at their peak, but they were still a decent team. It was a huge win for Dublin, coupled with the fact that it was my first year, that's what made it so special.

I got a point in each half, but my goal is the score I will always remember. Scoring a goal into Hill 16 in your first Leinster final is hard to beat. Johnny McNally hit a '45' that dropped to the left of the goal, and Ray managed to break it down to me to the side of the square. I threw one dummy and it sent about four of them the wrong way, for some reason!

I kind of stabbed it towards the far corner… and it went in off the post. Games are won on inches, and I got a bit of luck. It could just as easily have hit the post and come back into play. We needed that goal too, because Tadhg Fennin was after getting a couple of goals for them and we were rattled enough after having a good first-half. That wasn't dissimilar to 2000 when Kildare had hit us with two goals at the start of the second-half, so for me to get that goal in '02 just settled us down a bit and calmed the nerves.

We were only a point up at half-time, but Kildare came back and Fennin got that goal early in the second-half which might have derailed us in previous seasons. But we got those two goals of our own, and Ray's was a real striker's goal. It sat up in front of him and he side-footed it past the keeper. We always felt we'd get back into it and that was all thanks to the belief that Tommy had given us. If you look back at videos of 2002, we were up on the railings at Hill 16 celebrating. It's hard to overstate how big a deal it was at the time. The city was buzzing. We celebrated it like an All-Ireland.

What Tommy brought was huge momentum and belief. He got the crowd back onside too. He spoke after that Leinster final about how Hill 16 was unbelievable, especially after the Kildare goals, which was when we needed them most. He generated a huge amount of interest, and I think all Dublin fans who were around that summer will remember it very fondly.

I know we were beaten by Armagh in the semi-final, but it was a brilliant summer, especially when you consider where Dublin had been in the previous five or six years.

My role in the team was simple enough… get the ball, and take on my man. The open spaces of Croke Park suited me because I was very fit, and I was nippy. Tommy would have told me to turn and drive at my man's shoulder when I got possession. That was what I tried to do… open up space for others.

Johnny McNally is probably overlooked in terms of his contribution to the team that summer. He was a very selfless footballer, and he was happy to do a lot of the donkey work for me and Ray. I really enjoyed playing with Johnny, because you knew he was willing to make unselfish runs to make space for others.

It was pretty much one-on-one at the time. Sweepers weren't really being used and you often had to fight for your own ball. It was fierce. The game has gone quite measured in the last few years, whereas back then it was man-on-man… and you had to win that battle. It might have looked like there was a lot of space, but when you're going hammer-and-tongs for a ball with your marker, it didn't feel like that. It was definitely more enjoyable playing back then, because you got the chance to take on your man now and again. In my latter years, there were so many bodies around you when you got the ball that you had to get rid of it before you got smothered. That's not to say I didn't enjoy the success, but the style of football in my early days was certainly more enjoyable as a forward.

My role adapted a little as the years went by, and I moved out to centre-forward, but I always tried to move the ball quickly so that I might catch defenders out of position. When Bernard came into the team, I'd look for him because we had a good understanding. I became a bit more of a provider than a scorer, but I enjoyed that too. When Pat Gilroy took over, I had to focus more on my defending and improve my tackling. He knew I could do all the other stuff, but with teams attacking from half-back, he was concerned about whether I would be prepared to put in the work to chase lads down the field.

Something people often mentioned to me was my style of soloing, where I'd have the big high hop. I think some would have thought I should have been done for overcarrying! That's something that works in Croke Park, because you know it's going to bounce perfectly, but it doesn't work quite as well on a mucky pitch in the league!

I used to use that to build up a head of steam, bounce the ball in front of myself so that I'm running onto it. I didn't actually realise I was doing it until people pointed it out to me. It probably did help me steal a couple of yards because it looked like I was playing the ball, but it was in my hand for a while before I hopped it. I'm surprised the referees weren't discussing it, but I was never blown!

Back around 2002, we used to meet in Parnell Park before games and get the bus in. We'd come down through Fairview and you'd have the crowds outside Kavanagh's pub. From Fairview in, the place would be rocking. It was a great time to be playing for Dublin. When I think back to the atmosphere around the place and in Croke Park back then… supporters tend to be more engaged when you haven't won something for a while. There was a lot riding on that 2002 Leinster final for the players and the supporters, and that really hit home to me in the build-up and in the drive down to Croker. There was an unbelievable atmosphere that day.

As the years went by and we won more and more provincial titles, of course you're delighted to be winning them, but nothing ever quite tops winning the first one. It was similar to 2011 when we finally won the All-Ireland. No matter how many I won after that, nothing was ever going to beat 2011. Nothing can replace that feeling of winning the first one.

2002 as a whole, although it ended with that loss to Armagh… the overriding feeling for me and for the squad was pride. Our main goal that year was to win Leinster. We *had* to get over the line in Leinster that year. Anything after that was a bonus. I know that's a cliché, but getting that monkey off our backs in Leinster was the big goal that summer. Everyone was happy with how the year went.

As a new player in the dressing-room, I felt very welcome and settled in very quickly. We went away on a few trips for league matches, and we had a team holiday to South Africa at the end of 2002, so I would have said we were a very tight group. There was a very strong bond. You'd have expected us to build on that in the couple of years that followed, but unfortunately it didn't turn out like that… we lost to Westmeath and Laois.

A lot fell for us in 2002, particularly Ray's form. It would have been very hard for him, or anyone, to repeat that the following year. When he stopped getting the scores, we didn't really have anyone to step into his shoes.

Tommy Lyons had his critics in the subsequent years, but nobody can take away that he delivered us that first Leinster in seven years.

It's hard to put your finger on what went wrong in 2003 and '04. They were two tight games we lost, and we could easily have won them. If we had, then *everything* is different. I was young at the time, so I didn't pay much attention to the politics, I just wanted to play football. Maybe that was a bit naïve. It was difficult, particularly for me and some of the other guys who came in under Tommy, because he was so good to us. I was disappointed the way it ended for him. After what he did for us in 2002, I thought he deserved better than that.

Ray had such a good year, and we had nobody else to help him out after that. That was probably the case until Bernard came along. I'd chip in with a goal here and there and a few points in each game, but I wasn't a poacher. I tended to play out the field, and I wasn't an out-and-out sharpshooter, so we missed Ray's scores in those couple of seasons.

For all the heartbreak we suffered over the years, I never thought... *This is never going to happen for us.* I just wanted to play football, and I never got too hung up on what happened before or after. We'd analyse games and see what we could learn, but I just wanted to get out on the field and rectify it. I never thought too far ahead. If we lost, I just wanted to get back out training and go again.

Playing for Dublin becomes your life. When you lose, you wallow for a few weeks, then you're back with the club... then the club is done and you're thinking about getting back with Dublin. I never dwelt on things for too long, and I'd never watch games back unless we were analysing them as a group. Maybe that was naïve too, maybe I should have taken more lessons from games we lost, but that's just the way I was.

To finally get the All-Ireland win in 2011 was just incredible.

I was fortunate enough to be involved in the goal. I got a short free around the '45' and when I looked up, I just saw the space. I don't remember thinking... *There's a goal on here!*... but I just attacked the space. When I saw Kev Mc... knowing he's a good man to get a goal, I got it to him. To be fair to Kev, it might have looked like an easy finish, but it definitely wasn't! It was a huge goal, not just in that game, but in the history of Dublin football.

The last 10 minutes of that game was really high-quality stuff, and we just came out on the right side of it.

For my career as a whole, I have to be very happy. There are a couple of games where you wish things had gone differently, and I would love to have reached an All-Ireland when Pillar was in charge. That's probably my biggest regret with Dublin. That group of players put so much work in and didn't manage to get across the line. But overall, I was happy with my Dublin haul.

If anything, losing three county finals with the club is something I really wish I could change. But that's sport. I would have to be very happy with how things went, particularly kicking a point against Kerry in my last game in 2015. Not too many players get to sign off on that kind of high, so I can't really complain.

PADDY CHRISTIE

Paddy Christie wins the ball against Kildare's Martin Lynch in the 2002 Leinster final win, a game which finally silenced the doubts in the mind of the Dublin full-back and propelled him to Ireland selection and All Star honours.

66

COMING INTO THE 2002 championship, we had lost three Leinster finals in-a-row. Meath beat us in 1999 and 2001, and Kildare had beaten us in 2000 in a replay. That was a killer. Kildare got two goals at the start of the second-half after we had played all the football in the first, and were well ahead.

Tommy Lyons arrived in 2002, and he was talking a good game as he liked to do. Tommy was very positive. I don't know if he can make someone believe, but he can certainly help them to believe. His positivity really benefitted us, because the atmosphere around the camp at the time was quite dour. We had all this media stuff about how Dublin were no good, yet we were getting to Leinster finals, we were very close to beating Kerry in 2001… and we probably should have beaten Meath in that year's Leinster final.

We just couldn't score to save our lives.

All this pressure was very annoying, because we weren't far away. We were just a little bit off. I personally got very down... you're wondering if there's any light at the end of the tunnel. Then all of a sudden, you're in this fourth consecutive Leinster final. Tommy had been nothing but positive in the lead-up to the game. He wasn't saying we were going to hammer Kildare or anything, but he would just have said that we had a very good chance of winning the game and we could go further in the championship. That belief started to come, especially off the back of beating Meath in the semi-final.

I'm a teacher and I remember being in the school the week of the game. It was closed for the summer holidays obviously, but I was just in there tipping around trying to pass the time. The week of the match was a long one, so I would do anything I could to make the days go quicker. We'd usually train on Tuesday, Thursday and Saturday. But Tommy had this thing that, on the week of a game, we'd skip the Thursday session.

On the Saturday we might just go for a light session with some shooting drills and talk about a few tactical things. From the last proper session on a Tuesday to the game on a Sunday was a long time.

I was fluting around in the school, doing a few bits in the classroom. The game inevitably came into my mind. I remember thinking... *Imagine if we lose this again?* I had arrived there in a Tommy Lyons state of mind, looking at the positives. We had the confidence, lads were on form... we'd a lot of things on our side.

Next thing, I find myself thinking about how bad it would be to lose four in-a-row. A Leinster title back then, I'm not exaggerating, but it wasn't far off an All-Ireland. When Meath were winning Leinsters, they were often winning All-Irelands. Kildare weren't far off it either. You were a top team if you were winning Leinster.

That day in the school really stayed with me. I started going into overdrive then and I was thinking about what the week after the game would be like if we lost. Now, it wasn't *quite* as bad as before, because the backdoor had come in in 2001, so I knew we'd have another game. But it was still something that worried me, because winning a Leinster Championship at that time was such a big deal.

The irony now is that GAA fans in their teens or early-twenties probably think a Leinster is *nothing*. It meant the world, which is why I'm talking about this game. It was just elation when we won.

I don't remember much about the game itself… I've never watched it back. I'm probably weird like that, I don't watch games that I've played in. I suppose it's one of those things from a sports psychology point of view, where I just think it's in the past and you can't change anything.

I remember they showed the game on RTÉ in December, and I was still living at home at the time. My father – a Meath man – said, 'Ah, you're just in time, they're showing the Leinster final'… he couldn't wait to see this, even though he was raging that we beat Meath in the semi-final! But he was happy enough to support us in the final.

I looked at it for around 30 seconds… then I just said, 'No'. It was just one of those things. I was always into sports psychology, and I was always reading up on stuff around high-performance. One of the things that resonated with me was to be a *tomorrow person*… don't be looking back. Look forward, think about what's ahead of you because what's behind you, unfortunately, isn't going to change. It's liberating in a way, and it took me a while to start thinking like that.

I'd had a very bad experience the year before in that All-Ireland quarter-final in Thurles. Maurice Fitzgerald got the famous point to level it up the first day. It was lashing rain the second day, and I was wearing new boots. I slipped at least three times, and on one of those occasions it cost us a goal.

I was marking Johnny Crowley, and he got in behind me one-on-one with Davy Byrne and stuck it in the net. It was a killer, and it had a huge impact on the game. I came out for a ball and just misjudged it slightly. When I tried to turn, my feet went from under me and when I looked up… yer man had it buried.

I took a long time to recover from that. I had played consistently well for Dublin at full-back for a number of years and was a mainstay. I was reliable. Suddenly, I felt totally at fault for us losing that game… even though in hindsight Kerry were a better football team. The first day we had nearly robbed them, but they had much better forwards than us, and that was a common theme over the years.

Meath always had much better forwards and only needed half the possession that we needed. We had the likes of Dessie Farrell and Ian Robertson who were dangerous, and one or two others who would chip in, but when you look back on it, we had fellas playing in the forwards who just weren't a threat.

I'm not being disrespectful to any of those lads, it was just one of those things that they didn't produce for us. That's why I felt that it was my fault that we lost that game, because I knew that we would have to work really hard to get those three points back. And that's why, going into the 2002 Leinster final, I got that shiver when I thought about losing. I still probably hadn't cleared my mind of the Kerry game.

But when we won that game, I think my mindset started to change a bit. I remember Tommy talking to me after we won. He said, 'I'm delighted for you. I saw you coming off the pitch against Kerry last year and you looked like a beaten man'… which I was!

I had the weight of the world on my shoulders, and the whole squad felt like that too. Tommy Carr had been getting a lot of criticism from the media and I think that started to get in on him, and then got in on us too. I let it take over my life completely, to the point where it dictated whether I was in good form or bad form.

Everything revolved around it. Friendships, relationships… my professional life. If we had won, I'd be in great form in school. If we'd been beaten, pity the poor kids in the classroom! That was something that I had to change.

When I look back on it now, I'm obviously older and more experienced, and I've seen a bit of the world. I'd tell people, and it's not to disrespect football in any way, but it has to be kept in its place. It's a part of your life, you get a lot more out of it than you put in… but it can't dictate everything. If it does, then there's probably something inherently wrong with your life that you're allowing that to happen.

There were two NFL coaches whose books I read, and which really resonated with me. One was Bill Walsh, who coached the San Francisco 49ers. His book is called *The Score Takes Care of Itself*. It was all about putting everything in place before the game comes around, so you don't need to worry about the actual game itself, or even tactics. It really struck a chord with me, and I found that it summed up all my thoughts on coaching and management.

The second was Chuck Noll, who was the Pittsburgh Steelers' coach when they won four Super Bowls in the 70s. He always talked about when players finished playing, it's time to move on to your life's work as he called it… because your playing career is very short and it's just one chapter.

For me, I'm teaching here now in north county Dublin, I'm coaching the DCU Sigerson team, I'm involved with Tipperary, I've two kids… there's loads of other things that I've gone on to do since I finished as a player. It's very easy to get caught up in the bubble when you're playing, but when I look back on it, post-Kerry 2001, I went into almost a mini-depression for those three or four months, and I couldn't really get myself out of it.

I remember thinking all the time… *People are saying this, people are saying that.* The reality was *nobody cared!* People had forgotten all about it two days after the game! They'd moved on.

I was the only one carrying this around.

I look back now, and I wonder what I was thinking? I had only just started out with Dublin and had a full career ahead of me. I'd such a nice life, and I was getting bogged down because I had one bad day where I slipped a couple of times. *Big swing!* That's life. If you don't want those things to happen, then don't play sport.

For that 2002 Leinster final, things fell into place. I played well.

When Tommy Lyons came in, he was a breath of fresh air. I know some people would have thought he had too much to say for himself, but I loved that, and I thought that he was way ahead of the GAA at the time in terms of his ideas around management.

Some of the things he did would be commonplace in the game now, but they weren't at the time. He was a businessman, and he had a really good handle on how to deal with people. He was straight with people too.

That's very difficult at times when you're involved in football. It can be hard to have conversations with people and tell them the truth. I found Tommy very honest and open, and he managed to do that and not fall out with too many people. There was a group of players near the end in 2004 who were against him, but early on, he was key to the reinvigoration of things, and he gave new players a chance.

Case in point is Ray Cosgrove. Ray had been around for a few years… you wouldn't have said he was a young lad, but he was seen as someone who wasn't up to it. Tommy got him motoring and he shot the lights out in 2002.

For me though, it was Alan Brogan who made the difference. Ray was important, but Alan was just a class apart, as he went on to prove over a long period. We were training out in St David's in Artane which was very handy for me. When I think about it now, I still get a warmness in my stomach. It was a great time.

I think of that grass pitch, and I can see it in my mind's eye. We were playing an A vs B game, and I would have been on the A team. Alan was corner-forward up the other end. We had just struggled past Wexford, and Alan hadn't had a great game – none of us did really – but people were talking about him and how he could be a great player. I was looking at him and I knew he had something. I knew he'd cause problems for teams.

Before we played Meath that year, we were out in Artane, and he got a ball out in the wing forward position. He took off on a run, and I was just watching on from the other end… there were lads tackling him and bodies criss-crossing. Next thing, he's in on goal, and I think he stuck it in the net. I just remember thinking… *This lad is going to cause havoc. This is the first time Meath are going to have come up against anyone like this.*

Dessie, don't get me wrong, was a fantastic player, but he was well-known, and he had a few miles on the clock at that stage and had suffered a few injuries too. We lacked pace in the forwards, but when Alan came along, I knew he was going to cause Meath problems, and he did. He gave Mark O'Reilly a torrid time.

For the first time, with Ray and Alan, I felt we had a couple of new faces that were going to cause the opposition defenders big problems. Then you had Johnny McNally too, who never really got much of a run after that season, but he was a good player and a decent free-taker. In a very short space of time, it looked like a completely new team.

Against Meath in 2001 for example, we had the same faces. I could just imagine Darren Fay and Mark O'Reilly saying… *Here we go again, I'm not really too worried about these Dublin forwards.*

I'd have thought like that myself about certain lads. It's not being cocky, but you know you have their number.

Those three lads were all different players too. Alan and Ray had the pace, but I'd mark Johnny in training sometimes and he was a really awkward guy to handle. You'd find it hard to win a ball off him. Meath got a bit of a rude awakening that day… they were probably on the slide by then too, but we had something new for the first time in a long time.

To see that Meath defence looking a bit at sea was fantastic, because I'd been playing against them for a few years, and they'd always looked in control. Even in 2001, we had plenty of the ball, but we couldn't score. But in '02, things were different, and that was down to Tommy Lyons.

If I'm being honest about it, I think Tommy Carr would have put a lot of the same fellas in again. With due respect, we needed something new. Tommy Lyons took a massive gamble, because people were slating him, particularly after the Wexford game… but the Meath game gave everyone a boost and when we won Leinster it vindicated Tommy's decisions. Even though we went on to lose to Armagh in the semi-final, I felt very happy that we'd moved up a couple of notches.

It was a great year for me personally. I played International Rules for Ireland, and I captained Leinster to a Railway Cup. That might not seem like a big deal to anyone and there were only a couple of hundred people at the game, but it was a *big deal* for the players. We beat Ulster in the final… they had dominated the competition for a while. Luke Dempsey was manager and asked me would I be captain – I was delighted with myself!

It'll tell you how important it was, because we played the final down in Salthill, and Brian McEniff came into the dressing-room after the game and he said, 'Well done lads, but the referee was a disgrace!' Kieran McGeeney was standing beside him, and he was raging. I was delighted that we'd pissed these lads off.

They were great for years when they were winning, but when you turned it around on them, they didn't like it! I really enjoyed it, because my father had told me stories about the Railway Cup from years ago when it got huge crowds. There's a photo at home of the Leinster Cup, the Railway Cup and the All Star I won that year. My dad was looking at it years later and saying, 'I never thought my son would captain Leinster to a Railway Cup'.

Also, playing with lads from other counties was a big thrill for me. Playing with Graham Geraghty for Leinster and in the International Rules was brilliant. I always liked him… a lot of the Dublin lads didn't, but I always did. I always wished he played for us! I always thought that if we had him, we'd have won three or four All-Irelands, and if Ballymun had him, we'd have won a few Dublin championships.

He was just a serious player, and I always liked the idea that he didn't give a shit what anyone thought. He did what he wanted to do. We had loads of fellas who were very dedicated, but they just didn't have that class that he had. I would have craved one or two lads like him. But even he needed good players around him. In 2002, when that Meath team was on their way down, Graham wasn't getting good ball in and I think he might have had a knock too… he wasn't himself.

Tommy Lyons' whole rationale was about being positive, attacking… scoring. Don't worry if it goes wrong… *We'll recover from that*. That was very different from Tommy Carr. To be one hundred percent clear about this, I hold both of those guys in the highest esteem, but I think the person in charge needs to be positive. I think that, maybe from years of being hammered, Tommy Carr felt that we constantly had to prove ourselves, and sometimes it felt like we were beaten before we started, whereas Tommy Lyons was always… 'We can do this!' So that was one big difference right away.

He brought life with him, that's the best way I can describe it. It was infectious, like a positive virus if I can use that term given all that's happened in the last year! That positivity spread throughout the squad.

He had this expression… 'Look good, feel good, play good'… and he would always arrive with more gear for us. Training tops and the like. The wives and girlfriends would be giving out that there was more gear coming home in the bag every night! But this was Dublin, and we were on a bit of a run, so I think Tommy was able to use his business connections to bring a few quid in and get us extra bits and pieces. He had a massive amount of contacts and was able to get things done.

I would have taken that into my role with Ballymun. I'd kit the lads out in the best gear, so when they are walking around the area in their Ballymun tops, they feel good about themselves, and it instils it into lads that we're serious about this.

Some of the players might have felt he was a bit tactically naïve or didn't have the football knowledge to go with the management skills, but I always enjoyed playing under him. He didn't believe in sweepers. Every man had to go out and win their individual battle. He'd always talk up each individual and make them believe they were good enough to go out and get the better of their man.

I would always have been one for driving a nice car. Tommy would always be slagging me about the fast cars, but then one evening he was having a joke about it… then he said, 'But seriously, you're wasting a lot of money on those cars… they're only depreciating! Do you have a property? You'd wanna start thinking about that!' I was only out of college! But I did start thinking about it, and I bought an apartment a couple of years later, and Tommy put me in touch with someone who got me furniture. It saved me a fortune. I thought that was really impressive.

He wasn't doing it to save me money, he was doing it because he cared about people. When he said that something would be done, it would be done. That might seem like nothing, but it's really important for building a culture, be that in sport or in life. I took a lot of that into my life since then. Simple things like time-keeping, treating people with respect… doing things right.

Tommy's attitude to the media was probably in stark contrast to how things are done now. He would always encourage us to talk to the press if we wanted to. He had done a bit of media before he got the Dublin job, and he would have been of the view that… These lads have a job to do too. So, he'd tell us to talk away, be clever about it, don't say anything crazy. But he would tell us not to be running scared from the media. *How can you go out and be brave on the field on a Sunday if you can't answer your phone to a journalist?*

I remember having a couple of serious rows with journalists during Tommy Carr's time when he didn't want players to talk, and he did that for the right reasons. But then journalists would be getting mad with me when I told them I wasn't allowed to talk. They'd nearly be saying… Oh, are you not a big enough man to be able to make up your own mind?

It got very messy at times. It wasn't like I was going to say we were going to beat Meath by 20 points… or I was going to laugh in Graham Geraghty's face! I was going to say stuff that people already knew. Meath are a great side, it'll be tough… All that stuff. It was actually more stressful not doing interviews and arguing with journalists than it would have been to just chat for 10 minutes about a game.

Even if we did the interviews, Tommy Lyons would say to us not to read it. *Why would you need to? What do you care what some fella sitting at a desk thinks?* It's one person's opinion, and just because it's in the paper, doesn't give it any extra weight.

The bottom line was that we needed to get results on the pitch, which we did. All the foundations were being put in place. But beating Meath and then winning the Leinster was massive... then beating Donegal in the quarter-final after a replay with a brilliant performance. I've a lot of positive memories from that time; a lot of it was probably because I was playing well, but I'd like to think it was also because I can look back now and say that a lot of things were done right.

Some of the training was a bit of a slog and a bit dated, but that's only one aspect of everything that's going on, and most other teams were doing the same thing at the time. I don't think the success in 2002 would have happened without Tommy Lyons.

I scored a point before half-time against Kildare. I wandered forward and nobody tracked me. I think it was Darren Homan who gave me the ball under the Cusack Stand. I was about 30 metres out and I stopped for a second to see if anyone else was open for a pass, because I didn't really want to be having a pop if Alan Brogan or whoever was free. There was nothing really on, so I decided to have a go. I knew the second I hit it that it was going over, and a big roar went up. We were ropey enough at that time, and we needed something, so that gave us a bit of a boost.

We got a couple of goals that day, but we were hanging on for dear life at the end. It's a sad thing to say, but we were probably waiting for them to get a goal to finish us off, because that's what we'd become used to. These moral victories, like the Kerry game where people were nearly patting us on the back saying... *Ah, fair play to ye, ye're great guys.*

The ball went out of play near the end and the crowd was whistling... I could see the guys in the orange jackets, so I knew time was almost up. But the ball was put back in play and there was no whistle and I'm thinking... *Is this the time where they get the score?*

We intercepted a ball or something, and the whistle went. The roar that went up... it was just incredible. Collie Moran said afterwards that he didn't know what to do for a minute or so after the game was over. I think that sums it up perfectly. We were so used to putting out the hand to congratulate whoever had beaten us. In those moments just after the game ended, I don't think there was much of a feeling of enjoyment at winning... it was really just relief at not losing. Then lads are jumping around, and we got the trophy and did the lap of honour. It was one of those things where, in light of the year before, I could say that at least I had this. I had won nothing at underage with Dublin, nothing with Ballymun. Next thing, I had a Leinster title, a Railway Cup and played for Ireland.

I remember going back training in January 2003, and the difference was huge. I was back doing the hard slog, but this time I knew what it was for. Before that, you'd be back training and you'd be listening to all these speeches about why you were doing this. I'm not Einstein, but I'm not stupid. I'd be listening to all this talk, but I'd be thinking… *Hmm, yeah, but we're just not good enough.*

We'd be talking about running harder on the hills in the Phoenix Park, doing our gym work… *but we weren't good enough!* In 2003, I had something I could point to where I could say… *I know what this is for now. I know why I'm doing this.* I was always brutal at the long-distance training, and I really suffered. It wasn't even of much benefit to me, because all I needed to do was run from here to the wall… 10 metres. If I could beat Graham Geraghty over that distance, job done. If I couldn't… *goodnight.* If I didn't have that speed over a short distance as a full-back, I was gone. *When would I get to run non-stop for 30 seconds?* Hardly ever. But the training was a one size fits all, and that was the same for every county… I'm not criticising the Dublin management.

We'd play games in training a lot, which was brilliant from my point of view. Pillar was a selector at the time, and he'd do a few drills. He'd have the cones set up and then Tommy would come over… *Right, let's get two teams picked!* That was far more beneficial for me than running laps of the pitch or the Phoenix Park. Playing games sharpened me up, where you're doing loads of running without even realising it. If he thought I wasn't doing much running, he'd put me out to midfield or at No 6.

Coaching now is all about game-based stuff and getting away from drills that have no meaning. That's what Tommy was doing back then. Often, he'd put the six starting forwards on the six starting backs. So, I'd be on Ray or Alan. That would fairly keep you on your toes and kept you at a high level.

To go back to the books, Bill Walsh used to talk about standard of performance. You don't need to be roaring and banging tables. You train at a high level. You get used to doing that week in, week out. *Quality stuff.*

Then when it comes to matches, you just continue that on. Your aim is to almost be like a machine. Churn it out to the same level every time, to the point where it becomes normal behaviour. That means you don't have to ramp it up for a big game. You just get into the habit of doing what you do every day.

A manager's job then is to get things to a level where there's no need for any Al Pacino speeches. If you haven't been training well, or you've been out boozing when you shouldn't have been… no amount of speeches are going to lift you up to that level.

CIARÁN WHELAN

DUBLIN 1-14 DONEGAL 0-7
All-Ireland SFC Quarter-Final Replay
Croke Park
AUGUST 17, 2002

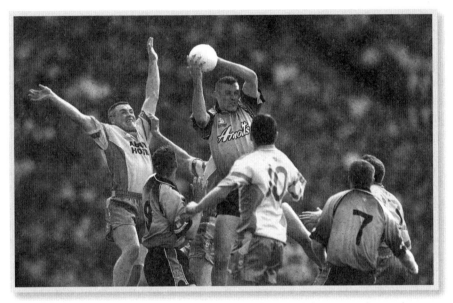

Ciarán Whelan, after spending the entire week in his sick bed, claims possession against Donegal in the All-Ireland quarter-final replay in 2002.

★ **DUBLIN:** S Cluxton; B Cahill, P Christie (0-1), P Andrews; P Casey, J Magee (0-1), C Goggins; **C Whelan (0-4)**, D Magee; S Connell (0-2), J McNally (0-1), C Moran; A Brogan (0-2), R Cosgrove (1-3), D Farrell. Subs: J Sherlock for Farrell, S Ryan for Moran, P Curran for McNally, D Homan for D Magee, E Bennis for Connell.

★ **DONEGAL:** T Blake; S Carr, E Doherty, N McGinley; R Sweeney, D Diver, K Cassidy; J Gildea, J McGuinness; C Toye, M Hegarty (0-1), B Roper (0-1); A Sweeney (0-2), B Devenney (0-2), P McGonigle. Subs: K Rafferty (0-1) for McGuinness, B Boyle for Gildea, C McFadden for Toye, R Kavanagh for Roper, C Dunne for McFadden.

THE ACTION

TOMMY LYONS WAS back on the sideline, Ray Cosgrove found the net again, and the Hill sang about winning Sam. After allowing Donegal to snatch a replay at the death two weeks earlier, Dublin made no mistake second time around with a clinical display in the Croke Park sunshine.

The throw-in time was delayed by 15 minutes in order to give tardy fans time to drink up, which forced both sides to abort their warm-up and head back to the dressing-room. Hardly ideal preparation, but it had little or no impact on Dublin, who dominated from start to finish.

Donegal couldn't repeat their heroics from 13 days earlier, but this was due in the main to the fact that their opponents raised their performance by a couple notches from the drawn game. Central to their success was Ciarán Whelan, who gave one of his best displays in the sky blue shirt and kicked four superb points from play... two off each foot.

The Dubs led by just a point after 15 minutes, but between then and half-time they left Donegal for dust. Three further points were added in the next 10 minutes, before the key score arrived. Darren Magee won Tony Blake's kickout and carried the ball forward before finding Dessie Farrell on the 20-metre line. Farrell transferred the ball quickly to Ray Cosgrove, who neatly side-stepped Blake to net his sixth goal of the summer.

Whelan capped off a magnificent first-half performance with his third point of the day just before the break, which put his side six to the good as they headed for the dressing-room. Any hopes Donegal had for a comeback were snuffed out early in the second-half as Dublin pulled clear, thanks in part to two superb points from play by Senan Connell. When Whelan knocked over his fourth point in the 57th minute, there were 10 points between them and the Donegal fans were headed for the exits. Undoubtedly, some of the players in gold and green wished they could have done the same. On a day when everything went right for Dublin, full-back Paddy Christie stepped up to drive over a '45' for the last score of the game.

The Dublin juggernaut rolled on then, and Ulster champions Armagh awaited in the semi-final.

★★★★★

66

WHEN YOU LOOK at the context, you might say now that it was only an All-Ireland quarter-final. But for me at that point, it was certainly the biggest game of my career. I had started in 1996 and we lost in the Leinster final that year… and we continued losing… first round '97, first round '98, Leinster finals in '99, 2000 and 2001. You're thinking… *When are we going to get a break?!*

When I started with Dublin, they'd just won the All-Ireland, but they were getting to All-Ireland finals and semi-finals in the years before that. Then I come in and we went seven years without even getting *out* of Leinster. We were going through a lot of transition, but we just didn't have a good enough team. It was as simple as that.

After losing the All-Ireland quarter-final replay to Kerry in Thurles in 2001, the season ended in a strange way. John Bailey, who unfortunately passed away in 2019, was chairman of the County Board. He came into the dressing-room after the game. Bertie was there too to say how proud he was, even though Kerry had beaten us.

John gave Tommy Carr a strong endorsement that he would be continuing as manager. Two or three weeks later, it went to a vote in Parnell Park. The delegates were split down the middle and John had the casting vote. He decided to vote against Tommy. That was him gone as manager.

Tommy Lyons came in and he invested in a few of the younger lads like Alan Brogan, Stephen Cluxton and Barry Cahill. He also got Ray Cosgrove playing to his potential and the year was a massive one by virtue of the fact that we won Leinster at last. It was a big weight off my shoulders having lost four provincial finals. We played Donegal in the quarter-final and drew.

We were probably lucky enough to come out of that the first day. Ray got two goals, we could have won it… but in the end, we were happy enough to get another go at it.

Tommy missed the first game due to illness, which had an impact for sure. Pillar was on the line, which maybe threw us a little bit. We only scored 2-8 and, even though we were ahead coming down the stretch, I thought we hadn't really played well enough to deserve the win. We had arrived at Parnell Park on the morning of the game, and word came through that Tommy wasn't going to be with us… that he was in hospital.

Our immediate reaction was… *Is it serious? Is he going to be okay?* When you arrive at Parnell Park three or four hours before a game and your manager isn't there, naturally it has an impact on everybody. Pillar stood in and he was experienced enough to know how to handle it. He had been heavily involved with Na Fianna and obviously went on to manage Dublin in his own right.

But it was odd, because it was a different voice in the dressing-room in Croke Park. It's important again to remember the context. We'd had a great run through Leinster, the city was buzzing, the Hill was hopping. This was a massive game and, all of a sudden, your manager is gone and someone else has to step in. Anything that upsets the preparation isn't ideal. We nearly got the job done, but we didn't.

One of the interesting things between the games was that Donegal stayed down after the draw. I think a few of them went on the lash in Dublin on the Monday and Tuesday. They got a lot of stick at home about that after the replay… *What were they doing? They should have been back up home getting ready for the next day.* But that was real hindsight stuff.

There was almost a two-week gap between the games. We would have had a few on the Sunday and Monday too… we wouldn't have done anything different from the Donegal lads, but they got a lot of grief about that. We weren't aware of it at the time, but after the second game it all came out, and it was an easy thing to use in the blame-game because Donegal hadn't performed.

The reality was we did the same, they just got the hassle because they lost. I suppose the only difference is we were back on the training field on Tuesday night after the drawn game… when maybe a couple of their lads were only making the long trip home at that stage!

On the middle weekend between the games, I came down with an awful bug. I've never been as sick in all my life. I was violently ill for a few days… I was in bed literally from the Saturday all the way through the whole week. I remember talking to Tommy Lyons on the Tuesday or the Wednesday.

'I'm goosed here,' I told him. 'I'm not going to make this game'. I'd lost a lot of weight, I hadn't eaten in days… I literally couldn't get out of bed. My wife Fiona was giving me Dioralyte to keep me hydrated. Even on Thursday and Friday, when I started to feel a bit better and got some food into me, I was still thinking… *80,000 people, Saturday evening, Croke Park… This is not going to happen.* I had almost resigned myself to the fact that I wouldn't be playing. But we kept it quiet… nobody knew about it in the media, and I just tried to get as much fluid into me as possible.

We had a meeting on the morning of the game out in Citywest. I arrived into the room, and it was the first time I'd seen the squad in a while. I had missed all the training and all the prep. Tommy came over to me.

'What about starting?'

'Jesus, I dunno Tommy. I really don't know. I've been very sick all week.'

He said, 'Let's give it a go, and if your legs are failing after 15 minutes, we'll pull you'. The rest is history as they say! It was a strange sort of day, but I went out and had one of my best games ever in a Dublin jersey. I look back on it now and think… *How did that all happen? How did it all come together?*

Because, genuinely, on the Wednesday and Thursday of that week, I was full sure there was no way I was going to be playing. No way. It was mad stuff really.

It's hard to explain it. It would probably be fair to say that, psychologically, you're not caught up worrying about the game because you're thinking… *I haven't a hope here…* but maybe there's an element of it feeling like a free hit. I really thought I'd be going off after 15 minutes, but I played the full game.

I was always nervous before games, particularly as I got older. When I was young, I played with a lot more freedom. Later in my career, I put a lot more stress on myself. I would have been 26 in 2002, so I was in my prime. For that replay, I possibly had written myself off, so I was only focused on trying to get myself right, rather than focusing on the game itself.

I got my first point after about six minutes from under the Cusack Stand off my right. We were playing well but weren't scoring and hit a few bad wides, so it was tight enough for the first 25 minutes or so. I got another point around then from the same side, but off my left. I was getting on a lot of ball at that stage, and I was in that zone where I felt I was going to win every kickout.

Ray got the goal soon after that, and I popped over another point before half-time from around 40 metres. I got another point then in the second-half when we were cruising.

I invested a lot of time in kicking with both feet. I'm right-footed naturally, but at one stage in my career I nearly felt more comfortable kicking off my left. Strangely, when I played minor and under-21, I wouldn't have had a strong left foot. It was only later on that I developed that.

I had a groin injury in 1997, and it was giving me an awful time, but I was only a young lad in my second year on the panel, so of course I didn't say a whole lot to the physios. I had that for about six or eight weeks. Once I got warmed up, I was fine, but for the first 20 minutes I would struggle. We used to go out about 20 minutes before training started, and during that period I'd only be able to use my left foot. That was the default way I became strong on my left. I probably should have worked on it sooner, but the lesson there is you can work on these things at any age. Some young lads would think if they aren't good at something by the time they are 16 or 17, then it's too late. *It isn't.*

It was a different time. There wasn't any video analysis going on really. I didn't watch the drawn game and nobody would have communicated with me the whole week I was sick in bed. I just rocked up on the morning of the replay! It was just a case of... *Get out there and play...* and the game plan was fairly simplistic. The level of analysis was minimal. I can only imagine if it was now and I was out of the camp for 10 days... I'd be inundated with Zoom calls, stats and video clips. But then maybe I wouldn't have gone out and kicked four points, so maybe there's a lesson in that!

I was surprised when Tommy Carr got removed, because if you had been in the dressing-room in Thurles in 2001, you'd have said that that certainly wasn't going to happen. Tommy was a popular manager among the group. He had come in at the end of 1997, and he was trying to break that duck and win a Leinster, but we were up against a very good Meath team that won the All-Ireland in '96 and went on to win it again in '99.

In 2000 we felt like we left one behind us against Kildare, and in '01 Meath beat us quite convincingly in the Leinster final. The Kerry game came next, and it's one of the few games that I've watched back because it has been on television quite a bit lately. I watched it recently with my young lad, who's a teenager now. We were eight points down the first day, and he turned around to me and asked, 'How did ye draw this game? Ye were bleedin' useless! Then I kind of looked at it and I thought… *Jesus, we were bleedin' useless!* That's looking at the game coldly 20 years later.

We got two goals, there was a massive momentum shift, and we could have stolen it. It would have been a real smash-and-grab job if we had. *Were we good enough though?* That's the question. The euphoria around those two Kerry games and the trip to Tipp and all that went with it… that was probably enough for people to think that Tommy was making progress and should get another year.

I know Dessie Farrell went to the meeting and spoke on Tommy's behalf, so that decision came as a surprise. Ultimately though, the County Board does the hiring and firing. Players don't decide who the manager is, and that was made very clear to us at the time. *Suck it up and get on with it.*

Tommy Lyons came in off the back of his success with Kilmacud Crokes and Offaly, and he was a very different character to Tommy Carr. One of the things that was obvious straightaway was that he was going to give young lads a go. Another thing that became apparent fairly early on was that he didn't fancy me as a midfielder.

He made it clear that he saw me as a half-forward. I played a lot of that National League at wing-forward or centre-forward, and it was a frustrating campaign. I always struggled in the half-forward line, particularly at No 11. Centre-forward is one of the hardest positions on the field to play in my opinion, and I had gone from facing the play… to having my back to it, and the game can bypass you. I was never comfortable there.

There was a game in the latter part of the league – I can't remember who it was against – but he put me back in the middle and I did well. Tommy changed his mind after that. I could have been on a very different path in 2002, but I managed to get that midfield position back.

With the years passing by and Dublin struggling to even win a Leinster, never mind compete for All-Irelands, I felt a huge amount of personal pressure.

It was tough at times, and there's much more scrutiny nowadays… but the narrative seemed to be that if I played well, then Dublin had a good chance of winning. That's not trying to sound arrogant, but that's how it was framed. Then if I played badly and we lost, I got hammered for it. That was the downside of it.

This was at a time before the short kickouts… everything was coming long. As a midfielder, your game was based around how you did in those battles for possession. Traditionally, the opposition kickouts were where you had the upper-hand, because you were coming in from behind the man or from a better angle… and if you won the ball, you were putting your team on the front foot.

On our own kickouts, I had someone trying to distract me. I found a lot of the time that teams would try to keep the ball away from me. I could see goalkeepers looking up to see where I was, and then going to the opposite side. That happened against Tyrone in 2005 for the whole second-half. Then the story is told that you just went out of the game.

There were many games where I found myself trying to live off scraps. You're trying to get on balls and make runs… and it's not working out.

There were games when I wasn't in it and wasn't getting on the ball as much as I'd have liked, and what happens then is you try to force it when you get possession. I'd end up making a mistake then and it impacts negatively. Before the Kerry game in 2001, we decided that if I carried the ball, then I could draw tackles and open them up. I got a little bit bogged down by that and every ball I got, I tried to carry it. In hindsight, that wasn't the right thing to do. Fair enough, when the opportunity and space is there, that's the time to run with it, but I should have mixed my game up a bit more. Upon reflection, we were fairly headless at times, but equally, I don't think we had the personnel.

In some ways we might have been overachieving in 2001 and maybe a little bit in '02. We got caught on a bit of a momentum wave after coming out of Leinster… we had the win over Donegal, then we're a kick of a ball away from a replay against Armagh. There were loads of little things in that game that could have gone differently for us, and we could have been in an All-Ireland final, but we were definitely a stronger team in 2002 than in '01. We had the new faces in the forwards, and we moved the ball a lot quicker.

There were a few new voices on the training field in 2002 as well. Dave Billings and Pillar came in, so it was really just that bit of freshness and a slight change in direction. Tommy changed how he wanted us to approach the media, and it was similar to Tyrone this year (2021) in ways… he wanted to change the image of the team and get the fans on board. It worked in 2002, but I think Tommy maybe got caught up in it himself a little bit. We had got to a semi-final and there was a sense that we had achieved something.

Okay, we had won Leinster, but we hadn't really achieved *anything*. That hype of 2002 went a little too far in my view. What also happened was that some of the older personnel who weren't getting a look-in began to become unhappy, and it went downhill fairly quickly. Ultimately, for all the changes, winning is the bottom line.

On the day of the Donegal replay, the throw-in was delayed by 15 minutes. Pillar used to slag me because we were involved in a few games that got delayed, and I would have been giving out hell in the dressing-room! You are ready to go, and you're built up for the game… then you've a 15-minute delay. In hindsight it didn't impact us, but at the time you're thinking… *Why can't they get in here on time?*

It was a Saturday evening game, and the lads were down the road filling themselves with juice! But look, you just had to deal with it. In terms of the hype and the crowds that year, Croke Park is the sort of ground that will swallow you up on a bad day and carry you along on a good one. That buzz and energy around the team in 2002 created a brilliant mood going into the Donegal and Armagh games. You're on the back of seven years of losing big games, so to start winning them and to feel that energy around the place and in the ground, that was a different dynamic.

We pulled away in the second quarter against Donegal and we were six up at half-time. It wasn't exactly done and dusted at that stage, but it felt like it almost was. They didn't really perform. They weren't quite at the same level as they had been the first day, but a lot of that was probably down to the fact that we squeezed them.

I was marking John Gildea for a while, but he had to go off injured at some stage. Jimmy McGuinness was on me for a bit too. It was one of my best performances for Dublin without a doubt. I don't think I could have performed better, particularly considering where I'd come from that week.

When we came back in 2003, we had to do it again, but things came apart really quickly. Where I felt it really came off the rails was after we played Louth in the Leinster Championship. We won that game comfortably, but Tommy made three changes for the next game against Laois. I felt like they were strange changes.

I'm not sure if it was a case of thinking we'd be okay and we could afford to change things around or what… but Laois turned us over. A few of the older lads were again left out which added fuel to the fire, and that followed on to the Armagh qualifier game. Cluxton gets sent off and Tommy said a few words about that after the game which wouldn't have gone down too well.

Those two games, in my view, broke all that momentum from 2002 and set the team on a different path. If you've older lads who aren't playing and you're not keeping them onside, that's a dangerous combination.

My last season was 2009. I played throughout the National League, but I picked up a hamstring injury just before the championship. I was back for the Leinster final and came on in that game and was sitting on the bench for the Kerry quarter-final… the 'startled earwigs' game. Pat brought me on after 15 minutes, but the game was nearly gone, even at that early stage.

We were seven behind and only had a point on the board. My daughter was born that weekend… our second child. I was struggling for that yard of pace, and I was getting crankier… so I'd made up my mind that it was the end of the road.

We came so close a few times… 2002 was obviously one, where we almost got by Armagh. Kerry might have been beyond us in the final, but you never know. The momentum would have been huge and with the hype around a first Dublin-Kerry final in years… *Who knows!* We might have done it. But 2006 and '07 are the two years when I felt we were closest. In '06, things were too comfortable for us. We were hammering teams coming into that Mayo game… then we were seven points up. That's the one that still gives me sleepless nights. *Seven up with 20 minutes to go.* We only have ourselves to blame for that one. In 2007, we ran Kerry to a couple of points, and we had them on the rack a few times. That would have been a great opportunity when you look at what Kerry did in the final. We were definitely more ready in 2006 and '07 than we were in '02.

At that time, lads would try to unsettle you and you could get away with a bit more than now, where cameras are hunting everything down. I came up against lads like John McDermott, and plenty of lads on the International Rules trips who knew how to handle themselves, so you learned pretty quickly that you had to become the bully… rather than getting bullied. You had to lay down a marker early on that nobody was going to get the better of you. That was really what midfield play was like at the time, and you had to learn your trade quickly if you were going to stick around.

RAY COSGROVE

ARMAGH 1-14 DUBLIN 1-13
All-Ireland SFC Semi-Final
Croke Park
SEPTEMBER 1, 2002

Ray Cosgrove shoots against Armagh in the All-Ireland semi-final in 2002, in the blistering summer when he kicked an amazing 6-23 in six games in the championship.

★ **ARMAGH:** B Tierney; F Bellew, J McNulty, E McNulty; A O'Rourke, K McGeeney, A McCann; J Toal, P McGrane; P McKeever (1-2), J McEntee (0-3), O McConville (0-5); S McDonnell (0-2), R Clarke (0-2), D Marsden. Subs: K Hughes for McCann, P Loughran for Toal, B O'Hagan for Marsden, C O'Rourke for McKeever.

★ **DUBLIN:** S Cluxton; B Cahill, P Christie, C Goggins; P Casey, J Magee, P Andrews; C Whelan (1-1), D Magee (0-1); S Connell (0-2), D Farrell, S Ryan; A Brogan (0-2), J McNally, **R Cosgrove (0-6)**. Subs: C Moran (0-1) for Ryan, D Homan for Magee, J Sherlock for McNally, D Darcy for Moran.

THE ACTION

THE WIDTH OF a post separated Dublin from a replay in this dramatic All-Ireland semi-final. Armagh, who had been knocking on the door for several years, led for only eight of the 74 minutes played but, crucially, had their noses in front when Michael Collins blew for full-time.

A game that was expected to be tight lived up to its billing. The meeting of Armagh's battle-hardened side with Tommy Lyons' free-wheeling Dubs provided a real contrast in styles, which made for fascinating viewing. It was the Boys in Blue who came out of the traps faster, racing into a three-point lead while Armagh sought their first score. The Ulster champions eventually settled and opened their account on 11 minutes. Moments later, Stephen Cluxton reacted brilliantly to prevent a deflected '45' from hitting the net. Dublin led for most of the half, but two points before the break from Oisín McConville sent the sides in level at six points apiece.

Paddy McKeever's goal seven minutes after the restart put three between them, but Dublin responded in kind within a minute when Ciarán Whelan fired a ferocious shot to the net after a typically marauding run through the centre of the Armagh defence. That score lifted Dublin's spirits once again, and they led by two points on three subsequent occasions. They found Armagh impossible to shake off though, and Ray Cosgrove's point in the 61st minute – which made it 1-13 to 1-11 – was to be their last.

Ronan Clarke cut the gap to one, and John McEntee then brought the sides level for the eighth time, before McConville slipped inside Paul Casey on the end-line and fisted over from a tight angle. Alan Brogan and Collie Moran both kicked wides for Dublin before the last chance arrived. Enda McNulty fouled Cosgrove around 30 metres out, slightly to the left of the posts.

It was the perfect angle for a right-footer such as the Dublin full-forward, but his shot didn't quite curl enough and came back into play off the post. Armagh gathered the loose ball and seconds later the final whistle sounded. It was unfortunate that the man who lit up Dublin's summer was ultimately responsible for missing the kick that saw them depart the championship, but on such fine margins are big games decided.

★★★★★

66

I CAME ON the scene in 1996. I was in the squad with Mickey Whelan, and I played a few league games. At the time, I was in college in Waterford, so I was commuting up and down for matches and training. In the lead-up to the Leinster final in 1996, there was an A vs B game, and I was shooting the lights out. I was really flying it, but I was very raw. I didn't know if I'd start but I was sure I'd make the bench.

In the end, I didn't, and I was disappointed because I was showing that I was close to making the team... to not even make the bench was a bit of a tough one to take.

In 1997 and '98 I was injured. I had an ankle injury first, then I pulled my hamstring, so I didn't get a good run of it for those two years, but I was back in in 1999. That was a year to forget too! I actually came on in the Leinster final for Dessie Farrell after about 15 minutes and I was kind of wandering around out the field, but I couldn't get into the game.

Then I went into the corner and Jim Gavin came out to centre-forward. I didn't get on much ball and the game bypassed me, so I got the curly finger with about 20 minutes to go! I'd have no regrets... it was just one of those days and things didn't go for us. It's not something I spent a lot of time thinking about.

Tommy Carr asked me to go back in 2000, and I told him that I'd felt a bit hard done-by and that I was just going to go back to the club and focus on that. I walked away after that. On reflection, it was probably the wrong thing to do and maybe I threw the toys out of the pram a little.

For 2000 and '01 I wasn't around.

The famous drawn All-Ireland quarter-final against Kerry in Thurles in 2001... I was in Portugal watching that.

Tommy Carr was ousted at the end of the 2001 season and there was a lot of controversy about that... Tommy Lyons was given the job. So even though I had played a few league games in 1997 and '98, 2002 was the year my championship career took off. Tommy getting the job was massive for me personally. I'd played under Tommy for the club in the mid-90s, so he knew me inside out.

From day one, I knew he was going to back me. I still remember the phone call I got from Tommy not long after he got the job. I was working in Bank of Ireland in Montrose, and the call came through. He just said, 'Cossie, I'm going to give you a fair crack of the whip here. I don't care how poorly you're playing. I'm going to stick with you. So don't be worrying and looking over your shoulder that someone is going to be coming on for you. You've got what it takes to wear the Dublin jersey… now just go out and do it'.

I'd like to think I paid him back in spades, but it was his man-management that got the best out of me. Tommy's not everybody's cup of tea, but he was absolutely brilliant for me in 2002. He got the city behind him, and he brought the swagger back into Dublin football that summer. Dublin had really missed that.

We hadn't won a Leinster title since 1995 remember. A seven-year gap was a massive amount of time to be in the wilderness, and Tommy had a massive part to play in ending that barren spell.

My form in the league gave me a bit of momentum going into the championship. I got a goal against Galway down in Tuam, which got us the draw we needed to stay in whatever division we were in… so that gave me a bit of a pep in my step going into the Wexford game.

We had a lot of younger guys coming into the panel… Clucko, Alan Brogan, Darren Magee, Johnny McNally, Paul Casey…we were very much a young outfit and there was no fear of anyone. That was something which Tommy instilled. We were a new squad in lots of ways and because of that, we weren't dwelling on defeats to Meath, or the Kerry games in Thurles the year before. Dessie, Paul Curran, Jayo…they were still important for us, but I would say they weren't the central figures they had been in the years gone by.

I don't mean that to sound like I'm running those lads down because I'm not for one second, but we had new leaders coming through like Paddy Christie, Coman Goggins and Johnny Magee. There had been a fair bit of change, even from the previous year, and it was very much Tommy Lyons' team now. There was a confidence in the team that wasn't there in the few years before that.

Pillar Caffrey was a selector at that time and he always said that Dublin footballers are judged on how they perform in big games. We played Meath in the Leinster semi-final and it was basically said to us… *If you can't produce it against Meath, that will be held over you.* Meath games back then were massive, and every time we played them, I would always think to myself… *How you're remembered, and how you look back on your Dublin career will depend on how you play in this game… This is the yardstick.*

So going into that game in 2002, I had that in mind. Fayser (Darren Fay) was marking me, and I would have looked up to Darren as one of the best full-backs in the country.

Walking off the pitch that day having won first of all, but also having got 2-3 against one of the best in the business, that gave me *massive* confidence moving forward to the next game. That was a huge game in my career, and I thought… *Yeah, now I'm in the big-time and I've proved I belong here.* I mean, you can look back on National League games, but championship is what you're going to be judged on. I felt there were still big question marks over me.

I got the breaks that day, don't get me wrong, but the history books show 2-3 beside my name! After that, I could stick my chest out a bit knowing that I could compete with the best of them.

Looking back on it now, I can see how that summer for me was huge and I obviously got a lot of headlines and media attention. At the time though, it's all happening so quickly, and you're caught up in your own little bubble, so a lot of it passes you by. You don't really realise the impact it's having when you're in the middle of it. You're oblivious to a lot of it, and I was trying to keep my feet on the ground.

It's only when I look back at what I did – kicking 6-23 in six games in the championship – there aren't too many lads who do that any summer. It's something I'm really proud of, because we were playing quality opposition every week.

The Leinster final was a huge occasion for me. Not just to get a goal but to finally win a provincial medal was massive for me personally and obviously for the county as well given it was seven years since we had won Leinster. The relief for the likes of Whelo, Paddy Christie, Darren Homan… those guys had been around for a few years with nothing to show for it.

There's a great photo after that game of myself, Jim Gavin – who was a sub that day – and my mate Tom Mulligan, who's sadly no longer with us… all of us in front of the Hill. The lap of honour afterwards… those memories will stay with me until my dying day. It really was a boyhood dream.

We got over Donegal in a replay in the quarter-final. Tommy Lyons missed the first game because of gallstones, if I remember rightly, so Pillar wore the *Bainisteoir* bib. We were lucky not to lose the first day, but we won the replay comfortably enough. I got a couple of goals in the drawn game and one in the replay, which were nice to get, and it kept the thing rolling along.

Armagh then in the semi-final in the new Croke Park! You're running out of the tunnel and the noise just hits you. In fairness to Armagh, their supporters are *loud*. The atmosphere that day was second-to-none.

That Armagh team had been on the go for a few years and they were seasoned. The likes of Kieran McGeeney, the McNultys, Francie Bellew, Diarmuid Marsden, Benny Tierney... they were further down the development road than we were, and they were on a mission.

Francie Bellew was on me for most of that game and he was one of the toughest guys around. In no way dirty or nasty, just tough and so brave. I know it's a cliché, but he'd put his head where some lads wouldn't put their hand. I won't say he was reckless, but he was fearless. He'd go hammer and tongs for every ball.

Francie used to get a bit of stick for being slow, but I can tell you that he was as quick over 10 yards as any full-back. He'd get a paw in, he'd put you under pressure... so yeah, that was a massive tussle.

Why did I pick this game if we lost? I thought my overall game that day was really good. I kicked six points which was fine, but my running off the ball, my touch... everything just fell into place, and I just felt everything went right for me. The scores in the other games probably got more headlines, but I watched that Armagh game back recently and I was just on the top of my game and my contribution that day exceeded anything that I had done in the games before.

Obviously, everyone will remember me hitting the post in added time, but the one thing I'd like to refer back to is... I'd gone and won the free. It wasn't as if I took the ball off someone and wanted to be the hero... I had won the free in the first place. Unfortunately, it came back off the post and we weren't alert to the rebound.

But someone had to stand up and take it, and I was as confident as you could be that it was going to sail between the posts. *Small margins*. It didn't, and the rest is history. It was disappointing to not have an All-Ireland final to look forward to, but there was some small consolation in the fact that I had played well and got Man of the Match.

Before the game, there was a bit of talk of a Dublin-Kerry final being bandied about in the media. It wasn't something that we talked about at all. We didn't take our eye off the ball – we definitely weren't looking ahead to the third Sunday in September even though a lot of people all over the country were getting excited about the possibility of a final that had such history to it.

Because it was the first semi-final for a lot of us, we didn't really think about the final, whereas to be perfectly honest, in 2006 when Mayo beat us… I came off the pitch with about 20 minutes to go and I thought… *That's it, we're heading for an All-Ireland final.* We were seven points up at one stage, we were flying, and the belief was there that we could get to a final.

Now, obviously things went badly wrong for us, and Mayo came back to win, but in 2002 I don't think that mentality was there. I don't think we really believed we could make the final in 2002 because it was a younger group. Of course, you could say we didn't make the final in '06 either, but I do think the belief was there by then… we just didn't close out that Mayo game.

It didn't feel to me that we left the Armagh game behind us.

It was nip and tuck and we had spoken a lot about making sure we weren't rolled over by Armagh. They were a big physical team… you don't get out of Ulster if you don't have that as we know, but we were determined not to be intimidated and not be bullied. That was one of the key things that we discussed before that game. *Let's get out of the traps quickly. Let's not give these lads any confidence early in the game or allow them to get any momentum.*

Coming in level at half-time, we knew we were right in it and felt we had a right good chance to kick on in the second-half, especially as we were shooting into the Hill. Generally, Dublin play better when kicking into the Hill… I was confident we'd push on and finally get over the line.

To go back to Francie… he's quite similar to Darren Fay. They're both big, imposing guys, but there'd be no lip or messing from them. They wouldn't have been in your ear giving it all that. It's important to note that, because Francie would maybe be viewed by some as a hard man. He was hard, but he was always fair, and he went out to win the ball. *Unfortunately, we just weren't good enough on the day. We finished with 1-13. Was that going to be enough to win a championship game?* Probably not… 2-13 would win most games, 1-13 is probably just a little short of what you'd need, and it wasn't enough in this game.

I was on the frees and I remember one of the papers mentioning that Dublin's lack of a consistent free-taker cost us. I would usually have kicked frees off the ground, but I had damaged my medial knee ligament. That's not an excuse, that's just the fact of the matter. I got two cortisone injections into my knee during that season.

But in saying that, I don't think I missed a huge amount of frees out of my hands that summer anyway. Certainly though, if the knee was right, I would have been much more comfortable kicking from the ground.

It might surprise people to know this, but it didn't feel like a devastating end to the game or the season for me. Initially, of course you're disappointed that you're not heading to an All-Ireland final… I don't want to be in any way dismissive of that. But when I looked back on the year in its totality, from what I achieved throughout the year, the pros massively outweighed the cons.

I had a great summer with Dublin… I won a Railway Cup and I also represented my country in the Compromise Rules. I was top scorer in the championship and I won an All-Star. Yeah, I lost a football match and Dublin fans might say… 'If he'd kicked that free, we could have won an All-Ireland!' Absolutely we might have, but would we have beaten that Kerry team in 2002? On paper, they were a far stronger team and would have been roaring hot favourites to beat us. Anything can happen and yes, potentially we could have won an All-Ireland, but I don't know if we would have been ready to take on that Kerry team.

It was an unbelievable year, and I don't beat myself up over any one part of it.

When I look back over my career, there are other games that I have nightmares about. We were beaten in a Leinster club final after three games by Éire Óg in 1999. After that third game, I didn't sleep for days, and I blamed myself for not winning a Leinster club that year. In the replay I won a free in the half-forward line, into injury-time, a wet day down in Tullamore. I thought I'd be the smart fella and put the ball into the corner towards Paddy O'Donoghue. The corner-back wins it, they come up the field and kick the equaliser.

It goes to a second replay, and we lose that. I blamed myself wholeheartedly for that one from a game management perspective. If one of my players did that now, I'd be livid with him. I should have put the ball on the ground, slowed things down… let Johnny Magee come up and kick it 40 yards out onto the road or whatever. That was one I really took to heart, because I felt I really let the team down that day by taking a wrong option.

I was lucky enough to win five Dublin championships and three Leinsters with the club, but that was another one that we could have won. That was a sickener. If I could go back to one game in my career, it would be that game with Crokes. We should have won the first day and it was in our hands – my hands specifically! – the second day.

After the Armagh game, we went to Seán O'Casey's, then on to Jury's in Ballsbridge. I don't have a huge recollection of that evening, but the following day we went down to Ballymore Eustace. Johnny McNally's brother is down there so we said… *Right, let's get out of dodge!* We rolled down there on the Monday evening around 6pm. Myself, Tom Mulligan and a few other friends went into Mick Murphy's pub… and the RTÉ news was on the television. The sport comes on and, of course, there's a look back at the game from the day before and they showed the missed free.

Next thing, the barman says to one of the locals, 'Jaysus, I really feel sorry for that poor bollix'… and one of the lads goes, 'Tell him yourself, he's just after walking in the door!' So that was the most abuse I got from anyone over it really!

PAUL GRIFFIN

DUBLIN 0-14 LAOIS 0-13
Leinster SFC Final
Croke Park
JULY 17, 2005

Dublin captain Paul Griffin lifts the Delaney Cup after Dublin's win over Kildare in 2009, but it was a Leinster final four years earlier that was the Game of his Life.

★ **DUBLIN:** S Cluxton; **P Griffin**, P Christie, S O'Shaughnessy (0-1); C Goggins, B Cahill, P Casey; C Whelan (0-1), S Ryan; C Moran (0-1), B Cullen (0-3), C Keaney (0-1); J Sherlock (0-2), A Brogan (0-1), T Quinn (0-4). Subs: P Andrews for Christie, S Connell for Goggins, D Homan for Ryan.

★ **LAOIS:** F Byron; A Fennelly, D Rooney, J Higgins; C Begley, T Kelly, P McMahon; P Clancy, N Garvan (0-2); R Munnelly (0-5), B Brennan, B Sheehan; C Conway (0-4), K Fitzpatrick, B McDonald. Subs: D Brennan (0-2) for B Brennan, M Dunne for McDonald, D Conroy for Rooney.

THE ACTION

DUBLIN MADE AMENDS for two years of provincial disappointment with a dramatic win over Laois in this Leinster final, which had the record crowd of 81,025 living on their nerves right up to the final whistle.

In typical Dublin fashion, they didn't make it easy on themselves or their fans. The first-half had been almost exclusively one-way traffic, as Ciarán Whelan dominated around the middle to give his side a platform that they should have made more of. Bryan Cullen's switch from the wing to centre-forward was causing Tom Kelly problems, while Alan Brogan and Jason Sherlock also added to the intense pressure that the Laois defence came under in the opening 35 minutes. Dublin's shooting was erratic, however, and although they led by five points at the break, they should have had considerably more than seven points to show for their first-half efforts.

Quite what Mick O'Dwyer said to his side at half-time is anyone's guess, but it's fair to say that the Kerry legend's words had the desired effect. Laois were a team transformed in the second period, while Dublin suffered another of their all-too-common barren spells. The O'Moore men were level by the 52nd minute, and though Dublin rallied with three unanswered scores, Laois then rattled off five of their own to lead by two with seven minutes remaining.

It was a severe test of Dublin's resolve, one which they were equal to on this occasion. Step forward Mossy Quinn. The St Vincent's man had endured a difficult afternoon, missing two frees and a '45'. Whatever doubts those misses placed in Quinn's mind, he had clearly banished them as the game entered its crucial closing stages. With a minute remaining of normal time, he floated over a free from 43 metres to level the scores. Moments later, after Dublin forced a '45' from Joe Higgins, Quinn again steered the ball between the posts to put his side in front.

Laois's composure deserted them in the two minutes of added time that remained, with Ross Munnelly and Tom Kelly both missing chances to force the game to a replay.

★★★★★

"

THE 2005 SEASON was my first one actually playing. I came onto the panel in 2002, so I was around when we beat Kildare in the Leinster final in Tommy Lyons' first year. Armagh beat us in the semi-final. At that stage it was a pretty young squad and we thought that we'd kick on the following year and go one step further, but then we had two seasons where it was really difficult.

Laois beat us in 2003 in a Leinster semi-final, then Westmeath beat us in the quarter-final in '04, so we lost the bit of momentum. Tommy left at that stage. There was a gap for a while in terms of who would come in... before Pillar was confirmed.

Leinster finals at that stage were such big occasions. Even the one in 2002... that was our first win since 1995. I was only 19 at the time, so I didn't have the baggage that a lot of those lads were carrying from the previous few years where Kildare and Meath were dominating. 2005 was similar in that sense in that we'd had a bad couple of years, and we needed to move forward.

Coming into that game, we were possibly favourites but there wouldn't have been much in it. We beat Meath and Wexford on the way to the final, but they were both fairly close games. Laois had hammered Kildare in the semi-final, so there was probably a bit of pressure on them. They had won it in 2003 and probably should have beaten Westmeath in '04, so they felt that they should have been going for three-in-a-row in '05. We started pretty well and from a defensive point of view we were really solid. I remember at half-time... we had played really well, but I didn't think we'd put up the scores that we should have. We were very dominant but that wasn't reflected on the scoreboard. We felt like we had gone flat out but only had a five-point lead to show for it. We missed a lot of chances.

The second-half, we started off fairly well but then we had this wobble. We were a team who, at that time, couldn't control the tempo of games. If things were going well, we were flying forward at 100 miles an hour... but if a team got a run on us, we couldn't control it that easily. Laois managed to get themselves back into the game and they went ahead by a couple of points coming into the closing stages... it probably wasn't looking great for us at that stage. Collie got a point, and then Mossy Quinn hit a free to level it up.

It was a really tense finish to the game. The winning point came from a '45' by Mossy, but there were still a few minutes to go at that stage and Ross Munnelly got a free before the end, which I fully expected him to score. Fortunately, he missed it… we got over the line by the skin of our teeth. Not to repeat myself, but I think it's worth reminding everyone that Leinster titles were a big deal for us at that time.

That's not to say they aren't important to the current players, but they weren't as frequent back then as they are now. I think it was Darren Homan who won the last ball when the whistle went, and there was a great photo of him celebrating. We played Tyrone a few weeks later and we should have beaten them the first day, but they pulled away in the replay… and that was the year gone.

Looking back on the years that preceded that win, the reaction towards Tommy Lyons at the end was unfair, I thought. Tommy was brilliant for bringing through younger guys. He had done that with Kilmacud in winning a club All-Ireland in 1995, he did it with Offaly… and then he did it with Dublin. He probably had a much more difficult transition too, because he was trying to bridge that gap from Tommy Carr, where a lot of that group would have felt that Tommy (Carr) was hard-done by.

They would have felt that they were close to getting over the line, but they probably weren't as close as they thought. When Tommy Lyons came in and brought in a lot of youth, there was always going to be a lot of kick-back from some of the more experienced lads. The first year went brilliantly, because the confidence that Tommy gave you as a young player was fantastic. He'd be like… *Of course you can go out and play at this level… Of course you can go out and win.* Age wasn't a barrier for him at all.

The tricky thing was when it started to turn against us. We probably should have beaten Laois in 2003, but having lost that, and then losing to Westmeath the following year… it made it very difficult.

Laois and Westmeath both had really good teams at that stage, but Dublin as a county – rightly or wrongly – would have had an expectation that we should be beating Laois and Westmeath. Pillar coming in allowed us to hit reset to an extent really, and Paul Clarke coming in was a huge thing too… Clarkey was such a tonic in terms of his love of football. He was a new voice, which was important because it was awkward enough at first. I remember the first meeting we had out in DCU, and there had been a bit of a gap in time after Tommy stepped away.

I think there were three or four weeks where it wasn't clear who was going to get the job. There were whispers of Mick O'Dwyer for a while... I'm not sure how far that went. Brian Mullins then looked like he was going to get it, and then there was a last-minute u-turn. But time was ticking by and there was no sign of a new manager being appointed... then Paul got the job.

Because he had been involved with Tommy Lyons, he wasn't a completely new face.

That first meeting was a bit difficult, and I'd say Pillar found it a bit awkward too, but Clarkey was in the room, and he was like... *What's the problem? You're here to play for Dublin. This is a good thing. Lose the long faces!*

That set the tone in terms of reminding us all why we were there.

Ski Wade came in too and he was brilliant. He was the first guy I'd worked with who was a real defenders' coach. He picked up on little things in the technique of defending, and our training that year was so different to anything we'd done before. Before, the backs would nearly be standing behind the goals while the forwards were shooting, and it'd nearly be... *We'll give ye a shout when we're having a game!*

But with Ski, we worked a lot on our body position when defending and tackling... where we needed to stand, when to try to win the first ball... we worked on getting blocks in, tackling technique. Nobody was really doing anything like that at that time, not in Dublin at least.

Some lads are naturally tight markers, but that coaching in terms of how to get better at it was great.

That Leinster final, I was picking up Donie Brennan. Laois had a lot of similar players at that time... they seemed to produce these small, fast forwards. I was winning most balls that came in and our full-back line as a whole was fairly dominant in the first-half. We were able to keep them at bay at that stage. In the second-half though, Ross Munnelly started to come into it a lot more. He was drifting all over the field, in and out of the full-forward line and he was their most efficient forward.

It was a time in Dublin football where we always seemed to be part of the best games of the year, but we were always coming out on the wrong side of them. We probably didn't learn enough from those games as we went along, and it carried forward for a long while. Like, even in Pat Gilroy's first year, we were going along well and then got hockeyed out the gate by Kerry.

We had a few of those years where we were flying along, but ultimately when we came under pressure – particularly against the top sides – we crumbled. The three top teams at that time were Armagh, Tyrone and Kerry. They were really brilliant teams.

If you looked at Kerry, for example, man-for-man we'd probably have stacked up fairly well against them, but they were a much more cohesive group. They played together much better, and they worked collectively much better. We tended to rely on individuals playing well, but if that didn't happen, we didn't have much else to protect us or support us. So, when we came up against those top sides, if they got on top of a couple of our key individuals, we'd be snookered in terms of… *What else have you got?* We had no Plan B to try to keep ourselves in the game, and games ran away from us.

In that Laois game, they got a run on us at the start of the second-half. Ross Munnelly started to get into it and kicked a couple of points… Padraig Clancy made a run and won a free which was converted. They were level with around 10 minutes of the second-half gone. That would have been a time for us to slow the game down and gather ourselves, but with that group, we were one speed and one direction only. If Laois came out at 100 miles an hour, our attitude would have been… *Okay, we'll go at 110!*

There was no reset button. We got away with it that day because we got a couple of breaks and Laois weren't able to punish us enough.

I'd have been relaxed enough beforehand. You always felt pressure going into a big game with Dublin, but it didn't get in on me. You were aware that it was an important game, and for me being at corner-back, I'd have been very conscious of where I stood in terms of that last line of defence because Laois had very good forwards. But we'd prepped so well, and everyone's form was good, so we were all confident that we'd be able to go out and cope with whatever was thrown at us.

On top of all that was basically being glad to have the opportunity to play in a Leinster final again after what had happened in the two previous seasons. You start to think about playing for Dublin on those big days... and having success with Dublin. For me in 2005, I felt like those opportunities were starting to come... to win Leinsters and move beyond that towards All-Ireland semi-finals and finals.

Before games, Ski would take the defenders as a group and go through our key match-ups. We played really man-on-man, so playing corner back at that time... you were on your own! Nobody was coming to help you, so if I was struggling then I had to figure that out myself. We didn't have a sweeper, and that wasn't down to a sense of bravado or anything... it was a case of everyone being confident that they could win their own battle.

The odd guy dropped back when the need arose, but that would mainly have been if they were following their man. Most guys' natural inclination was to look forward. There wasn't a system in place, and often times in the full-back line there'd be a big gap and the next fella you'd see could be up around the halfway line.

If we were on the front foot, that was fine, because even if a ball was played in, it was coming from so far away that you could really go and attack it. If we didn't have pressure on the ball though, you could be in for a long day.

We'd always get caught out by runners, because when you're playing man-on-man with no protection, once one fella got beaten or let his man go... you'd then have overlaps. We'd get away with it against some teams because they mightn't take their chances or we'd be able to get the scores back at the other end, but against the likes of Kerry and Tyrone it was a different story because they were so efficient.

Laois played very orthodox, like us. Mick O'Dwyer was still over them at the time so they played a traditional game. Comparing it to now, it was totally different. End-to-end. There were no short kickouts in that match. Clucko put the ball down and banged it out to Ciarán Whelan and Darren Homan or Shane Ryan. They had Noel Garvan and Clancy, and Fergal Byron was doing the same with his kicks. Hit it as far as you can and let the midfielders contest it.

Nobody was trying to slow the game down... when you got the ball, you moved forward. There was no such thing as holding the ball and trying to move it over and back, and set up attacks. Of course, that meant there were a lot more mistakes, because players weren't as cautious, but it probably made it more exciting for the fans.

The reason I picked this game is obviously because it was my first Leinster, but also because of what had happened in the two years before with the difficult defeats and all the negativity that went with that. To go from that, to then having that really positive experience was a huge weight off everyone's shoulders. After the game the fans were still allowed onto the pitch, and we were looking out on this sea of people.

These things really stand out. There were games later that we won, but the expectation had shifted. At that time, just getting back to a Leinster final and winning it would have been our primary focus. *Were we good enough to win an All-Ireland at that stage?* Certainly not. But in the years that followed, the focus changed. Obviously winning Leinster was still a target, but we were looking at trying to get over that quarter-final hurdle that we got stuck at for a while… then trying to get over the semi-final hurdle that we got stuck at. The goalposts moved a bit and I'd probably remember some of those defeats more readily than games we won.

For all the chaos that went on in some of those game around that time, it was bloody enjoyable. The experience of the occasion is what stays with you. You have to enjoy it to be able to play well, to perform and to cope with being in those situations. It's not that it was always easy, but playing with Dublin was always enjoyable.

It was something you wanted to do. It was never onerous. It never felt like a burden. That team had a brilliant bond. The days after games, when we'd catch up or go and play golf or whatever, it was a great group, and everyone loved being part of that shared experience.

While the fans would be intense in their support during a game, and there is the famous photo of someone shouting at Tommy Lyons after one game, playing for Dublin is probably easier than any other county in Ireland because of its size. Nobody knows who you are when you're walking down the street!

The abuse Tommy got, he didn't get that at home or when he was out and about. But lads in Laois or wherever, it's a much smaller community so if you go out to the shops, you probably have everyone asking you about the game that's coming up… or the game you just played. You can't do anything without someone commenting on it. Even the most successful footballers Dublin ever had… they can still live normal lives. They have that option to be as prominent, via promotional or media work… or as anonymous as they like.

To win that game the way we did, with Mossy kicking the last two scores from a free and a '45' was incredible. He'd had a really difficult day with the frees, so for him to stick both of those over showed massive character. That's the sort of guy he is though… he would always put his hand up. Always. He would never say… *No, I don't fancy this one.*

It looked like we'd blown our chance a little bit. We'd had our spell of domination, but we didn't kill it off and kicked a lot of wides. The winning '45' came from Alan Brogan kind of nudging Joe Higgins over the end-line, so we robbed it a little because that could have been a free on another day.

After the game, we went back to DCU, then we used to go to the Sunnybank Hotel near Glasnevin. The place was mobbed, and we were in this tiny room out the back. It was a sweatbox because there were 35 of us on the panel, plus family and friends all milling around. But it was fantastic.

We'd spend a few hours there and then it'd be into town for as long as you could last. The next day we went to Hollystown to play some golf… then there'd be a bus into town. The Monday was just the players.

I was still around in 2011 when that group finally got over the line, but I was injured that whole year. I got injured at the start of 2010 during the league, so missed that whole year and then I had a couple of setbacks. I had a procedure in the summer of 2011, so I was just staying around the panel and helping out in different roles. That was a massive release for a lot of those guys who had been around for a few years like Clucko, Barry Cahill, Alan Brogan, Mossy… Paul Casey. Everything has taken off more than any of us would have thought at that stage. If anyone had told you in 2005 that Dublin would dominate Leinster to the extent that they have, I don't think you'd have believed them, because Kildare, Meath, Laois, Westmeath… those teams were all fairly close, but they faded away.

I've my medals upstairs somewhere. The kids would take them out sometimes and look at them. I never got too bogged down with medals, to be honest. It's usually months later when you get them and by then, you've moved onto the next season, so I wouldn't be too bothered about them. It's more the experience and the memories you have.

SHANE RYAN

MAYO 1-16 DUBLIN 2-12
All-Ireland SFC Semi-Final
Croke Park
AUGUST 27, 2006

Shane Ryan races away from Pat Harte in the heart-breaking All-Ireland semi-final defeat to Mayo in 2006.

★ **DUBLIN:** S Cluxton; D Henry, B Cahill, P Griffin; P Casey, B Cullen, C Goggins; C Whelan, **S Ryan**; C Keaney (1-3), A Brogan (0-4), R Cosgrove (0-2); J Sherlock (1-0), K Bonner (0-1), T Quinn (0-2). Subs: D Magee for Cahill, S Connell for Cosgrove, D Lally for Ryan, M Vaughan for Quinn, C Moran for Bonner.

★ **MAYO:** D Clarke; D Geraghty, D Heaney, K Higgins; A Higgins (0-1), K Nallen, P Gardiner; R McGarrity, P Harte; BJ Padden, G Brady (0-2), A Dillon (0-4); M Conroy, C Mortimer (0-5), C McDonald (0-2). Subs: B Moran for McGarrity, K O'Neill (0-2) for Conroy, D Brady for Padden, A Kilcoyne for B Moran, A Moran (1-0) for Nallen.

THE ACTION

A GAME FOR the ages. Dublin and Mayo played out a modern classic in this All-Ireland semi-final at Croke Park. When the dust had settled, Dublin's latest crack at bringing Sam Maguire back to the banks of the Liffey had been reduced to rubble in the most dramatic way imaginable.

The tension of the occasion had been ratcheted up before a ball had even been kicked in anger. Mayo, out first, decided to proceed to the Hill 16 end to go through their warm-up. Dublin emerged minutes later and were clearly in no mood to cede what they view as their patch, and also made their way to the Hill, much to the delight of the crowd. How much value either side got out of their warm-up in such a crowded space is open to question, but it set the tone for the game.

Mayo backed up their pre-match defiance by getting much the better start. Conor Mortimer opened their account after four minutes, and they had three more points on the board before Conal Keaney got Dublin off the mark in the 17th minute. The same player found the net six minutes later as Dublin eased into the game. The sides were level on four occasions before Mortimer edged Mayo in front just before half-time.

Dublin's start to the second half was in stark contrast to the first. Jason Sherlock found the net just two minutes in and, from there, the blue wave looked set to crush the Connacht champions. Mayo had no answer to the power and pace of their opponents, and with just 11 minutes gone in the second period, Dublin had opened up a seven-point lead (2-11 to 0-10). Brogan, Keaney, Quinn and Bonner all contributed scores and it looked a certainty that a first All-Ireland final appearance since 1995 was there for the taking.

Then the wheels came off in scarcely believable fashion. The Dubs were outscored 1-6 to 0-1 in the final 22 minutes as Mayo pulled off one of the greatest comebacks of all time. Substitute Andy Moran got a vital goal on 51 minutes, which cut the gap to just two points. They were soon level, and Mortimer's free with 15 minutes to go edged his side in front, before Brogan got Dublin's first score in over 20 minutes to level it again with three minutes remaining. Mark Vaughan then hit the post, and moments later Ciarán McDonald made a decisive and memorable intervention, curling over from a tight angle to win it.

★★★★★

❝

I WATCHED THE game back recently and I went through serious trauma. I realised very quickly just why I hadn't watched it before. I don't know quite why I picked this game. There are other games that I remember more fondly, like the 2008 Leinster final when we gave Wexford a hiding. I played well, we won Leinster, and it was great… but there was nothing particularly memorable about the game. The Mayo game was certainly memorable because it was exciting…and very, very painful.

It's the one game from my career that sticks out like a sore thumb. There are unhealed wounds there and re-watching it didn't do me any favours at all! We only lost by a point and looking at all the small things that went wrong or we didn't do properly… if any one of them had gone our way we would have won, or at least drawn.

But the game was so different back then in terms of how it was played. So, *so* different. One thing stood out… the amount of aimless long balls that went into the forward line. Both teams were guilty, but particularly Dublin. You just don't see that anymore… it was something that annoyed me watching it back.

I'd have strong enough memories of the game itself but when I looked at it again, that was something which really stood out. I found myself shouting… 'What are ya doing?' at myself and other lads… several of whom have All-Ireland medals now. Just booting the ball away when we had time. It made the game really exciting. But I'm watching it back… I know what happens, I know how it ends… and I'm still excitable and shouting and roaring at lads!

It was edge of the seat stuff, because you've high balls going in around the goals and nobody knows where it's going to go. *Are you going to pick up the break… are you not?* There was no certainty about it, so that made it great to watch for the neutrals, but not for me!

In the 2002 All-Ireland semi-final against Armagh, I thought we were ready to make the next step up to a final. I had watched them on TV a few times and they had only scraped by Sligo in a replay in the quarter-final, but then I actually realised… *Oh, these lads are a little further down the line than we are.* They were fitter, stronger and just a little wilier than we were at that point.

In 2006, I really thought we were ready, but we obviously weren't when you see what happened Mayo in the final that year. We were spared that hiding, albeit I don't think we'd have done as badly as they did.

We changed our training when Pillar came in… it became more scientific at that stage. Before he took over, strength and conditioning consisted of a couple of months in pre-season, then it stopped. Then suddenly when Pillar came in… it *didn't* stop in January. We were doing it throughout the year and maintaining what we'd built up during the winter. That's probably why we were able to dominate Leinster, because we were ahead of every other county in the province in that regard, whereas Armagh, Kerry and Tyrone were ahead of us. Mayo would have been up there too.

We just couldn't quite get to that level in those few years.

Under Pillar, we had a strength and conditioning coach, Daniel Tobin. He went on to work with Leinster Rugby and I think he's with Gloucester now. He was top quality. It took him a while to win players over, because he was coming from an athletics and sprinting background. He was trying to do a little bit with us on the pitch to change the way we run and help us run more efficiently.

A lot of us – myself included – used to laugh and scoff at this, because we were thinking… *We're not on a track here, there's fellas trying to tackle you when you run… This is nonsense!* One thing he used to do was to get us to focus on our arms, get your arms swinging to improve your running. He had a few of us lined up, sitting on the pitch, swinging our arms. You can imagine the look on Ciarán Whelan's face, or Darren Homan's face when this was going on. *What the hell is this?*

The lads would be laughing, and I felt bad for Daniel because he was only 21 at the time and he was trying these things out. We all thought it was crazy, but lads came around to it soon enough.

Very quickly I started to notice a difference in matches. I'd play a game and I'd come off after thinking… *Hang on a second, I was able to run away from that lad. There's something to this. It works!* I guess it became part of your muscle memory and it got into your head. How the conditioning side of it worked in practice was, we did our gym work twice a week, and then before training we'd do another 15 minutes in the gym. Just light stuff, topping up and maintaining what we'd done on the other nights.

2005 was the first year we noticed a difference, so in '06 we were building on that again. I'd been on the panel seven years by the time Pillar came along, and we'd never done anything like that before. In fairness, most counties weren't doing it at that time either. Nowadays you've club teams doing it. We all got on board quick enough, and Daniel was based in DCU which was where I trained anyway, so he was there to motivate us, to show us how to do it… to push us on. It was really important. A gang of us used to go and I loved it. You had the craic with the lads, you felt great afterwards, and you knew it was going to make a difference when the games came around. If we were in any doubt as to the benefits, we got tested and I know that I saw improvements in my sprint times. I was half a second faster over 10 metres after say a year, which meant that over 40 metres in a game, you're two seconds ahead of a fella that you were alongside the previous year.

We could see it on the page, and we saw it in our results on the field.

The first thing everyone probably thinks about from that 2006 semi-final is the pre-match stuff. Mayo went out onto the pitch first and went down to the Hill 16 end. We had no knowledge of this until we came out ourselves. I can't speak for anyone else, but I know when we came out and I saw Mayo down at that end, my first thought was… *This is fantastic, this is great, let's get stuck in!*

I felt like it made it even more of an occasion. When we came out, I think Mayo were jogging across the pitch in a line as part of their warm-up. I remember I was holding a football and I just lashed it up to that end without looking. I followed the flight of the ball, and it whacked some Mayo lad on the top of the head!

We went straight over to get our photograph taken… so we had 30 seconds or so to adjust to what was happening. I remember someone saying, 'We're not backing down, we're warming up down there!'… which I was happy to do.

From the stands, it must have looked very odd. We're making our way down and, of course, the crowd is going mad… both Dublin and Mayo fans, and we're trying to go through our normal routine. I'm kicking some Dublin footballs… I'm kicking some Mayo footballs…it didn't matter.

There was no real aggro between the players, everyone was doing their own thing. Some people have said that maybe we'd have been better off going up to the Canal End and doing our warm-up without any distractions but, to my mind, that would have given Mayo a little psychological win before the game started.

They would have been slapping each other on the back saying, 'Yeah! Look what we did to the Dubs, we kicked them off their patch!'

I think after the first few minutes of chaos, both teams just focused on their preparations, because you're thinking… *We still have to play a match here.* They obviously tried to get in our heads, but I don't think they did… not for me anyway because I thought it was great.

Mayo went four points to no score ahead, which wasn't really a reflection on how the game was going because we had started well and had loads of possession… we just couldn't score, and they couldn't miss. But that was nothing to do with the warm-up, it was just our execution and probably our shot selection wasn't good enough.

The game had started at one hundred miles an hour. It was end-to-end stuff and Mayo got some fabulous scores. We missed a few frees and kicked a few more bad wides. Mayo went in a point ahead at half time, but we should have been six or seven up. We scored a goal… could have had two more, had several bad wides. In fairness, Mayo also had a decent goal chance, but if we had been a little more clinical, we could have been ahead by a few points at half-time.

I don't really remember what was said at half-time, but I can imagine it was along the lines of… *We're playing fairly well, we've missed a lot, but we're still only a point down.* There would probably have been a mention of fixing a few small things but, overall, we would have been happy enough with where we were. I always felt Pillar was a player's manager, and he'd always be very conscious of keeping calm and motivating lads. He'd always be positive, and he'd try to reassure fellas.

I never really took in much of what was said at half-time really, I was just using it to get a rest and get ready for the second-half.

Myself and Whelo were midfield, and Ronan McGarrity was having a good game for Mayo, but I think we had the slight upper-hand. Ciarán was having a good battle with McGarrity. Back then, pretty much all the kickouts went long. I don't think there was one short kickout in the game. Stephen Cluxton, while he was sending all of his kicks long… they would still be specifically targeted at certain lads.

He hit Kevin Bonner with a few, and he hit me too with balls into space. I wouldn't call them short kickouts as such, not like what we see now, but that was possibly the start of the shorter kickouts. It came about naturally really. Whelo was the main man in midfield... a six-foot plus fielder of the ball, whereas I was the short one, the runner. I wasn't going to be competing with Ronan McGarrity or whoever, so if I was going to be an option for kickouts then it needed to be a ball into space. It just evolved naturally rather than being anything that was planned.

For the start of the second-half, we reshuffled things a bit. Darren Magee came on in midfield, I went to wing-back, Paul Casey went to full-back, and Barry Cahill came off. Darren had come on for Whelo as a blood sub in the first-half and had done well, so the management decided they wanted to leave him on once Ciarán was ready to come back in. I didn't mind at all going back. I was on Billy Joe Padden which I thought was fine, because I had him for pace. Unfortunately, they took him off and I found myself marking someone I didn't have for pace in Aidan Kilcoyne. He was a little flier, and at that stage I was getting a bit tired.

I remember feeling a bit giddy looking at the scoreboard when we went so far into the lead. You're telling yourself there's still 20 minutes to go, which was a long time and, as it turned out, was plenty of time for Mayo to make a comeback. I would definitely have allowed that thought to come into my head for a few seconds... that we've one foot in the final if we can continue playing the way we're playing.

We played brilliant football in the third quarter. We were on top everywhere, we got some great scores, we were defending well... it was all looking good. In hindsight, we possibly should have scored a little bit more during that purple patch. But any game I've lost in my career, I always console myself with the thought that the team that deserves to win, will win. Unless something completely crazy happens, that's how it is. We had our purple patch, Mayo had theirs, and they took enough of their chances to win... whereas we didn't.

When Andy Moran got the goal, that was where I started to think we were in trouble. It was a double blow for me. Firstly, it brought it back to a two-point game but also, I blamed myself for the goal because I was the one tackling Andy and I felt that I should have blocked it. It was a bit of a sickening blow because, all of a sudden, they have the momentum.

We never really got back into it after that, which was a bit weird because we were still in the lead and there was plenty of time to go. But that's the way sport is. Momentum can make all the difference.

I came off after an hour or so and Declan Lally came on. We were a point behind at that stage. I was pretty much gassed out by then. I was thinking that if I hadn't been marking someone who was full of running, I might still have had something to offer the game. But I wasn't annoyed to be coming off or anything, it was the right decision.

I had put in a huge effort, and it was hard work chasing around after Kilcoyne! That was the difference in moving to wing back. When I was midfield, I got to dictate the pace more than my opponent… there's a bit more freedom to play and I always backed myself to be fitter and stronger than the lad I was marking. At half-back, I found I was reacting more to what my man was doing. I could try to dictate things, but my first job was to defend, so it was different.

Sitting on the bench for the last 10 minutes or so was tough. When Alan Brogan equalised, every ounce of me was just urging Dublin to get one more score. *Just one!* You're giving it everything you have on the bench to will the lads to get that winning score. At the same time, I'd happily have taken a draw. I didn't think that Mayo were going to win it at that moment, which probably contributed to how upset we all were at the end.

When Ciarán McDonald floated that score over… my heart sank.

But I thought… *Okay, there's still time… There's still time!* There were still five minutes left when that score went over, and we had chances. Mark Vaughan had a '45' which David Clarke stopped from going over, and then he had a free from about 55 metres right at the end, but unfortunately that went wide. Sin é.

For me personally, it was the worst I've ever felt after a match. I didn't want to talk to anybody for a long time. I put my earphones in and put my head down for I'd say a good two hours after the game. I wouldn't even talk to the players. I had a bunch of songs by this band called Zero Seven. It was kind of laid-back, chilled out music… which didn't chill me out at all!

I had five or six songs in-a-row, and I just kept listening to them over and over. The reason I remember this is because every time I hear those songs now, it brings me back to that day. I haven't really listened to them much since then. So that was me for a few hours after the game. Out of the shower, headphones in, head down… not talking to anyone, not looking at anyone. On the bus, back to DCU for a meal… the same. I just didn't want to engage with anyone.

Little things keep coming back to me.

I would usually arrive to training fairly early. I'd do a bit of catching or kicking or a bit in the gym. Stephen Cluxton would always be there early too, so we might do a few little drills. The week of the game, I arrived about an hour before training and Paul Clarke, one of the coaches, was putting a bunch of suits back into the boot of his car.

'What's going on here?'

'Oh, just checking out a few suits in case we get to the All-Ireland final.' Now, this wasn't arrogance, this was just something that would have to have been in place if we did get through. Paul was there early because he didn't want anyone to see. I was kind of excited to see the suits and imagine getting to a final, and then after the game I remember that I saw the suits… and I was even more depressed!

We were so close to having that All-Ireland build-up that I never got to experience, and little things like that come back to you and you're like… *Ah Jesus!*

What made it even worse was that I was invited to a wedding down in Mayo a month after the game. I was in the depths of despair after losing the game, and then I'm remembering I've to go to this wedding… and the lad getting married was good mates with Kevin O'Neill, who came on that day and played really well.

The only thing that dulled the blow a bit was that it was the week after the All-Ireland final, and Mayo had been hammered by Kerry. If Mayo had won, I don't think I could have gone! The funny thing was the Mayo people were so nice and nobody said a word to me all night. The only person who said anything to me about the game was a Dublin fella. He made some comment, and I really had to bite my tongue! He wasn't really into football, so he didn't know what he was saying, but I had to work hard to keep my cool!

Looking back on the game as a whole, there were certain things we did that cost us. Looking at myself first, I should have blocked Andy Moran for their goal. And Conal Keaney was through on goal twice and stuck it over the bar. At the time you're thinking… *Great, you made sure of the score,* but when you look back, you're thinking… *Why didn't you go for goal?* Now, the keeper was on top of him for one, and the other might have been saved, so the right decision might have been to go for a point.

Really though, there's nothing to be gained from thinking about things like that because you'd drive yourself mad. Plus, Mayo had lots of similar chances that they didn't take.

One of the things Pillar always pushed was that, when we lost, as far as we were concerned the better team won. He would have drilled it into us that he didn't want to see any Dublin player in the papers moaning. We had to accept our defeat, because it's not going to change.

That was a big thing with the management. Accept your defeat with dignity no matter how you feel about it. We didn't want to be the team that was going straight to journalists giving out about x, y and z. We had to look at ourselves first and the message from Pillar was... *If I see anyone whinging in the papers, don't expect to play for me again.* I thought that was really good leadership, because I've seen other counties before and since, be it players or managers, complaining. Sometimes it's justified, but I think you're better off to just hold your tongue... because it'll just seem like sour grapes.

Analyse your own performance first. *Did you do everything perfectly?* Look at that before you start blaming referees. We were disappointed, disgusted, we made mistakes, but we're going to come back at it next year... that was the way we looked at it.

It took a while to get over that one, but I don't think it impacted me in games in the future. When I came back in 2007, I was ready to go again. From when I was a kid I always wanted to play in an All-Ireland final, and that remains the best chance I ever got to fulfil that dream. Kerry beat us the following year, but they were just better than us and I wasn't able to point to as many mistakes as we made in the Mayo game. So that was an easier loss to accept.

I wouldn't talk to anyone about the Mayo game for years. In the week after it, people would ask me about it, and I'd just shut off. Lads in the club would be like, 'Why did they move you out of midfield?' and that kind of thing.

I'd nearly walk away from someone if they brought it up. That lasted for about a year. Once I heard 'Mayo'... my eyes would glaze over. It's 15 years ago, you'd think I'd be over it by now!

Then I think about it... and when I compare my hurt to the hurt of Andy Moran or Donal Vaughan or Keith Higgins, there's probably no comparison, but I can only go on what I feel myself. I'd love to have played in a final, even if we lost.

I played in four semi-finals with the footballers and hurlers. I think I lost two by a point and two by two points. Then again, it's never enough. You always want more. My first three years with Dublin footballers we lost three Leinster finals in-a-row. I remember saying to myself... *If I just win one Leinster, I'll retire happy!*

But you win one, and you want more.

If you had told me at the start of my career that I'd win six Leinsters and play in four All-Ireland semi-finals, I'd have bitten your hand off. But you always want more. That's why Mayo keep coming back, that's why Dublin keep winning... that's why Kerry are always there.

These lads always want more.

JOHNNY MAGEE

KILMACUD CROKES 3-6
ST OLIVER PLUNKETT EOGHAN RUADH 0-13
Dublin SFC Final Replay
Parnell Park
OCTOBER 27, 2008

Johnny Magee is surrounded by Plunkett's defenders in the 2008 Dublin senior final replay, but two goals from the veteran secured victory and (inset) he lifts the winning trophy with his daughter Lauren.

★ **KILMACUD CROKES:** D Nestor; K Nolan, P Griffin, N McGrath; A Morrissey, C O'Sullivan, B McGrath; D Magee, N Corkery; L McBarron (0-1), M Vaughan (0-2), P Burke (0-1); B Kavanagh (0-2), **J Magee (2-0)**, M Davoren (1-0). Subs: C Lamb for N. McGrath, B O'Rourke for McBarron, R O'Carroll for Corkery, K O'Carroll for Vaughan.

★ **ST OLIVER PLUNKETT EOGHAN RUADH:** E Somerville; R O'Connor, C Evans, P Curtin; M Brides, T Browne, J Brogan (0-1); R McConnell, D Matthew; A Darcy, D Sweeney, G Smith; A Brogan (0-2), J Sherlock, B Brogan (0-10). Subs: N Murphy for Browne, P Brogan for Curtin, K McDonnell for Darcy, R Glynn for Sweeney.

THE ACTION

KILMACUD CROKES PULLED off what could best be described as a smash-and-grab raid in this replayed Dublin senior football final played on the October Bank Holiday Monday. The sides had met four days earlier and Plunkett's wayward shooting in the second-half let their opponents off the hook.

The script for the rematch didn't differ hugely from that of the drawn game. A Bernard Brogan-inspired Plunkett's were the better team for large parts of the game, but they never quite finished Crokes off and, ultimately, paid the price for that lack of ruthlessness.

Kilmacud recalled veteran Johnny Magee, and placed the former Dublin stopper on the edge of the square, where he played a central role in the outcome. Magee scored his side's first goal of the evening in the 14th minute, diving to finish from close range after good work from Mark Davoren and Niall Corkery.

That score helped Paddy Carr's men to a 1-6 to 0-7 half-time lead, but Bernard Brogan shot five unanswered second-half points to give his side a 0-12 to 1-6 lead with just 10 minutes remaining. At that stage, it looked like Brogan's influence would see his side clinch their first ever Dublin senior title. Then came the twist in the tale.

Magee got his second goal of the evening with nine minutes to play, when he palmed a long delivery from Rory O'Carroll towards the goal. The ball was scrambled clear, but Magee appealed that it had crossed the line. After consulting with his umpires, the referee agreed, and suddenly Crokes were level.

Plunkett's must have wondered what was happening? Before they had time to come up with an answer, the ball was in the net again, and the game beyond them. Another long delivery into the square dropped to Davoren who, among a sea of legs, managed to squeeze the ball into the net. Magee then dropped deep as Crokes looked to hold onto what they had while Plunkett's poured forward in desperation. All they could muster was a free from Brogan, whose performance will surely go down as one of the greatest losing displays of all-time in a Dublin senior final.

★★★★★

66

SOMETIMES YOU KNOW before a game that you're going to lose. We were out warming-up before the 2007 Dublin senior semi-final against St Vincent's and I turned to Ray Cosgrove and said, 'We're not right here… we're all over the shop'. The focus wasn't there. Lads were dropping balls… skitting and laughing.

We had beaten Vincent's by six points in the first round and also in a league game, and I think a lot of the lads thought we'd do the same again. Once that attitude gets into a team, it's almost impossible to pull it back. Pat Gilroy and Mickey Whelan were over them, and they had their homework done. They came out and they really put it up to us. They wanted it more, they worked harder than us, and I think they won by something like six points in the end.

It was a young Vincent's side at the time. The likes of Diarmuid Connolly and Ger Brennan were just getting going at that stage. They beat us, won the final, then went on to win the Leinster and All-Ireland championships! That was a big reality check for our lads, because we had won the Dublin Championship in 2004 and '05, and won the Leinster club in '05 also. Salthill beat us in the semi-final, but we had been away in Tenerife in January to celebrate the two in-a-row. It was meant to be a trip where we celebrated and also did a bit of training, but it just turned into a drinking session.

We took our eye off the ball for the Salthill game and while we only lost narrowly, we were miles off the pace. But the loss to Vincent's in 2007 played a huge part in what we went on to do in '08.

My last involvement with Dublin was in 2007. I'd been off the panel for 2005 and '06 under Pillar, then was brought back in for '07. I put a lot of effort into that season, but I didn't get much game-time. Pillar rang me at the end of that year to say he wouldn't be bringing me back in. I'd had words with him after the 2003 game with Armagh… I was one of the first to be dropped when he took over as manager. I had been taken off when Stephen Cluxton was sent off, and we had an exchange of words… let's just say that! Whether that was carried over and was the reason I was dropped, I don't know.

Paddy Carr took over as Crokes' manager and we had a meeting in the Stillorgan Park Hotel in December 2007. Lads were just asked what sacrifices they were going to make. At that stage there was a bit of a drinking culture in the team. There was a discussion as to what the time-frame might be for not drinking before the championship started. Some lads thought two or three weeks was enough… a few others like me, Cossie and Liam McBarron were saying… 'It's six-to-eight weeks, or nothing'.

Lads were asking… *Sure what's the harm having a few drinks after work on a Friday?* But it wasn't just a few drinks after work. It was a few, then a few more… then a nightclub, and the next thing is it's four in the morning! Then you're training on a Tuesday and it's only really getting the drink out of the system from the weekend… so you're missing doing a quality training session and you're only a couple of weeks out from a big game.

I wasn't leaving that room until we had a firm agreement as to what we were doing, because we had already wasted a couple of years. Some lads did break the agreement, but they were confronted about it, and I let Paddy know that I didn't think it was good enough. I had seen it from my Dublin days where I didn't feel we had that unity and you couldn't trust many fellas… and that's what Pat Gilroy sorted out when he came in. I felt that that's what we missed during my time playing with Dublin… that team ethic where everyone had your back.

I had been thinking about giving up playing altogether, but Paddy and Mark Duncan, who was a selector, told me that they still thought I had an awful lot to offer and that they wanted to make me captain. It was a no-brainer at that stage to keep playing. It probably would have been an emotional decision to retire then after being dropped from the Dublin panel.

It was important that we set down the standards during that first meeting, because I was getting on and had a lot of miles on the clock… and I didn't want to be wasting my time if everyone wasn't one hundred percent committed. There was no question about the talent and quality of player that we had, it was just about getting that consistency and work ethic.

We were always very good on the ball and could beat any team on our day, but the key factor was how hard we worked when we didn't have the ball. You can tell very early in a season how you're going to go… I saw that as manager too when we won the championship in 2018. I knew from the attitude of the players when we didn't have the ball.

That was the same in 2008, and it all stemmed from getting that fundamental buy-in as to what was expected.

What Paddy brought was a huge amount of positivity and be gave us great self-belief. He's a real people-person and he knows what buttons to press. He was exactly what we needed as a group. We had a lot of inter-county experience, and also some younger lads coming in like Kevin Nolan and Cian O'Sullivan. Paddy felt that we were missing a presence up front, and he asked me about playing full-forward. At the start of that year, he arranged for me to do extra training, so I was doing a bit of boxing in the National Stadium to lose a some weight. Then my work situation totally changed.

I went from working days to working night shifts in Terminal 2 in Dublin Airport for the first time ever. As well as that, I was planning my wedding. Working nights was a massive spanner in the works. It was 8pm to 8am, so sometimes I had to miss training… sometimes I started work a bit late and went straight from training. My body clock was all over the place and I was trying to maintain a level of fitness, which was difficult.

I played in all the games throughout that championship, with the exception of the semi-final. We beat Vincent's after a replay, and I had a battle with myself after that game. You're trying to lead by example and stick to what we'd spoken about at the beginning of the year. I went into the dressing-room and grabbed my bag. I was out the door, and I wasn't coming back, because I was really pissed off about not coming on.

When I was half-way out the door, Mark Duncan grabbed me. I had to check myself, and then I was a bit embarrassed that I was letting the lads down. I needed to look in the mirror and ask myself if I was in the right shape and the right frame of mind to come on. It was a bit of a watershed moment for me, because I had been preaching to lads about doing things for the collective after what I'd seen with Dublin for so many years… and now here I was throwing a strop.

As captain of the team, I had to be responsible for the role that I'd signed up to. That was the battle I had. I was a former Dublin player. I'd been a central figure for Crokes for many years, so having to swallow that bitter pill that you're no longer a main player was difficult. But I went back in, sat down… and bit the lip.

I came on in the drawn final and then I went to Paddy before the replay and said, 'Look, I can do a job for you here, if you trust me to do it'. I'd played midfield and centre-back for all of my Crokes' career, but I changed my game to play full-forward and win ball for the likes of Mark Vaughan, Mark Davoren and Brian Kavanagh. I was never going to beat a guy, round him, and stick it over the bar! But I knew how to play the game and make space.

I used all the tricks of the trade. I was angry then when I wasn't starting because I felt I had been really unselfish and changed my game for Paddy... and now I wasn't being used. Plus, I was battling with working nights, trying to keep the weight off and get some training in. I'm one of these lads that if I l even look at a menu, I put on weight! My daughter was only three at the time too, so there were nights where I wasn't getting more than four hours sleep. It was a difficult year for a variety of reasons.

Coming into the final, I knew there was no chance of me starting given I hadn't featured in the 'semi', but I had accepted that. Paddy wanted pace and mobility in the team, and we had plenty of lads who ticked those boxes. My job was to come on and close out the game if needed. Really, in those two games, we got out of jail.

Plunkett's were the better team both days. They hit the crossbar at the end of the drawn game when Nesty Smith was one-on-one with our keeper. Bernard Brogan was on fire in the replay... they had quality footballers. What stood to us was the resilience in the group, and the buy-in that we had where we never gave up. We kept going right to the end. It's clichéd stuff, but that's really what it was.

The honesty of the group and our work-rate off the ball kept us in it against Plunkett's, particularly the first day when they were by far the better side. We always used to talk about how there will be days when you go out and you're not going to play well, and things won't click. But the one thing you're in control of is your work-rate and your intensity. They were the things we focused on all through that year.

It keeps you in games that you shouldn't be in!

In the lead-up to the replay, I spoke to Paddy. I thought that Conor Evans, their full-back, had caused us a lot of problems coming forward with the ball. He was coming out of defence too easily. I wasn't named in the starting 15 that got released, but Paddy had told me earlier in the week that I would be starting. We knew they wouldn't be expecting it. I felt that I'd be able to curb Evans' runs a bit and be a leader in the forward unit.

We were creating opportunities but taking too much out of the ball at times. When we moved the ball quickly, that's when we created the most problems for them. It was trying to get the balance right, as to when to run the ball and when to kick it. We were struggling to find the right blend in terms of how we played, and I think it wasn't until the All-Ireland club final that we played our best football.

Against Plunkett's in the replay, we obviously did some good things and we got the three goals. In fairness, the second goal I got was a high ball into the square, but we had moved the ball quickly. The same for the first goal… it was moved quickly down the left side by Davo (Mark Davoren)… it came across and I punched it in. Moving the ball quickly was key, because we caught them out of position.

Our backs had such a job to do to contain the Brogans, Jason Sherlock and Nesty Smith. When you look at the likes of Adrian Morrissey, Cian O'Sullivan, Kevin Nolan and Paul Griffin… they're all brilliant ball-carriers and they are fliers too. We would always encourage them to bomb forward where possible. But when you're trying to keep an eye on forwards of the quality of what Plunkett's had that day, you're not going to get the same attacking support from your backs because they had to defend more.

You can't be leaving the likes of Bernard Brogan on his own. Griff would tell you he had a nightmare that day, but we left him exposed. Paul was arguably one of the best defenders in the country at the time, but he was left exposed because of the quality of ball that was going in. Bernard was unplayable in the replay.

We went a long time in the second-half without scoring which was a bit worrying, and I remember going down the field a bit to try to give the lads a bit of a gee-up. When the second goal went in, there was a bit of controversy over it because the Plunkett's lads were saying it was a square ball. I looked at the umpire and said, 'That's not a square ball!'… because I had made sure I wasn't in.

That was one thing with us, we were always confident of scoring two or three goals in a game. In fairness to Paddy and Mark, they would always have told us to go for it if a goal was on. We recognised when teams were open. People might say that the goals we got in that game were lucky, but we knew if we moved the ball at pace, we would cause teams problems. We did something similar in the Leinster final against Rhode, where we were eight down and got goals at vital times.

I didn't think Plunkett's were as mentally strong as we were and felt when I got the second goal to level it, that they were wondering what they had to do to win the bloody thing. They had dominated both games, and yet we were still there with them. I said to the lads that if we were close with 10 or 15 minutes to go, we'd win it.

We had that resolve from the drawn semi-final and also the drawn final. It was the confidence we got from not playing well, but still not getting beaten. We didn't play particularly well in the final, but we weren't going away. I knew that with the quality of defenders we had, we wouldn't cough up too many goals. Not conceding a goal in either the draw or replay was a big thing against that forward line… and keeping Alan Brogan to two points as well, that says it all about our defence that day.

The goal that won it for us was from another long delivery. We recognised that they were struggling with direct ball. We didn't do that half enough in the drawn match, we didn't let the ball in long as often as we should have. Playing diagonal balls into the square was something we worked on, and I think that was a key factor in our success that season. As soon as the third goal went in, I went straight back and sat in front of Davy Nestor. I did that in all the games I played in… I'd drop back if we were leading… and there were no goals going in, no matter what.

If a high ball came in, I'd be the only one going for it and Davy would stay on his line. We had been caught by a couple of late goals earlier in my career with Crokes, so it definitely wasn't going to happen again.

The change in mentality was such an important thing, and I wonder if Vincent's hadn't gone on to do what they did after beating us in 2007, would we have had the success that we then had. Go back to St Patrick's Day 2008. As captain, I'd organised that we'd all go into town. Brian Kavanagh had just joined us, so myself and Ray picked him up. I'd gotten a few quid and we all met in a pub to watch the All-Ireland club final.

Vincent's went on to win, and the conversation that whole night was… 'That's us in 12 months' time. It should be us today, but it's definitely going to be us in 12 months' time'. The bond really increased that day. I can say I definitely wasn't cheering for Vincent's, but them winning it gave us an extra bit of focus. I knew it was important, so I asked Paddy if we could go. It was going to be the last chance for a few drinks because lads were going to be back with Dublin and the other counties.

Could you say that was decisive in us going on to win the club All-Ireland in 2009? Not entirely of course, but I think it had a big part to play. Really, we won the All-Ireland at that meeting in the hotel at the end of 2007. We all agreed to something that was bigger than ourselves.

Once you have that commitment in place, you can narrow down the things that can go wrong and say... *Well, it wasn't because of this or that.* Any Crokes team I've been involved in, the aim is always to win the All-Ireland. That has always been my mindset, but it's about how you get there... and what people need to do. I always feel that we have the players to do it, but that's only half the battle.

I'm very lucky to have won five Dublin Championships as a player, one as a manager, three Leinsters and an All-Ireland. *Should we have won more?* Absolutely. I'm convinced we should be sitting on another two or three All-Irelands, but that's probably me being greedy. Where we've fallen down is we haven't been consistent enough, we haven't been ruthless enough in how we go about things. You look at what Corofin have done. People might disagree with me, but I thought we were capable of doing the same, but we just didn't have the right mentality within the club to go after it.

To go up and lift the trophy in the county final was a hugely proud moment. When the whistle went, Davy Nestor was the first person to grab me because I was right beside him. I had watched Kilmacud teams as a kid win Dublin senior titles in 1992 and '94, and I always dreamt of being captain when we won championships or All-Irelands. The same with Dublin. There's not too many people out there who can say they've fulfilled dreams. To be able to share that with my wife and my young daughters was fantastic. Lauren was able to come up and lift the trophy with me.

It was the first cup that I had lifted as a Crokes man because it was the first time I'd been captain. Being with Dublin for the guts of 10 years, you're gone from the club for most of the season. You want your captain to be someone who's there the whole time. The timing was good because I had learned so much from Dublin in terms of what not to do. It was very emotional given the struggles I had had across the year and everything that went on, both on and off the field.

To think that I nearly walked out after the semi-final! It was an exceptional time and I'm still hugely proud of it to this day.

99

GER BRENNAN
(& KEVIN NOLAN)

DUBLIN 1-12 KERRY 1-11
All Ireland SFC Final
Croke Park
SEPTEMBER 18, 2011

Ger Brennan runs out onto the field before the 2011 All-Ireland final victory over Kerry.

★ **DUBLIN:** S Cluxton (0-2); M Fitzsimons, R O'Carroll, C O'Sullivan; J McCarthy, **G Brennan, K Nolan (0-1)**; D Bastick (0-1), MD MacAuley; P Flynn, B Cahill, B Cullen; A Brogan (0-2), D Connolly, B Brogan (0-6). Subs: P McMahon for McCarthy, K McManamon (1-0) for Flynn, E O'Gara for Cahill, E Fennell for Bastick.

★ **KERRY:** B Kealy; K Young, M Ó Sé, T O'Sullivan; T Ó Sé, E Brosnan, A O'Mahony; A Maher, B Sheehan (0-4); Darran O'Sullivan, Declan O'Sullivan (0-1), D Walsh; C Cooper (1-3), K Donaghy (0-2), K O'Leary. Subs: P Galvin (0-1) for O'Leary, BJ Keane for Walsh, D Bohan for Brosnan.

THE ACTION

DUBLIN'S LONG, LONG wait for Sam Maguire ended in dramatic circumstances after a pulsating clash with Kerry at a heaving Croke Park. A low-scoring first-half saw Pat Gilroy's charges lead by just a point (0-6 to 1-2), with Colm Cooper finding the net on 19 minutes after a good run by Darran O'Sullivan. There was no indication of the drama that was to come! Having fallen short so many times in previous years, it was fitting that this Dublin team pulled a win out of the fire, something that looked unlikely after Cooper had given his side a four-point lead with just seven minutes of normal time remaining.

Then came the pivotal score of the game. Kerry, who were playing keep-ball in the middle of the field, coughed up possession and Cian O'Sullivan took a quick free which found Alan Brogan in oceans of space. Brogan carried the ball forward before releasing to substitute Kevin McManamon. The St Jude's man easily rounded Declan O'Sullivan, with the Kerry defence caught totally off-guard, before blasting low past Brendan Kealy.

Hill 16 erupted, and suddenly the prospect of a first All-Ireland title since 1995 was on the cards for the Dubs. The remaining minutes of the game must rank among the most dramatic ever seen in a title decider at Croke Park. Kerry appeared to be rattled, and the equalising score again came from a soft concession of possession from the Kingdom. Tom O'Sullivan's loose pass forced Anthony Maher to foul Michael Darragh MacAuley and, from the free, Dublin worked the ball to Kevin Nolan, who fired over from 40 metres.

With the momentum, and with Kerry in a tailspin, Dublin looked certain to claim the win, and this feeling was copper-fastened when Bernard Brogan put them in front on 68 minutes. The Kingdom managed to compose themselves, and patient play found Kieran Donaghy, who lofted over a superb point from under the Cusack Stand in the 70th minute.

A replay beckoned, but there was one final twist. Dublin pushed forward in numbers looking for the winning score, and when McManamon was fouled by Barry John Keane 40 metres out, Bernard Brogan immediately waved Stephen Cluxton forward.

The Dublin keeper sauntered up... put the ball down.

And slotted it between the posts.

★★★★★

66

TRYING TO REMEMBER specific moments from a game can be quite tough, because you're living in the present and the game moves so quickly. You're nearly thinking strategically. I would be anyway, about what's coming next. *What way are they setting up? Where do we need to be?*

My role in the team was quite strategic. One of my strengths was being able to see things that were happening and being able to communicate that to teammates or even get a message to the sideline to ask what they were seeing… because they don't always see the same thing a player is seeing. I'd all those thoughts going through my head the whole time as a player.

The stand-out memory from the game is obviously Kevin Mc's goal.

We were putting a lot of pressure on Kerry around the middle and getting a lot of turn-overs. I think Cian O'Sullivan came out from corner-back and got a press on, and he got a hand in on a loose hand-pass from Declan O'Sullivan. A couple of passes later, and Kevin had the ball in the net. I remember that very clearly.

Then, of course, the other main memory is Clucko's point. But what I remember about that was organising the defence. We were well used to Stephen sticking frees over, but we were conscious that we needed to be set in case the ball didn't go dead.

I was pushing back a bit and cheating between full-back and centre-back with Rory O'Carroll behind me, and I think Michael Darragh in front of me. If the ball had come in before Clucko was back, Rory would have gone in goal, I'd have gone to full-back… and one of the midfielders would have gone to No 6.

When the free went over, I didn't get wholly excited. I made my way back to No 6 and we all made sure we didn't give Kerry an easy out… and to give Clucko time to get back into goal.

But the cheer that went up when that ball went over the bar was something else. That crept in on you as a player, because it was so loud that it was hard not to pick up on it.

You could almost feel the stadium shake.

That was a cool moment, but it was only briefly lived because the next thing… the ball was being kicked out. Kerry only got a couple of passes away before Joe

231

McQuillan blew the final whistle. It was just euphoria, it was unbelievable.

No more than a fella winning a junior final or whatever, it means a lot because of all the work you've put into it. But when you've been getting well beaten in quarter-finals or semi-finals by the likes of Kerry, Tyrone and Cork over a long number of years, the relief that you feel when you finally get one over on them is immense.

I don't remember half-time at all. In the first-half, Paul Galvin came on for Kieran O'Leary after 25 minutes or so. We had spoken about that before… that if Galvin comes on, he's going to try to rile up the crowd, he's going to run into a few fellas to try to get things going… which is fine, you'd expect that.

We said that we wouldn't go near him… we'd let him expend energy running into nobody, which is kind of what happened. He came on in the half-forward line… but Kerry moved around a good bit. Declan O'Sullivan was inside a lot, even though he was named at 11. Darran O'Sullivan came into the middle and tried to have a run at me. Again though, we had spoken about this and the way we operated defensively was to not get pulled all over the place.

No 3 and 6 were the key cogs in anchoring our defence, so that was something that we had practiced well with Pat over the years. Now for their goal, in fairness, Darran O'Sullivan came through the middle and as any good coach would say… when you're defending running back towards your own goal, you're in trouble. You want to be defending facing out the field and holding a strong line.

For the goal, we were caught out and ended up running back trying to defend. Other than that, though, I thought we played well as a defensive unit. You're up against top footballers in Kerry, so holding them to one goal and a couple of points in a half was good going. Our forwards and midfield worked very hard to get a press on out the field to reduce the quality of the ball that was coming in, and I think we did that fairly well for the whole game… particularly towards the end when we got the turnover for the goal.

I won a breaking ball from a kickout near the end of the game and Kieran Donaghy put his big paw in my face… which is fine, it's all part of it… but I stupidly reacted, and the ref threw the ball up. Eamonn Fennell thankfully bailed me out and won the ball, and we broke up the field… and Barry John Keane fouled Kevin Mc. I was a relieved man because we could easily have lost that throw-up and who knows what would have happened.

I still say Donaghy went down a bit handy though! But, joking aside, it was a really stupid thing for me to do to react like that. It didn't cost us though, thank God.

It was a low-scoring game, and the amount of sloppiness in our kicking – in the first-half especially – was surprising. We were a team at that time who tried to move the ball quickly with the foot, but our passing quality wasn't as high as it should have been. The game has evolved a lot even since then, but we had lads like Bernard Brogan who was well able to win his own ball, Diarmuid Connolly likewise, Eoghan O'Gara… we had a lot of big men, so we were happy to take our chances with some of the kick passes.

From my own point of view, I'd a good burst for five or 10 metres but genetically, after that, I don't have the same power output as some other lads. My strength was always in reading the play and predicting – successfully a lot of the time – where things are going to be, so that obviously helps when you're in that central role. I would have known, most of the time, when to push up, when to drop back… when to follow a guy… and the way we were set up was, we'd just tag whoever came into our space.

But like I mentioned before, it's when someone gets behind you… and you're chasing back towards your own goal, that's when the defensive structure goes out the window and it's more like a scramble defence… you're just trying to not concede a goal. In situations like that, you're happy to get away with the ball going over the bar.

I think the Kerry goal was the only time they really exposed us and opened us up. There were one or two high balls that went in, where Donaghy caused a bit of trouble, but on the whole I think we contained them fairly well.

I got booked after 45 minutes for a foul on Declan O'Sullivan. It's something that gets said in the media and on commentary a lot that… 'Oh, he's going to have to watch himself a bit now', and there is a lot of truth in that. For that particular collision, in my opinion there wasn't a whole lot I could have done.

Declan certainly wasn't going to go past me, I knew that much, but he got a bit of a nudge from behind which didn't help his situation. He's a super player, Declan. He has a bit of Diarmuid Connolly about him in that he has a way of making you think he's going to pass it, but then he'll pull away from you with a solo or a hop. He was brilliant at riding tackles too. We were conscious of him getting in behind us, because he usually had goal on his mind.

I wasn't sure what was behind me, but I just stood my ground because we couldn't afford to let Declan in on goal. He collided with me as he was going down and had to get a bit of treatment.

After a booking, you have to be a bit clever in what you're doing. You can't be pulling and dragging, or at least you can't be getting caught doing it! I played in plenty of games in my career where I was booked after five or six minutes, so the challenge is there from that moment on to be a bit more skilled in your tackling and a bit cooler on the ball... and in your intimidation of an opposing forward.

When the incident happened with Donaghy at the end, I was worried for a second that I'd get a second yellow... but I was more annoyed with myself that I'd given up the free-kick which might have cost us dearly. I was just thinking... *You feckin' eejit.* But then, I was looking at the ref and wondering was he going for the pocket. He's a good ref in fairness, Joe McQuillan... we had him a good bit over the years.

We actually had him when we won our first All-Ireland club with St Vincent's in 2008 against Nemo. My da reminded me of that either before or after the 2011 final... that he seemed to be a good omen for us. All the top referees are sound lads... they chat to you normally and respectfully in spite of some of the abuse you're giving them. When someone talks to you in that way, it's very difficult not to respond accordingly as a player. Joe McQuillan, David Coldrick, David Gough, Pat McEneaney... all solid referees and normal fellas who are excellent to deal with.

Unfortunately, they can be few and far between, and some lads like the prestige of refereeing big matches and get a bit carried away with themselves. That said, if you've four or five Dublin or Kerry lads, all six foot plus, all 14 stone going at you... as a ref, you probably have to bite back in some shape or form.

My first year as a regular starter was 2009. I'd been knocking around since 2006 with Pillar trying to get in. My first start was against Meath, and I was a bit looser with my hand movements back then. I was very stupid. Brian Meade was checking my runs a few times, so I checked him! I was lucky on that one... I got away with one there!

I had the advantage, or sometimes the disadvantage, of being Pat Gilroy's clubmate at Vincent's, and he definitely rode the Vincent's lads harder than other lads… to my mind anyway. Maybe it was a bit like a father managing his son… he doesn't want to seem to be overly biased towards his son or, in this case… clubmates.

Mentally, we probably weren't tough enough when Pat came in and we maybe thought we were better players than we actually were. That can happen, because it's an amateur sport, and in a county like Dublin there's a decent bit of media attention on you! You've companies asking you to do stuff for them, whether it be opening a shop or whatever… and when everyone outside of the group is telling you how great you are, that can creep into your own psyche or subconscious. Then, when push comes to shove in the heat of championship battle, you're found wanting… and we were found wanting on several occasions prior to getting over the line in 2011.

One of the contributing factors in that – not *the* contributing factor, but one of them – would have been how we perceived ourselves outside of our on-field achievements. We all enjoyed a bit of attention and that was something that needed to be nipped in the bud. One of the things that Pat did was, he took control of the guys who were doing the media, he took control of guys doing ambassador roles or different gigs.

That was all managed effectively with the team in mind, so any lad that was going off doing something for a company or a business… that all had to be passed by the management and the players. Everyone knew what everyone else was doing, and from that system of managing external demands, I think that helped hugely in bringing the focus back to what we were doing on the training field.

For argument's sake, if I was still playing for Dublin and I got asked about doing this book, I'd have said I've no problem doing it, but here's the number of a guy that you need to run it past first… be that Pat or someone else within the backroom team. They'd decide what, how and when. It just meant that no mental energy was being wasted on external pulls. That was something which was fairly loose previously and was tightened up fairly well under Pat.

It took a couple of years to get a hold on that, but it helped massively in my view.

We're all human, and when a handful of lads are getting the bulk of the media attention, I'm sure some lads would be envious of that. The old thing of looking over at the neighbour and wanting something that they have, that you don't have.

It's not a good way to live, but I've no doubt that it existed on our panel and exists on many panels.

That's sport... the lads who are kicking the scores are the ones who are going to get the attention. There were two things that Pat did... now I haven't asked him this, but from knowing him I'd say this.

Number one, he wanted to remove the distractions from the big-name players, to manage that for them and to ensure that they were putting all their energy into the on-field performance.

Number two, he wanted to bring these lads down to earth a bit and bring them back to the goals and philosophy of the team, which was all about humility and playing for each other. Where it became a problem, was when we lost a game and the fella who's doing all the media appearances performed poorly... it became very easy to challenge him, which is unfair in a way. He takes umbrage then because he's thinking... *Lads are only jealous of me...* and his mates are probably telling him, 'Don't mind them, they're just ragin' because they're not getting any attention'.

Lads can get pissed off, and if that disgruntlement isn't channelled in the right direction, then the cracks are there... and they'll be exposed against the top teams. The success in 2011 was borne out of everyone working their asses off for each other. You were taking to the field with not just a team, but a squad that was in the same place and pulling hard in the same direction. That wasn't something that could always have been said about Dublin teams in the years before that, I believe.

It was something I could feel. From all the meetings we had and the places we went as a group, I remember a few lads ringing me to go for a pint... and I'd ring them to go for a pint. These are lads who I'd probably never have rung before about going for a drink, nor would they have rung me!

But there was a mutual love and respect there, because I could see their efforts and what they were doing for the team, and they could see mine. You're still going to have disappointed lads when you're carrying a panel of 30 or 40, and they probably have to swallow a lot more pride in order to contribute to training games and so on. As someone who was in the mix for selection more often than not, I can only imagine that was difficult for guys.

There was an education to be done in terms of making lads realise the result of their actions on the group. A bit like giving out to your two-year-old for having the cornflakes all over the floor! Sure, they don't know any better! Even though we were adults, some of us probably wouldn't have had the awareness that we should have had.

Mickey Whelan was a big driver in the background with David Hickey and a couple of others. They were all sound fellas who didn't take any shite, didn't waffle and didn't butter you up. They just gave it to you as it was, and that kept you grounded. It was great… very refreshing.

It was hard work though. My God, the training was tough.

The 6am sessions are all the rage now, but they were new at the time. A lot of how we trained under Pat was similar to what we had done with St Vincent's with Mickey as coach when Pat was still a player. The 6am stuff started with Vincent's, which helped us to win the club All-Ireland. I found myself going to bed around 9 or 10pm… because you're up at 5am for the 6am session.

But then you're overthinking things, afraid you're going to sleep in. Then, you can't sleep and the next thing… it's half one or two in the morning! For the first few weeks of those early morning sessions, I'd say fellas had feck all sleep. Physiologically, from a sports point of view, I'd say those sessions made very little sense. However, I'd say that the psychological element was at the core of it. I'm not sure I'd say it was 90%/10% in terms of the psychological/physical split, but it wouldn't be far off that. I enjoyed it though.

You're 25… I think I'd just started teaching, life was handy, I was paying my rent and I wasn't spending too much money on anything else because all I was doing was sleeping, eating and training. Some mornings were harder than others, but the mornings that you're not in the humour, the energy of the collective feeds you. That's the beauty of team sport. Hail, rain or snow the sessions took place, so it was certainly something that helped us, even if it was very tough.

We'd train on Alfie Byrne Road in Clontarf in the mornings on the astro pitches there, and we'd be out in Ballymun in the evenings a good bit as they had an astro pitch there also. In hindsight, doing double sessions on all-weather pitches probably wasn't great for the body, but it flushed out a lot of the shit. Most lads survived in fairness… a few lads dropped off alright, but you'll always have that. It was a real leveller though.

The big challenge for Pat was trying to bring a lot of egos from a lot of different clubs together... quite apart from the training and playing. I'd say it was done in a covert way in his communication with players, be that in one-to-one chats, or small group chats. On occasion he would have a go at a couple of fellas... and it didn't matter who they were, he was very comfortable in challenging lads in front of the group which was hugely important. In those group settings, it was usually performance-related... about lads doing their own thing. Pat would basically say to lads... *If you want to keep doing your own thing, you can f**k off. Here's what we're doing. What do you want to do?* It was as simple as that!

Those group discussions would often have been about eliminating that selfish culture which obviously fed into the team ethic. I know there was one instance where poor Mark Vaughan got caught out. We said we'd go easy on the drink because there was a decent drinking culture within the squad before that which had to be stamped out.

Mark was out one night in Dame Street or Dawson Street, and got spotted at the bar by Pat and his wife. It was a pity for Mark because he was a great lad and Pat was very fond of him, but it was just after one of these heated debates about where we were going and what we were doing... and cutting out the drinking would have been something that was discussed. Mark was out for a few quiet beers and was just unfortunate to get caught. That was him gone... he never played for Dublin again, which was a pity.

When the final whistle went, I was just hugging the lads closest to me. It's hard to describe. I've a couple of kids now and people ask me what's better... having kids, the club All-Ireland or the All-Ireland with Dublin? They're all different categories.

My first championship start against Meath in 2009 was special and the feelings I had that day were close to the feelings I had when the final whistle went in the final in 2011. The sense of pride that you have in representing your county... and thinking about your parents and family and how proud they are of you. Your da bringing you to matches all over the country when you're a kid. All those things go through your head.

I'd have been involved in the development squads from under 13, so it's just a wonderful feeling to finally get to the top. It's impossible to describe it in words.

When we won in 2013, that was very special too and I felt huge relief that we weren't going to be considered a great 'one-in-a-row' team which Cork would have had in 2010 and Armagh had in 2002. As good as 2013 was, however, it didn't come close to the feelings of euphoria I felt in '11.

The craic was unbelievable for the weeks after it… it's all a blur! The fact that it was Kerry we beat made it sweeter. Coming from St Vincent's, all the great Dublin teams of the previous decades had a lot of Vincent's lads playing, and they would always have said that it's not much of an All-Ireland if you don't beat Kerry.

The other thing which I admired about Kerry was they were great at talking up the opposition. They'd always say what a great team we were and what a great bunch of lads we were.

But I didn't think they really respected us behind all that. Now they do.

KEVIN NOLAN

Man of the Match Kevin Nolan celebrates after the historic All-Ireland final victory over Kerry in 2011.

"

AFTER MY SECOND year at under-21, a few of us were brought into the senior training squad. This would have been towards the end of Pillar's second-last year. Cian O'Sullivan and myself were picked up by Paul Clarke, and brought out to Darndale Boxing Club and we did a couple of sessions out there. Strength would have been a massive thing back then… if you looked at the likes of Bryan Cullen, Collie Moran, Paul Casey and Conal Keaney… they were all big strong fellas.

If you compare that group to the squad now… you're looking at leaner, quicker players in the current team, so that was the transition that we went through.

The following year in 2008, having finished first year in college, I was brought into the panel for the league. I didn't play much in that league campaign, but I was doing very well in the in-house games, so he gave me my debut in the Leinster final against Wexford. That was a special day for me. That first year was a bit of an eye-opener for me.

Dad always said to me at that time, not quite that I was there to make up the numbers, but that I was there to put pressure on lads. That was always in the back of my mind, so when I got picked for that Leinster final, I thought… *Jesus, I can't believe I'm playing*… because I was expecting to have to bide my time for a year or two more.

Maybe that feeling got the better of me, because 24 minutes into that Leinster final, I was taken off. I had been yellow carded and probably close to being sent off. I was man-marking Redmond Barry, who was probably their main threat. I was on thin ice fairly early on and the management decided to take me off. So that was my first experience of playing senior championship football for Dublin, and it was a big learning curve.

Tyrone beat us in the quarter-final in 2008 and I went back to the club, and we ended up winning the All-Ireland Club Championship. After that game, I had to have a hip operation which meant I didn't play with Dublin in 2009. I was on the squad at the start, but having played so much with Crokes, I had a labral hip tear. I spoke to the Dublin physios, and it was decided that I was going to have to be operated on. The summer of 2009 was the famous 'startled earwigs' game against Kerry, but I missed that whole year with Dublin.

In 2010, I'd had a good season with DCU – we won the Sigerson – so I was back in again with Pat Gilroy. He gave the lads another chance after the Kerry game in 2009… and then the Meath game happened. After that game we reviewed what went wrong.

We conceded five goals that day as many people will remember, and every goal we conceded, we traced it back on the video to where it started. It might have been a foul around the middle of the field… and four or five Dublin players were looking around them or shouting at the referee, while the Meath lads were taking the free… and the next thing the ball is in the net.

We went into the qualifiers and Pat gave the likes of myself, Mick Fitzsimons and a few of the younger lads a chance… and we went on a bit of a run and got a bit of momentum. If you talk to managers in any sport, they will often tell you that the younger lads are easier to mould, and Pat moulded us into a system that he wanted us to play. We beat Tipp, Armagh, Louth and then Tyrone in the quarter-final.

I remember chatting to Bryan Cullen after the Armagh game, and he said he had never beaten a northern opponent in knockout football. When he said that to me, it struck me that maybe the older lads had a bit of baggage and when they were coming up against the likes of Tyrone and Armagh, maybe there was a bit of... *We've never beaten these lads before, so how are we going to do it now?*... whereas the younger lads hadn't experienced that, and didn't have any hang-ups or fears. It's probably a bit like what teams playing against Dublin now are facing, most of them are beaten before they go onto the pitch.

We didn't have that at the start, with the teams that we had never beaten... we had to get over that, which was something we did in 2010 in beating Armagh and Tyrone.

We played Tipp in Croke Park in front of about 20,000 supporters, and they had Barry Grogan playing full-forward for them. He got a goal, and you could hear people giving out to the Dublin defenders... you could hear the insults being shouted! Cork beat us by a point that year in the semi-final... Donncha O'Connor scored a penalty and got 1-5 or 1-6. That was a game that we might have felt we left behind us, but we were pretty happy with how the year turned out given we'd been slaughtered by Meath in a Leinster 'semi'.

Cork beat Down in the final, but if we had gotten through and beaten Down, it wouldn't have been anything like the feeling of beating Kerry the following year so... silver linings!

I felt confident in my own ability in terms of being good enough to be playing for Dublin, but Pat would have tested that. I can only speak for myself, but I'm sure he did it to other lads as well. There were times in 2010 where the likes of myself and Dean Rock travelled down to the country to play the likes of Carlow or Westmeath on what was essentially a Dublin third team.

We were put in there to see how we got on with it. I remember travelling to Roscommon and I played the first-half and was taken off at half-time. I remember thinking... *Why the hell are they bringing me up here to play half a game?* With that, Mickey Whelan and Niall Moyna came over and said it was the best football they'd seen me play in a long while.

I worked my way into the team that way.

Gilroy would have challenged you like that, kind of like saying... *You're either going to travel up to Monaghan for a challenge match or you're not going to be involved.* That broke down a lot of personal egos, I think. It was a way of showing lads that Dublin aren't just a summer football team in front of the cameras. *Are you going to travel down to Iniskeen on a Thursday night for a challenge game? Are you going to be up for the 6am training session?*

That was all part of the mental challenge Pat laid down to everyone, and he tried to break down any cliques within the squad. It was a challenging time, but I don't remember anyone opting out, because it was such a privilege to be involved. Obviously, some lads were dropped for whatever reason, but I can't recall anyone actively walking away from it.

He challenged me in different ways.

Physical challenges, mental challenges. Here you were playing on a Dublin team – not the Dublin team with all the superstars – but a *Dublin* team nonetheless. *Let's see how you handle it.* I lived on campus in DCU for my four years and I got a phone call from Pat one night.

Sometimes you don't want to be getting those phone calls because it could easily be... *Good luck.* I was sitting in the common room in DCU... I'll never forget it, and he said to me, 'Listen Kevin, it's like this... you could be off the panel or you could be on the starting 15. That decision is up to you'.

This was between the league and championship in 2010. Now, the lads that were starting in the team the years before that...I have to be honest, and I'm not trying to sound arrogant, but I would have felt I was good enough to start ahead of them.

Along with that, Pat worked with Caroline Currid, who people will be well aware of. She has worked with ourselves, Tipp, Tyrone, Limerick... I think she has five All-Irelands at this stage! But I would have been mad into sports psychology at that stage, and I would have spoken to her a few times. She asked me what I could be doing differently... what could I bring to the team and so on. I would just have said that I thought I was good enough, so she challenged me to go and prove it... to show Pat I was good enough.

We were playing Cork in the league down in Páirc Uí Rinn, and the whole panel went down on the Friday, and played a challenge match against Cork's second team that night. I was picked to play in that game, and I did well. The next morning, Pat named the team for the league game… and I was picked on that as well, so I played two games in 24 hours.

They were the challenges that you had to get over to prove yourself. I wouldn't say I was close with Pat. I always tried to not get close to managers because you don't want people thinking you're a favourite. Pat was at my wedding, and we obviously achieved a lot, but that was all based on hard work as opposed to being friendly.

People will have their memories from 2011, but we scraped past Kildare in the Leinster semi-final. It was level coming up to the end of the game and we got a free in for a foul on Bernard, which was fairly controversial as people might remember. We just about got by Kildare, and in the Leinster final we got a lucky goal when the Wexford keeper punched a ball and it hit his own defender's head… and ended up in the net. We were a lucky team at times that year.

We had Tyrone in the quarter-final and we were going into that game to try to finish off that Tyrone team. We had beaten them the previous year and we felt like a few of them were coming towards the end. I was marking Colm Cavanagh, who did well in the game, but I felt like I had a decent game myself. Tyrone had given us a couple of tough days in the years gone by, so the motivation was there to finish them off. I don't mean that we thought we were better than them or anything like that, but we wanted to beat them so that some of the lads who were getting on a bit wouldn't want to come back for another year.

The famous – or infamous maybe! – Donegal game was next. I think everyone remembers that one. It was the first time we had experienced that ultra-defensive style. We did training sessions beforehand, where we had extra defenders in the backline… but not to that extent. If you look back at that game, there were times where there would have been five Dublin defenders back and only Colm McFadden up.

We had never prepared for that. Myself, Ger (Brennan) and James (McCarthy) wouldn't have attacked as much as would be the case now, we would have held our positions more.

We were 0-4 to 0-2 down at half-time, and thankfully we had the likes of Mickey Whelan who is a legend of the game, and Pat of course. They didn't need to say a whole lot, but I do remember one of the things that was said was that if I won a kickout from Stephen, maybe I was taking a hop and a solo before looking up… instead of sprinting with the ball and getting the ball moving before their defenders could get back.

That was at a time when the ball was moved more with the foot compared to now, but in that game, it got to the stage where we had to bide our time and stay patient. I mean, we went in at half-time and we weren't even tired. There had been in-house matches that had been more exhausting than that half of football. Donegal were a big, strong team and when you took the ball into contact you were lined up and hit. We had to move the ball more quickly, and Pat made a few changes that turned the game in our favour.

Diarmuid Connolly got sent off about 12 minutes before the end of the game, and I'm not really sure what the Donegal mindset was at that stage. It was like they had perfected their defensive game, but they weren't able to fully adapt their attacking game when they had the extra man. They obviously got that right in 2012, but at that stage it was maybe still in development.

We brought on Eoghan O'Gara and Kevin McManamon, and we got a two-point win – 0-8 to 0-6 – which is probably the lowest-scoring semi-final in GAA history.

We based our game on hard work, and how we measured hard work was in tackles. We always looked to out-tackle the opposition, and we only ever lost one game where we out-tackled our opponents. That was the 2011 league final. In every other game we won, we had more tackles than the other team. That Donegal semi-final was played on a wet day and people would have thought that that would suit them because they liked tackling… but so did we.

We did a lot of walk-throughs on the rugby pitch in DCU, where you weren't allowed to run. It was done to build understanding of the game. With Pillar's team, they were strong and fit, but maybe they weren't able to think on their feet when a team presented them with a different challenge. That's what Mickey Whelan was all about… teaching the game through understanding. Something might change in a game, but you can't wait for the coach or the manager to tell you, you have to be able to adapt. Mickey would have tried to instil that into the players. Mickey was a man before his time.

I remember seeing us playing games against the likes of Laois in Leinster in the years before that, and there were Dublin players pointing to the scoreboard and almost taunting the Laois players. That was all gone under Pat. There was a lot of humility there. That incident with Ger and Donaghy… Kieran was an unbelievable footballer, but he'd antagonise anyone! I'd say there was a bit of that, and Ger reacted and played into it. When the game is that tight, all those emotions come out. We don't see that as much anymore because Dublin aren't in that situation very often now. Thankfully, that throw-up resulted in Eamonn Fennell tapping the ball down and that's what he's remembered for in my head.

For all that time Eamo was on the panel, he was battling against serious midfielders. He'd tell you himself he was a bit of a party animal, but what he did in that final was phenomenal. If he didn't win that, then we don't get the ball and we don't get that winning point.

In years previously, I would have been thinking about the game too much. You're wasting energy thinking… *What if this goes wrong, what if that goes wrong…* so talking to sports psychologists really helped me. I'd be a massive fan of that. Not everyone is, but it would have helped me to focus the mind when it needs to be focused. Like, there's times when you go home after training and you're watching a movie… you shouldn't be thinking about the game then. In years gone by, I would have been guilty of thinking about a game far too much.

The final?

In the weeks leading up to it, you're talking about the suits being sorted, tickets being sorted and, thankfully, Pat had been through that in 1995, so he'd have known what to expect. It was a matter of getting the easily-managed things sorted as early as possible and then you could focus on the important stuff. The word we used before the Donegal game was *patience*.

The word before the Kerry game was *belief*.

It's not that we were looking at Kerry thinking… *These lads are over the hill…* definitely not, you were looking at lads who were legends of the game, like Marc Ó Sé , Tomás Ó Sé, Colm Cooper… all massive figures in the game. But we just had that belief. We had our gameplan and all we could do was stick to that and we knew it would put Kerry in a tough position.

Pat adopted an Ulster style of defence – only to a certain extent mind you – but he brought elements of that to our play, because it had been shown that Kerry struggled against that in the past. Pat felt that if we could implement some of that kind of football, that it would put Kerry under pressure.

The day itself finally came around. I know sometimes people love to think there's something different about All-Ireland final day… like you get up and go for a nice walk. No. It's literally the same routine as every other game.

You have a bit of breakfast, you might go back to bed for an hour after you've got a bit of fuel into the body. Then it was the drive to DCU for our pre-match meet-up. Pre-match meal… bit of a chat with the lads… read a book maybe. We'd have gone into a meeting room then to talk about tactics, pick out things that opposition players might look to do… and a guy from each line of the team might say a few words, 'This is what we have to do today'. Things like that. It's boring enough to be honest!

But at that stage, it's just a matter of keeping things simple. All the work is done. We met on the Saturday morning for a kickaround, and we had a chat then too. It's more just to reinforce the positive things. Rather than focusing on what could go wrong, you're talking and thinking about games when things went well.

One other thing that happened was, the weekend before we had a 'Probables vs Possibles' game. We did the pre-match parade and the handshake with Mary McAleese. Mary couldn't make it that day… she was booked out! But we would have had the line-up and the handshake because there is that delay for an All-Ireland final.

Usually, you do your warm-up in the green room in Croke Park and when you get out onto the pitch you've about 16 minutes before the throw-in. For a final, you might have four minutes less when you include the handshake with the President, the parade… so if you do that the previous week, it means that you're not caught off-guard when it happens on the day.

Once we got into our positions, I was picking up Darran O'Sullivan at certain times and Paul Galvin at others. We didn't have man-marking jobs, but I would have been left half-back… box No 7. I have to give Bryan Cullen massive credit because in the previous years, if an opposition half-forward came into my area, Bryan would follow him back and leave me free.

On the opposite side you'd have James McCarthy and Paul Flynn, who worked well together. When that happens, sometimes you're worried that players might get mixed up, but we had good communication and good systems so that didn't happen too often.

There might have been times where Mick Fitz or Cian O'Sullivan would have been picking up Gooch but, in the main, you picked up the man who was in your area. That was the main reason we won… we worked as a group whereas in the past maybe some Dublin teams and players worked individually.

I started the game averagely really. I had tried a couple of long passes and they had been cut out around the 'D'. Something which gave me a bit of a wake-up call and got me into the game was, I got a belt on the head off Declan O'Sullivan. I could be a bit stupid at times only looking at the ball when I'm going into tackles, and I got an elbow off Declan which kind of snapped me into action.

My game that day was centred on getting tackles in and giving the ball, and going whenever I could. It wasn't ever a case that either Dublin or Kerry were going to go miles in front, it was tit-for-tat. There was nothing or nobody lighting up the game. I know I got 'Man of the Match', but that was probably just for the 10 minutes at the end. There would have been other lads who had a good shout for it. I helped Ger Brennan out… he helped me out. You don't get a medal without the lads around you.

The only problem with Croke Park on All-Ireland final day is you can't hear what lads are saying to you. But the previous 18 months or so of playing with fellas… even the gestures are enough to tell you what you need to know. Also, you pick up players' habits and you almost know what lads are going to do at times. We were on the same wavelength.

To be a point up at half-time against a Kerry team – most of whom were All-Ireland winners – was a good position for us, especially having conceded a goal. They got a few goal chances. There was a high ball played in and Donnchadh Walsh got a start on me, got the ball and I got a tackle on him, and it ran over the end-line. There were other times where Darran O'Sullivan broke through and could have got a goal, so we had to be happy enough to have limited them to three scores in the first-half.

That word belief would have been mentioned again. We were in a happy place. We were leading and we hadn't even played that well. Nobody on our team had played in an All-Ireland final before… we were in uncharted territory against a really experienced team.

For me personally, it wouldn't be a case of dwelling too much on what had gone wrong for me. There were those couple of occasions when kick passes were given when they shouldn't have been. I'd be using that information to think… *Okay, next time I'll give it and go… I'll work the ball.* Things like that… obviously mistakes happen, but you're just using the information from what has happened to take into the next ball. In the first-half I was maybe sitting back too much, so in the second-half I was telling myself… *I'm going to attack more.* That allowed me to get on a lot more ball and it got my man thinking… *Right, this guy can attack as well…*

I'll go back to the psychology part of it again though… you're not beating yourself up. Everyone is helping everyone else out because we're sitting in our groups – in your numbered positions – so I'm next to Ger and the other defenders and we're communicating about what to do in certain situations… who to pick up and so on. It's all very positive. There's a lot of pride in the players and there's a lot of emotion in a dressing-room in the middle of an All-Ireland final.

If someone said… *Listen, you shouldn't have done that…* some lads might take that the wrong way. You're not saying things to lads to piss them off or make them feel shite. It's all to help them perform better.

To get into the psychology side a bit, one of the main things I take from it is, it gives me a focus. So, a simple example… if my goal is to pass the ball successfully ninety percent of the time, then I'm focused on that. But you still keep the positives in mind. If I give a bad pass, it's *gone*… there's nothing I can do about it other than make sure the next one is better.

I read something once about some professional golfers and if they hit a bad shot, they pick up a piece of grass and throw it behind them… and that's the shot gone… *forgotten*. It's that sort of mentality… it refocuses you and gets you thinking about what the important things are.

I think Jim Gavin might have moved this particular point on, but Pat had it too, and that was to move the ball on after one touch. You'd try to get the ball and move it as quickly as possible. The way we measured that was, if you got the ball and gave a pass immediately, that was counted in the stats as a good pass. In other words, you're not constantly going off on a mad solo-run and then passing it.

If I took a few solos and then passed it, that wasn't counted in our stats as a good pass. That was all done with the objective of moving the ball along as quickly as possible.

We played modified training games where we weren't allowed go into certain areas of the field or do certain things. If you're playing Tyrone, you don't want to be running the ball down the middle of the pitch, so in training we'd work on keeping the ball out wide and then moving it back in towards the 'D'. Without the manager telling you to not do something, you're training in such a way that the restrictions are forcing you to play in a certain way.

I'd have been mad for kicking the ball. Giving a nice kick pass and being able to set up a score… there was a bit of individual pride there. But it all came back to the team. If you're doing the right thing for the team, then you're helping yourself and helping the team.

When we got into the last 10 minutes of the game and Kerry were leading by four points, a lot of people probably thought they were comfortable and would close it out. Colm Cooper got the point that put them four up, but you're never thinking… *Shit, this is gone.* It's always just… *Keep battling away… Keep twisting the screw.*

When Kevin Mc got the goal, I didn't even look up at the screen. I genuinely wasn't aware of what time was gone and what was left. You're in the mindset that if the Kerry keeper takes a quick kickout, and it sails over my head because I'm looking at the scoreboard or the Hill celebrating, then we're in trouble.

When you look at the goal, it was Declan O'Sullivan who was the last man back. If that's Tomás or Marc Ó Sé, maybe they stand Kevin up better or put in a better tackle. Kevin was able to side-step Declan and stick it in the net. Kerry seemed to be all up field, and we caught them with Alan Brogan through the middle and he was able to lay it off to Kevin. There was nobody near either of them.

Whatever happened to Kerry in that transition, I don't know, but they were disjointed and we made the most of that. Having experienced the Hill when a goal goes in, it's just pandemonium. That goal set us on our way for the last eight minutes or whatever was left.

The league final against Cork in 2011 played a huge part in the closing stages of the All-Ireland final for us.

We were eight points up with around 10 minutes to go in that game and a lot of players would have been looking up at the scoreboard. At that time, Dublin hadn't won the league since 1993… almost 20 years. So that would have been a massive trophy for us. Lads would have been thinking about being out on the town that night with a trophy, going to whatever nightclub. We ended up losing that game.

Pat and the management really focussed on that in the lead-up to the All-Ireland final. It was drilled into us that if we got into the same position again, we weren't going to let it slip. When we looked back at the stats from that league final, it showed that hydration might have been an issue, but lads would also have admitted to looking at the scoreboard and thinking… *Brilliant… We've won a National League.*

After the goal, we're back to a point and I popped up with the equaliser.

I know it was said on the commentary, but it wasn't my first point in the championship. I scored against Wexford in the Leinster Championship in 2010! It obviously sounds better to say your first point was in an All-Ireland final, but that wasn't quite the case.

I was a soccer player when I was younger, and I was late to gaelic football. When I started out, I was a corner-forward and then eventually was moved to the half-backs. But I'd always have had an eye for a score. With the style we had at the time, I wouldn't have found myself going forward too often. On that occasion though, I just drifted forward, and I found myself with nobody around me.

Dermo gave me the pass, and I was coming in on my right foot in the ideal position. There was a bit of craic on the All Stars tour a few months later, because Bryan Sheehan was only centimetres away from getting a block in, and he was saying, 'F**k ya anyway Kevin… I nearly had you!'… so it's all those tiny margins. It's getting the ball off as quick as you can.

I was never one for a dummy solo… that was never going to happen. I was confident of kicking the ball over the bar, so I didn't over-think it… and took the shot. If it had dropped short or gone wide, I'd have had plenty of lads at me, but it was the right thing to do.

A few minutes later, I got another ball in an attacking position, but I gave the ball to Mick Macauley, and he took a shot and put it wide. When I watched it back, I was thinking… *Why didn't I shoot that time?* The reason was that Mick was in a better position than me and I didn't have as clean a shot as I did the first time.

Bernard put us ahead after that, which I think gets forgotten at times. A lot of people seem to think it went from my point to Cluxton's winner. But Bernard kicked an unbelievable point to put us ahead… and it was looking like we're going to do it. But no, Kieran Donaghy kicks an even more unbelievable score… the score of the game really. With everything that happened in the last 10 minutes, those two points get forgotten I think, but they were incredible scores to get in the circumstances.

I didn't know how close it was to the end when Donaghy got his score or when Clucko kicked the winner. Brendan Kealy kicked the ball towards Bryan Sheehan, and I got in behind him and tapped it down to myself. If I was thinking about the scoreboard or the time, there's a chance I don't get to that ball.

When Clucko kicked the free, I was fully prepared for the next ball because I was sure there was time for Kerry to have another attack. Luckily for us, it turned out the be practically the last kick of the game.

I'd been involved since the end of 2007, and we'd have trained out in St David's in Artane. Stephen and Mark Vaughan would have always been out kicking frees before training sessions. He'd been practicing this for years but because the likes of Mark and Mossy Quinn were there, there was never a need for Stephen to hit frees.

But earlier on in that 2011 final, he kicked one from about 50 yards right down the middle, straight over the bar. Now I think he missed one, but to have Bernard Brogan shouting at him to come up and kick that last free… he was the right man for that job. It was the right side for Stephen, and we all knew that.

When the final whistle went, I don't even remember what I did! There's was a picture taken by one of the sports photographers after the game of a group of the players all celebrating, and I'm just standing there looking for my family in the crowd. Standing there with my hands on my hips. Just because I wanted to share the moment with them.

The crowds couldn't come on to the pitch, and I'll never forget The Black Eyed Peas' song *Tonight's Gonna Be A Good Night* came on. Every single time I hear that song, I get goosebumps because it was the song being played as we were going around the pitch with the cup. I'll always remember that.

The whole place was an ocean of blue and it had been a long wait. I personally didn't have to go through the ups and downs of the previous years as much as some of the other lads did, but we were fortunate to get over the line in our first final since 1995. All the 6am starts had paid off!

The crowds not coming on was something that I know a lot of people were against because it was such a tradition for so long and made for a great spectacle, but it was great for us to be able to enjoy the win and get photos and so on. It made it a bit more personal and a bit more romantic – if that's the right word! – for the group to share it together without the crowds being on the field. Lads were able to bring kids on and get photos.

There was the picture with Pillar Caffrey and Bernard with his Garda hat on and all that, so that kind of thing is special to me. I remember once when he was still manager, Pillar dropped me home from training in St David's… all the way Dun Laoghaire. He only lived about five minutes from Artane, so he didn't have to do that.

I always had great time for him and it was great that he was there to celebrate a little bit with us when we finally got the job done.